DISRAELI
— v —
GLADSTONE

To Ken and Georgia

In many instances you will see titles in lower case letters — as in earl of Beaconsfield and prince of Wales. Like many other people I think that this is wrong but the publisher insisted. I won the argument and lost the vote.

I hope that you find the book interesting.

Roger Mason

DISRAELI
—v—
GLADSTONE

WESTMINSTER'S MOST BITTER FEUD

ROGER MASON

FONTHILL

Fonthill Media Language Policy

Fonthill Media publishes in the international English language market. One language edition is published worldwide. As there are minor differences in spelling and presentation, especially with regard to American English and British English, a policy is necessary to define which form of English to use. The Fonthill Policy is to use the form of English native to the author. Roger Mason was born and educated in England; therefore British English has been adopted in this publication.

Fonthill Media Limited
Fonthill Media LLC
www.fonthillmedia.com
office@fonthillmedia.com

First published in the United Kingdom and the United States of America 2020

British Library Cataloguing in Publication Data:
A catalogue record for this book is available from the British Library

Copyright © Roger Mason 2020

ISBN 978-1-78155-772-3

The right of Roger Mason to be identified as the author of this work has been asserted by him in accordance with the Copyright, Designs and Patents Act 1988.

All rights reserved. No part of this publication may be reproduced, stored in a retrieval system or transmitted in any form or by any means, electronic, mechanical, photocopying, recording or otherwise, without prior permission in writing from Fonthill Media Limited

Typeset in 10pt on 13pt Sabon
Printed and bound in England

Preface

This is my twenty-seventh book. Most of the others have been on the subjects of finance and company law, but others have been on history and railways. I have enjoyed writing them all and, believe it or not, this includes the ones on company law. This book is rather special, and I have not enjoyed writing any book more than this one. I have tried to tell the story faithfully, but at the same time, I have tried to make the book interesting and enjoyable. It is something that Roy Jenkins and Antonia Fraser have managed so well, and I hope that you think that I have succeeded.

Many years ago, I acquired a love of history while a pupil at Aylesbury Grammar School, and this love has remained with me since. My teachers were Mr Byford and Mr Dalby Ball, and I have much for which to thank them. I recall Mr Byford teaching us about Disraeli and Gladstone and how it sparked my interest. It is perhaps not too fanciful to think that it sowed the seeds for this book. He was an admirer of Gladstone but not Disraeli, whereas most of us boys held the opposite view. On one occasion in exasperation, he shouted that we were all nineteenth-century conservatives. We thanked him for the compliment.

Kenneth Clarke said that Gladstone thought Disraeli a charlatan and that Disraeli thought Gladstone mad. They probably did think this, and it is fair to wonder if each of them had a point. Even so, in their different ways, both were geniuses and very remarkable men.

Perhaps their bitter rivalry was a factor in bringing out the best in them. Rather like the middle distance runners Steve Ovett and Sebastion Coe—would each of them have done so well if they had not had the other to beat?

Finally, I would like to thank my wife, Dorothy, for her invaluable help with the photographs. I would also like to thank Geoff Wright, my wife's cousin, and my friend, Lal Banerjee. They found occasional mistakes and made helpful suggestions. Geoff Wright has a special insight because he is a former publisher and twice stood as a candidate for parliament.

Roger Mason
Leighton Buzzard, England

Contents

Preface		5
Part I: The Youthful Disraeli: 1804–1837		9
1	1804–1830	11
2	1830–1837	17
Part II: The Youthful Gladstone: 1809–1837		23
3	1809–1827	25
4	1828–1832	30
5	1832–1837	34
Part III: Conservatives Under Peel: 1837–1845		37
6	1837–1841	39
7	1841–1845	44
Part IV: The Feud: 1846–1881		51
8	1846–1847	53
9	1847–1851	59
10	1852	69
11	1852–1855	77
12	1855–1859	85
13	1859–1866	93
14	1866–1868	105
15	1868–1870	122
16	1871–1874	135
17	1874–1875	153
18	1876–1878	160
19	1878–1880	168
20	1880–1881	178
Part V: Gladstone After Disraeli: 1881–1898		185
21	1881–1885	187
22	1885–1893	194
23	1893–1898	199
Endnotes		202

PART I
The Youthful Disraeli:
1804–1837

1
1804–1830

Benjamin Disraeli was born in Bloomsbury on 21 December 1804. His birth place is now close to central London, but at the time, it was in Middlesex. At his birth, he took his father's name of D'Israeli, but when he was eighteen, he elected to drop the apostrophe and become Benjamin Disraeli. This is the name by which he is most commonly remembered. It is believed that he did it in order to distinguish himself from his father, who was well known. His sister and two brothers did the same thing. Part way through his second term as prime minister, he accepted a peerage and became the earl of Beaconsfield. This meant that from August 1876 until April 1880, he was prime minister in the House of Lords; then, until his death a year later, he was leader of the opposition in the same chamber.

As his name suggests, Disraeli was born a Jew, which is of great importance and there is more on this later. His family had a Sephardic Jewish, Italian, and mercantile background, and on both his paternal and maternal side, all his grandparents were born in Italy. His grandfather, Benjamin D'Israeli, had come to England in 1748; he prospered as a stockbroker and merchant, and he left a considerable sum of money to his son, Isaac. The future prime minister's mother was Maria Basevi, the daughter of another wealthy Jewish, Italian immigrant.

Isaac was a wealthy, successful, and prosperous man of letters, well known in literary circles. He loved books, had an extensive library, frequently visited the reading room of the British Library, and was an early and faithful member of the Athenaeum Club. He wrote a number of successful books and was a founder member of the *Quarterly Review*.

Benjamin got on well with his father, but he did not enjoy a close relationship with his mother who showed few maternal feelings towards him. Later, his close women friends, not to say his mistresses and his future wife, were almost exclusively older than him, and many people who think that they know about this sort of thing believe that he was consciously or subconsciously searching for a mother figure. He had the knack of attracting older women, so finding them was not difficult.

Benjamin was the second of Isaac and Maria's five children. His sister, Sarah (1802–59), was two years older, and they became very close. She gave him good advice and helped in his early career. There were three younger brothers, Nephtali (born and died in 1807), Ralph (1809–1898), and James (1813–68). The two surviving brothers both became civil servants. He got on well with them, but he was closest to Sarah.

When Benjamin was twelve years old, something happened that profoundly affected the remainder of his life and made his career as a politician possible. His father had been a member of the Bevis Marks Synagogue, but he had never taken his religion very seriously. However, his father's father (Benjamin's grandfather) was also a member and he did take it seriously. Isaac had fallen out with the synagogue in the past but had remained a member, probably out of respect for his father. Then there was another dispute and his father had recently died. This time, Isaac resigned and was henceforth not associated with any synagogue or religion.

Although not committed himself, Isaac accepted a friend's advice that it would be advantageous to his four surviving children if they were baptised into the Church of England. It seems cynical, but this was done. The future prime minister and his three siblings became Anglicans.

The United Kingdom was less anti-Semitic than many European nations, but there is no escaping the fact that anti-Semitism was a problem in many areas and would continue to be so. Just one example: Disraeli was not bound for a university, but Oxford and Cambridge were barred to practising Jews. Until 1858, only people willing to swear an explicitly Christian oath could be members of parliament. MPs had on a very few occasions turned a blind eye (or perhaps we should say a deaf ear) when one or two Jews had omitted the key sentence or muttered at the strategic moment, but this was very much the exception. It was done for a few respected, respectful, established, and moderately behaved men. They would not have done it for the flamboyant, eccentric, conceited, and outrageously-dressed Benjamin Disraeli.

Despite being a baptised Anglican, Disraeli did suffer discrimination throughout his life. He was proud of his Jewish heritage and had an obviously Jewish name. Before he dropped the apostrophe, it translated as 'Benjamin of Israel'. His hair and facial features were readily recognisable as being typical of the Jewish race. Indeed, they were typical to a pronounced extent. Of course, had his father not had him baptised, he might himself have had it done later, either due to genuine conviction or as a cynical step to further his career. Given his character and frequent opportunism, this possibility cannot be excluded.

In passing, it is interesting to note that quite a few people, mainly women, have found that their conscience allows them to adopt a different denomination or even a different religion in order to marry into royalty or make other advantageous marriages. Catholics have become Protestants and Protestants have become Catholics. Protestants and Catholics have become members of an Orthodox Church. People have been able to see their way to adopting Islam. In some cases at least, it has been a love match and a genuine conversion, so to avoid embarrassment, I will not name names. You probably can.

Disraeli's detractors looked for signs that his Christianity was not sincere, but they were very largely disappointed. It appears that it was. He became an active Anglican Christian who regularly attended church and took communion. When close to death, he spoke of redemption, and he and his wife and benefactress (who like him was an Anglican of Jewish descent) were buried together at Hughenden Parish Church. Having said all that, he was not a conventional Christian. John Vincent puts it as follows:

> Disraeli held no less than four religious positions, more or less concurrently. First, he rejected conventional supernatural Christianity. Secondly, he believed that modern thought might give Christianity a deeper meaning; so he rejected conventional materialism. Thirdly, he believed in the Jewishness of Christianity. Fourthly, he believed in the social necessity of religion. Of his scepticism there is little evidence.[1]

It should be noted that Disraeli thought that Anglicanism was an extension of Judaism and based on it. He did not see a contradiction. Many Christians and nearly all Jews would find this hard to accept. He once described himself as 'the blank page between the old testament and the new'.

At the time of writing, Britain has had fifty-five prime ministers and most of them attended public schools. In twenty cases, it was Eton College—David Cameron and Boris Johnson being the most recent to do so. Furthermore, most of them went on to university, mainly Oxford or Cambridge. This was true of William Gladstone, whose education was at Eton and Christ Church College, Oxford. Disraeli was one of the very few up to his time who did not do so. Finding the money would not have been a problem for his father, and his two surviving brothers were educated at Winchester. Despite his success in life, he strongly regretted that he was not given this opportunity. It seems that his mother played a large part in the decision, and that her main reason was fear that he would be bullied, perhaps because of his delicate health and obvious Jewish appearance. In an outstandingly vulgar sentence about his schooldays, Richard Aldous writes: 'What it did not provide was the often brutal "bugger-me-with-a-toasting-fork" initiation rites, that nearly all public school boys of the English governing class endured'.[2]

Disraeli first attended a dame school and then a boarding school at Blackheath. Following this, at around the time of his thirteenth birthday, he moved to Higham School, near Walthamstow. This was run by a Unitarian minister, the Reverend Eli Cogan. As noted in Marvin's *Disraeli's Reminiscences* (p. 145, 1975), Disraeli later wrote:

> I was at school for two or three years under the Revd. Dr Cogan a Greek scholar of eminence, who had contributed notes to the A[e]schylus of Bishop Bloomfield and was himself the editor of the Greek Gnostic poets. After this I was with a private tutor for two years in my own County, and my education was severely classical. Too much so; in the pride of boyish erudition, I edited the Idonisian Eclogue of Theocritus wh. was privately printed. This was my first production, puerile pedantry.

Be of good cheer if you are not familiar with the Aeschylus of Bishop Bloomfield and the Idonisian Eclogue of Theocritus. I had never heard of them either.

Shortly before his seventeenth birthday, Disraeli was articled to a firm of solicitors, for which his father paid the sum of 400 guineas. A career in the law was not to his liking, but the following two and a bit years were not wasted. He worked diligently, learned well, and was respected by his employers.

Then his life changed dramatically and things became controversial, exciting, and, in some ways, disastrous. He travelled and became a novelist, and he wrote in other ways as well. He borrowed money, speculated disastrously, and lost a lot. He was co-founder of a newspaper that failed, and he adopted an outrageous, dandified style of dress. He became a man about town who knew a lot of people. He became a hard man to ignore.

In May 1824, when he was twenty years old, he submitted a manuscript to his father's friend, the publisher John Murray, but it was not published. He then turned his attention to the prospect of making a fortune by speculating in South American mining shares, and he borrowed a lot of money to do so. The modern term for this is being highly geared. It is a way of becoming very rich if the shares do well, but also a way of becoming severely financially embarrassed if they do badly. At this time, he wrote three anonymous pamphlets promoting the shares in which he had invested. John Murray, who had also invested, published them. He joined Murray in forming a new newspaper. This failed after just six months, and at the same time, the value of his shares in the mining companies crashed. He had lost £7,000 and was financially ruined. His debts were a severe embarrassment, and it was 1849 before he finished paying them off.

Disraeli's talents included writing, and in particular writing novels. After politics, it is this for which he is most remembered. His first novel, *Vivian Grey*, was written very quickly and published in four volumes in 1826–27 when he was only twenty-three years old. It portrayed high society and the people who moved in it. The portrayals were distinctly unflattering and seriously upset many people, including some who thought that they could recognise themselves in the writing. Their number included John Murray, who Disraeli blamed for the failure of their newspaper. The novel was not very good, but it sold a lot of copies.

The novel's publisher was persuaded not to put the writer's name on the cover, and for a while neither he nor the readers knew who it was. This led to a frenzy of speculation about who it might be. Many thought that it must be someone well-connected and upper class. Eventually, the truth came out and everyone knew that this was not the case, and that it was in fact the flamboyant, uppity, absurdly ambitious, conceited, and very irritating man of Jewish descent and appearance, Benjamin Disraeli. His critics fell upon him and he was greatly embarrassed. He wrote afterwards:

> With what horror, with what supreme, appalling astonishment, did I find myself for the first time in my life a subject of the most ruthless, the most malignant, and the most adroit ridicule—I was sacrificed, I was scalped—The criticism fell from my hand, a film floated over my vision; my knees trembled. I felt the sickness of heart that we experience in our first serious scrape. I was ridiculous, it was time to die.[3]

Gladstone read the book nearly half a century later and said that it was trash.

Despite the disaster, he published a further fifteen novels during the remainder of his life. Some of them were very good, famous, and influential. He also wrote some non-fiction, poetry, and drama.

Disraeli was often attracted to women older than himself and an early instance was Sara Austen. The 'affair' started when he was twenty-one years old and she was nearly thirty. The lady was the wife of a worthy but rather boring solicitor. It is not certain whether or not she was his mistress, but it is certain that she was enormously attracted to him, gave him a great deal of motherly affection, bright companionship, flattery, and practical help with his novel *Vivian Grey*. She negotiated the publishing contract, and to avoid the writer's identity being discovered, she copied it out in her own handwriting. When his identity as the author was discovered, she bolstered and consoled him.

Sara persuaded her husband to lend him some money, and after he had been unmasked as the writer of the book, the three of them took a continental holiday. Her husband must have been a very tolerant man. Sara did not tire of Disraeli, but after the holiday, he tired of her and called the affair off. He found her rather too demanding and not able to match his intellectual abilities.

The next three and a half years were the worst of his life. He had lost a very large sum of money in stock exchange speculation, and his new newspaper had failed. As a result, he was seriously in debt. His book had resulted in opprobrium, with anger and derision being heaped upon him. The result was a severe nervous crisis—the term nervous breakdown would not be out of place. He became severely depressed and lethargic. He did little. During this awful period, he was supported by his father and by his sister, Sarah, to whom he remained very close.

By 1830, he was emerging from this terrible interlude, and in the spring of that year, he finished a new novel with the title *The Young Duke*. As he recovered, people sought his company. There is an interesting account of a dinner party given in 1830 by Edward Lytton Bulwer.[4] Disraeli arrived wearing green velvet trousers, a canary-coloured waistcoat, silver-buckled shoes, lace cuffs, and his hair in glossy ringlets. The sparkle of his talk astonished them all. To the women, he made particular appeal, and they appealed no less to him.

Lytton Bulwer was Disraeli's friend and contemporary, with considerable achievements as a novelist, poet, playwright, MP, and government minister. He served with Disraeli in Lord Derby's 1858 administration. In 1862, he was offered the crown of Greece, which was vacant following the abdication of King Otho. He declined the invitation. As a young man, Disraeli was noted for the flamboyance of his dress. He did not continue the practice into middle age.

His recovery was complete by the time that he took a sixteen-month tour of the Near East in 1830–31. This is covered in the next chapter, as is his developing life and his entry into politics, culminating in his joining Gladstone in the House of Commons in 1837.

2
1830–1837

Starting in May 1830, Disraeli travelled for sixteen months in Southern Europe and beyond, and his experiences profoundly affected his interests, opinions, politics, and outlook on life. His future novels, political beliefs, and actions are included in this list. In particular, they influenced his attitude to the 'Eastern Question', which loomed over much of his political career, and of the political career of his rival William Gladstone. The issue was the decay and weakness of the Ottoman Empire and the expansionary ambitions of Russia. Although the journey had a sad ending, it rejuvenated him.

He set off with William Meredith, who was the fiancé of his sister, Sarah. It seems odd that a young man would choose to leave his intended bride for such a long time, but Meredith's uncle was opposing the marriage because of Sarah's Jewish background. We might well think that this was a reason for William not to go. For part of the journey, they were joined by Meredith's friend James Clay. According to Jonathan Parry Clay's buccaneering temperament, raffish habits and sexual experience fascinated Disraeli.[1] The journey encompassed Spain, Malta, Corfu, Albania, Greece, Cyprus, Turkey, the Holy Land, and, finally, five months in Egypt.

In his later years, Disraeli customarily dressed in a restrained way, but that was in the future. During the tour, he frequently dressed flamboyantly, or as many would say outrageously. To take just one example, when he left Malta, he was dressed as a Greek pirate, with a blood-red shirt, huge silver buttons, a sash crammed with knives, a red cap, red slippers, and sky-blue pantaloons. We are told that the officers' mess had long since stopped asking him to dinner.[2] He took two canes to the garrisons in Gibraltar and Malta, one for the morning and one for the afternoon, and he ostentatiously changed them as the guns fired at noon. He was not popular with the officers that were stationed there.[3]

The tour was tragically cut short after the final five months in Egypt. Meredith contracted smallpox and died. Disraeli returned home with a venereal disease, which was successfully treated with mercury. His sister,

Sarah, remained unmarried and was a great support for her brother for the rest of her life. She died in 1859, and he missed her badly. They frequently wrote to each other and he poured out his thoughts, political and other, in his letters.

Shortly after his return, Disraeli wrote two novels, both of them having obviously autobiographical undertones. Indeed, the first of them was subtitled 'A Psychological Romance'. This was *Contarini Fleming*, published in four volumes in 1832, and it depicted the conflicting elements in its hero's character. The other was *The Wondrous Tale of Alroy*, which was published the following year. This portrayed the conflicting emotions of a medieval Jew in choosing between a large empire and a small, exclusively Jewish state. After writing this one, he decided that his writings would no longer be about himself.

After his return from the tour, and in addition to expending considerable efforts on his writing, Disraeli turned his attention to politics. He had ideas and wished to make his mark and contribute, but a large part of Benjamin Disraeli's motivation was conceit and the wish to achieve the advancement of himself. He was still weighed down with crippling debts, and cynics have commented that serving members of parliament could not be imprisoned while parliament was sitting because of debt. It was, though, 1911 before MPs who were not ministers were paid. It was an exciting time and the great issue dividing the parties and the country was parliamentary reform. The Great Reform Act became law in 1832 and this increased the size of the electorate. It also went a considerable way to abolishing the rotten boroughs. The most extreme example of these was 'Old Sarum', where one man chose two MPs.

The political parties were in a state of flux. The Tories who traditionally supported the monarch and the Church were split into three factions. The Whigs were closely associated with the relatively small number of great families that had compelled the Bill of Rights in 1689. In many cases, the leading Whigs were related to each other. Lady Antonia Fraser wittily called them the cousinhood. Supporting the Whigs were the Radicals, who were a minority. As their name suggests, they espoused more radical policies.

During this time, Disraeli's amorous life was active, interesting, and complicated, and it helped him progress with his political aspirations. As he confirmed in a letter to his sister, Sarah, he had no intention of marrying for love. If at all, it would be for money, to advance his career, or perhaps both. He wrote: 'As for "love", all my friends who married for love and beauty either beat their wives or live apart from them. This is literally the case. I may commit many follies in my life, but I never intend to marry for "love", which I am sure is a guarantee of infidelity'.[4]

In 1832, he started an affair with Clara Bolton, the wife of a doctor, but a year later, his attentions switched to Lady Henrietta Sykes. She was four years older than him, married to Sir William Sykes, and the mother of four children. It would get complicated. Henrietta was voluptuous and highly sexed, and Disraeli enjoyed this aspect of the relationship, but she was also another paramour who could be described as something of a mother figure. Indeed, she often signed her letters to him with the words 'your mother', and they frequently included homilies on such subjects as the importance of brushing his teeth.

Henrietta had been having an affair with Lord Lyndhurst, the former Lord Chancellor, but she switched her attentions from him to Disraeli. At the same time, Sir Francis Sykes, Henrietta's husband, started an affair with Clara Bolton, Disraeli's former lover. As already stated, it was complicated. Then, after three years, Henrietta started a parallel affair with an Irish painter, Daniel Maclise. This caused Disraeli to break off the relationship. He had certainly been very fond of her, but not as fond as she had been of him.

In 1834, Henrietta had introduced Disraeli to her former lover, Lord Lyndhurst. It was all very amicable and this included Sir Francis Sykes and Clara Bolton. Disraeli and Lyndhurst took an instant liking to each other, and Disraeli became Lyndhurst's private secretary and his political protégé, which helped Disraeli's career.

At the same time, Henrietta lived openly with Disraeli. The two of them moved freely in the easy going society of the 1830s. Disraeli was received by the great Tory hostess, Lady Londonderry, and he met luminaries such as Lord Hertford, Lord Durham, and the duke of Wellington. At Mrs Norton's salon, he met the future Whig prime minister, Lord Melbourne. 'Well tell me what you want to be,' asked Melbourne. 'I want to be Prime Minister,' answered Disraeli.[5] The two men would later become Queen Victoria's favourite prime ministers. Gladstone, followed by Palmerston and Russell, all Liberals, would be her least favourite.

It is rather hard to discern the true nature of Disraeli's political beliefs at this stage of his life, but his first three attempts to become an MP were conducted as an independent radical. He was firmly anti-Whig and remained so, but he had radical ideas and some sympathy with elements of the Tory party.

He was a candidate in the 1831 and 1832 general elections, his chosen constituency being High Wycombe, which was not far from the family home at Bradenham. Both attempts were hopeless. It customarily returned two Whigs, and Lord Carrington had a great deal of influence. One of his sons was one of the candidates. Disraeli was the only opposition to the two Whigs.

The future prime minister famously opened his first campaign by speaking from the top of the portico outside the Red Lion inn in High Wycombe High Street. It was topped by a large red lion, and pointing to it, he indicated first the head then the tail. 'I shall be here and my opponents will be there,' he said, but he was wrong.[6] He came third out of three both times. His third and final attempt in High Wycombe was in the 1835 general election. By now, he was moving in Tory circles, but once again, he stood as an independent radical and, once again, he came bottom of the poll.

Following this, Disraeli realised that he needed the formal backing of a political party. The Whigs were anathema to him so he chose the Tories, which were closest to his ideas. He had been moving in Tory circles and had met and socialised with leading Tories. In 1836, he was admitted as a member of the Carlton Club. Before this, there was one more political campaign. In the spring of 1835, he was the official Tory candidate in the Taunton by-election. Again, it was a hopeless campaign. The constituency was firmly Whig and the Tory had no chance. For the fourth time, Disraeli was bottom of the poll.

Immediately following the Taunton by-election, a vituperative quarrel erupted between Disraeli and the Irish leader Daniel O'Connell, a man who had been a leading campaigner for Catholic emancipation and for a number of Irish causes. At the time, he was an MP and would be lord mayor of Dublin in 1841–42. The quarrel was a discredit to O'Connell and, we may or may not think, to Disraeli as well.

Campaigning at Taunton, Disraeli had said 'The Whigs have seized the bloody hand of O'Connell' and continued by saying that they were in power only by 'leaguing themselves with one whom they had denounced as a traitor'.[7] Misled by inaccurate press reports, O'Connell thought that Disraeli had denounced him as a traitor. Disraeli had come close, but he had not actually done that. As noted in Hurd and Young's *Disraeli* (p. 57, 2013), O'Connell launched a deeply offensive anti-Semitic attack:

> His name shows that he is of Jewish origin. I do not use it as a term of reproach; there are many most respectable Jews. But there are, as in every other people, some of the lowest and most disgusting grade of moral turpitude, and of those I look upon Mr Disraeli as the worst. He has just the qualities of the impenitent thief on the cross, and I verily believe if Mr Disraeli's family herald were to be examined and his genealogy traced, the same personage would be discovered to be the heir at law of the exalted individual to whom I allude. I forgive Mr Disraeli now, and as the lineal descendant of the blasphemous robber, who ended his career beside the founder of the Christian faith, I leave the gentleman to the enjoyment of his infamous distinction and family honours.

Not surprisingly, Disraeli took violent offence and challenged the sixty-year-old O'Connell to a duel. When O'Connell declined, he followed it by challenging his son, who had recently fought a duel as a substitute for his father. However, on this occasion, the son also declined. Duelling was illegal and could lead to charges of murder or attempted murder. The threat of the duel caused Disraeli to be temporarily detained by the authorities. Exchanges of insults included Disraeli's claim that O'Connell's supporters had 'a princely revenue wrung from a starving race of fanatical slaves'. No duel took place, but the enmity would continue into parliament after Disraeli's 1837 election victory. Disraeli was very pleased with the progress of the dispute because it gave him much public attention, something that pleased him mightily.

The term moral turpitude, a phrase used by O'Connell, seems subjective and can mean what people want it to mean. In modern times, visitors to the United States have been asked if they intend to commit acts of moral turpitude in the country. It is said, perhaps unreliably, that the late writer Keith Waterhouse would answer 'sole purpose of visit'. He was never refused entry.

William IV died in June 1837 and was succeeded by his niece, Victoria, who was barely eighteen years old. The law at the time required that a general election be held shortly after the succession of a new monarch, and this was held in July 1837. It was the last one held for this reason—the requirement was abolished by the 1867 Reform Act, which is sometimes termed Disraeli's Act. The Whigs led by Lord Melbourne lost forty-one seats and the Tories led by Sir Robert Peel gained forty-one. However, the Whigs still had a majority of thirty and continued in office. It was the fourth election in six years and the Whigs won all of them.

This time, Disraeli was one of the two Tory candidates nominated for the two-seat constituency of Maidstone. His running mate was Wyndham Lewis. The two men issued a joint address (policy statement), which was unusual at the time. It pledged support for the 'protestant constitution' and opposition to the 'heartless new poor law'.

Lewis, who was wealthy, paid Disraeli's expenses. He was still financially embarrassed and heavily in debt. These expenses included what we would now call bribes, and were indeed clearly bribes at the time. Until 1872, voting was done in public and bribery was common practice. A reading of Charles Dickens's *Pickwick Papers*, published in 1836–37, is very instructive. It gives an account of corruption in an election in the fictional borough of Eatanswill.[8] Gladstone's election in 1833 was helped by questionable practices, some of which he did not know about.

Both Disraeli and Lewis were elected. Thirty-two-year-old Benjamin Disraeli had reached the House of Commons at his fifth attempt in six years. He remained an MP until 1876, for most of the period as a member for Buckinghamshire. Then, for the rest of his life, he served in the House of Lords as the earl of Beaconsfield.

PART II

The Youthful Gladstone:
1809–1837

3
1809–1827

William Ewart Gladstone was born on 29 December 1809 at 62 Rodney Street, Liverpool. This made him just under five years younger than Benjamin Disraeli, who was born on 21 December 1804. Despite this, he became a member of parliament more than four and a half years before the older man. Gladstone was elected in 1832 and Disraeli was elected in 1837. The fact that both of them were born in late December has frequently led to their ages at the time of important events being overstated by a year. A review of books and articles will confirm this. To take just one example: Gladstone died on 19 May 1898, which meant that he was eighty-eight at the time. It is often put at eighty-nine.

In 1809, the population of Liverpool was around 94,000. By today's standards, that does not seem very much, but at the time, it was one of the very largest towns or cities in the United Kingdom outside London. It was also one of the most important. Liverpool was a town and did not become a city until 1880. No. 62 Rodney Street was a very good property in the Toxteth district. Toxteth is now remembered for the Toxteth riots in 1981 and being very run down. This was not the case in 1809, when it was a sought after area. William did not live in Rodney Street for long; in 1815, his wealthy father moved the family to a new house at Seaforth, which was 5 miles away on the edge of Liverpool. He had this built and it was set in a 100 acres.

Both William's parents were Scottish and of Scottish descent. His father, John, was forty-five years old at the time of William's birth, and his mother, Anne, was thirty-seven. Anne was John's second wife, the first having died childless after six years of marriage. William was the fifth child of John and Anne, and followed sister, Anne MacKenzie, and brothers, Thomas, Robertson, and John Neilson. Sister, Helen Jane, followed four years later. There were six children in all.

William's mother, Anne, was very religious and enjoyed delicate health. She was self-effacing and there was no doubt that her husband was the dominant person in the marriage. Like her husband, she was an Evangelical member of the Church of England. Richard Shannon disparagingly wrote: 'She found the duties in an alien land of running two large houses distasteful and the obligations of being the hostess of a rising business and political luminary quite terrifying. For her, ill-health became a way of coping with pressures she could not otherwise deal with'.[1]

William's father, John Gladstone, was a very successful self-made man. Born in Leith, near Edinburgh, he was the second of sixteen children and left school at the age of thirteen. He then joined his father's corn and grain trading and provisioning business. At the age of twenty-two, he moved to Liverpool, and in this town, he set up a trading partnership that was very profitable. A close friend at the time was William Ewart, and the future prime minister was named after him.

John Gladstone's trading activities extended abroad and in particular to the West Indies. This made him very rich indeed. He was worth £145,600 in 1812 and £502,000 in 1828.[2] In 1815, there was only one Church of England building in Liverpool, and in that year, he financed the building of two more. With his wife, he was an Evangelical. Like his parents, William was a lifelong and very committed Anglican, but he was much more 'high church'.

John Gladstone did not trade in slaves, but the plantations that he owned used slave labour, and a large part of his very considerable fortune was derived from this source. He was generous with his family and, in time, the money passed to his children, including William. The future prime minister was wealthy, and, one-stage removed, the source of some of his money was slavery. To put it mildly, this was controversial. It is worth mentioning that, over time, William gave considerable sums to charity, including schemes to help fallen women. There is much about his work with this deserving cause later in this book.

At the relatively late age of fifty-four, John Gladstone became a member of parliament, and he was an MP from 1818 to 1826. He was returned again in 1826, but his election was overturned due to a successful petition alleging corruption. He continued to try to be elected to parliament and his last unsuccessful attempt was at the age of seventy-seven. During his time at Westminster, he was noted for speaking in defence of the rights of slave owners, of which he was one. William's brothers, Thomas and John Neilson, also became members of parliament, so four Gladstones sat in the House of Commons at different times. William was the only one to distinguish himself. His other brother, Robertson, was active in Liverpool politics and served as mayor of the town, and one of his brothers-in-law became a member of parliament.

It was a political family. William was introduced to Liverpool politics and national politics as a child. His father became an MP when he was still a young boy, and both father and son were supporters of the Liverpool MP and future Prime Minister George Canning. William was upset when Canning died in 1827 after just four months in 10 Downing Street.

William's very strong religious feelings developed during his childhood. Like both his parents, he was an Anglican, but, as already mentioned, more 'high church' than them. The service of God was extremely important to him for the rest of his life, and he devoted a great deal of his time to it. In fact, he was perhaps the most religious of the country's prime ministers. He certainly ranks in the top three or four. His politics were subordinate to the aim of serving God. Of course, then as now, sincere and active Christians took different sides on political issues, but William's politics were always conducted with God in mind. In passing, it is perhaps fair to say that his father's defence of the rights of slave owners is hard to reconcile with his religious convictions. Disraeli too was an apparently sincere Anglican, but on religious matters, he thought that Gladstone was rather a humbug. He thought the same on other matters too.

From 1816 to 1821, William was one of just twelve boys attending a preparatory school at a vicarage close to his home in Seaforth. It seems that his experience was unexceptional. Roy Jenkins wrote: 'He had been taught, but not very much or very skilfully, by the Evangelical vicar of St Thomas's, Seaforth, the church which his father had built and entered in his balance sheet'.[3] In 1892, in his unfinished autobiography, William wrote: 'I suppose I learnt something there. But I have no recollection of being under any moral or personal influence whatever'.[4]

At the age of eleven, William followed his three older brothers to Eton College. His father's position and money secured their places at what was then (and arguably is now) regarded as Britain's most prestigious school. It is rather presumptuous to ask, but I hope that you will accept a personal and amusing anecdote from the writer. Harold Macmillan's first government contained no fewer than thirty-five Old Etonians and seven of them were in the cabinet. Sometime afterwards, I took a German girl on a trip to Windsor and Eton (which I did not attend) and I mentioned this to her. I was later told that she had written to her mother and told her that she had been taken out by a boy who had attended the same school as a quarter of the cabinet.[5] It is not relevant, but it is a nice story.

Twenty of Britain's prime ministers have been educated at Eton College, and their achievements and experiences have been varied. The 3rd marquess of Salisbury is among those that were unhappy. He was very badly bullied, and when he was fifteen years old, he persuaded his father to take him away. Despite this, he later sent his four sons to the school. He delivered the first two there himself, but the memories of his experience were so upsetting that he left it to his wife to take the other two.[6] William Gladstone was one of the ones who did well (or indeed very well) and on the whole enjoyed the experience.

The headmaster was Dr John Keate, who held the position for no less than twenty-five years, from 1809 to 1834. This man, who was only around 5 feet tall, was generally respected and successful. He was, though, a headmaster who had no compunction about beating his charges. Discipline was in a deplorable state when he took over as headmaster, and the use of the birch was one of the ways that he asserted his authority. Two years before William's arrival at the school, and following a riot, he beat eighty boys in a single day. It would not be acceptable or indeed legal now. William was beaten a small number of times, but there was a good mutual regard and respect between the two.

William was not especially popular with the other boys, but he had friends and one very close friend in particular. He was certainly not unpopular. One of the younger boys allocated to do menial chores for him—they were known as fags—later described him as 'a good-looking rather delicate youth, with a pale face and brown, curly hair, always tidy and well dressed'.[7] He took little interest in games but enjoyed sculling on the river. He also took many exceedingly long walks, partly because he enjoyed them and partly because he (no doubt correctly) thought that they would be good for his health. Taking fearsomely long walks was something that he continued throughout his life. Just two of many examples are instructive. In 1863 (at the age of fifty-three), his diary very precisely records a walk of 25¼ miles in North Wales. In 1884 (at the age of seventy-four), while staying at Balmoral, he climbed Ben Macdui. This was 4,300 feet high and the highest point in the Cairngorms. It took him seven hours and forty minutes to do the 20-mile round trip.

William worked hard at Eton, accounted for his time, and did not waste it. This too was something that continued for the rest of his life. He was a good scholar and mastered Latin and Greek among other things. This could be said of many nineteenth-century prime ministers because they were staple parts of the curriculum at Eton and other public schools. The 14th earl of Derby translated the whole of *The Iliad* into blank verse. This was done for fun in his spare time.[8] *The Iliad* is a poem written in the eighth century BC in Homeric Greek and contains 15,693 lines. Although William worked long and hard, there was time for some relaxation. His father sent him parcels of wine, which he appreciated. A consequence was that he acquired the nickname 'Mr Tipple'.

Before going to Eton, William had acquired firm religious beliefs, and on his arrival, he was dismayed to find that this aspect of life was somewhat neglected. This did not deter him from regular bible reading (sometimes from a Greek text), nightly prayers, and seeking out sermons, though when he listened to them, he was frequently disappointed. His sister, Anne, was a great source of strength and spiritual encouragement. She was seven years older than him and was his godmother as well as his sister. She suffered from ill health during his later years at Eton, probably tuberculosis, and she died soon after he started at Oxford University. He was very upset.

Anne had also provided religious guidance for William's younger sister, Helen, who was aged fifteen at the time of Anne's death. William stepped into the void and attempted to take over the role that Anne had played. This proved irksome to Helen and he did not get far. Helen's life was destined to be troublesome and included drug addiction and conversion to Roman Catholicism. This mattered a great deal to William.

In July 1825, at the age of fifteen, William started to keep a diary, which substantially consisted of an account of things that he had done and how he had spent his time. He maintained it for more than seven decades, making entries almost every day until December 1896. It reflected his strong wish to use every minute of his life productively and keep a record of it. He certainly achieved this—at Eton and for the rest of his life. He had extraordinary physical and mental energy. When he finished, his diaries covered forty-one closely written volumes and are a very useful insight on the man, his life, and the times in which he lived. They throw light on his motivation in helping prostitutes and this is examined later in the book.

In his diary, he kept a faithful record of the books and pamphlets that he read. Roy Jenkins comments that it is possible to see the whole vast sweep of his literary input: theology, politics, history, science, poetry, and fiction—all the main controversial subjects of the year.[9] An example of a diary entry is instructive. The following is for 28 February 1826 when he was just sixteen: 'Read Memoirs of Sir Rt Walpole in Biograph. Dict; finished L'Avare; read a speech of Huskisson's on Silk Trade. Capital. Began Lyrics (Greek iambics instead of usual) and read about 160 lines of the second Georgic'.[10]

In October 1825, William was elected to the debating society, and he devoted much time to its affairs. He became secretary and then president, took his responsibilities seriously, and was successful. He got members fined—for example, 'Got Pickering maj fined for taking a paper out of the room without leave and Doyle for not filing the papers nor entering the question on time'.[11] The subjects of the debates were very wide-ranging and included questions such as 'Was Virgil as great a poet as Shakespeare?' and 'Was Cranmer admirable?'

William left Eton in December 1827. His destination was Christ Church, Oxford, which he joined in October the following year. On leaving his school, he described it as 'my long-known and long-loved abode.'[12] It is sometimes said that schooldays are the happiest days of our lives, though many would dispute it. As mentioned earlier in this chapter, the 3rd marquess of Salisbury (prime minister 1885, 1886–92, and 1895–1902) would have been among their number. One who would have taken a different view was Sir Alec Douglas-Home (prime minister 1963–64). He had a happy and successful time at Eton, and married one of the headmaster's daughters. William's memories were happy. When he left Eton, he wrote that 'the happiest period of my life is now past.'[13] Before going, he carved his name on a stone wall and on a door. On the latter, he very uncharacteristically made a mistake with the spacing of the letters.

4
1828–1832

Gladstone joined Christ Church College, Oxford, in October 1828. He would have liked to have done so sooner, but this was the first available date. Before going, he spent some time being coached by the rector of Wilmslow and rather mournfully, but perhaps unjustly, recorded that his classics were in a bad way. During the interim before Oxford, he remained close to his sister, Anne. As told in the last chapter, she was his godmother and a source of religious challenge and inspiration. Her health was declining and she died soon after his start at Oxford. He felt the loss deeply and sometimes compared himself unfavourably with her. On 24 December 1830, he wrote: '… dearest Anne's day of birth in the human state: I the hypocrite, and the essence of sin, am indeed deceitful above all things and desperately wicked, desperately wicked'.[1] One wonders what Disraeli would have made of that.

Christ Church had a strong claim to be the premier college in Oxford, and indeed England. So Gladstone went to an elite establishment and enjoyed the company of some elite people. In doing this, he was accompanied by a number of friends and colleagues from Eton. One of them was the earl of Lincoln, who soon afterwards played a part in launching his political career. It is not certain that the option was open to him, but Gladstone's father did not pay the extra fees to give him the status of gentleman-commoner. When Gladstone graduated, six of Britain's then twenty-one prime ministers had passed through Christ Church. The future Prime Ministers Peel and Derby had done the same, so with Gladstone himself, the total is nine. It is a remarkable number.

No study of Gladstone is complete without an account of his helping prostitutes over a period of half a century, and consideration of his motivation and temptations. This is included later in the book, but his diary records possibly his first interest on his very first day in Oxford. He wrote: 'Met a woman and had a long conversation with her'. On the next day, he wrote: '… met the poor creature again, who is determined to go home'.[2]

Gladstone was a connoisseur of sermons at both Eton and Oxford. He listened to and read many of them, though he was frequently disappointed. He was philanthropic and, not surprisingly, this often had a religious connection. For one Oxford day, his diary records that, with a cousin, 'they visited a poor blind invalid. She seemed in a most happy state. We each read her a sermon'.[3] We must hope that she found the experience inspiring and valuable, perhaps even enjoyable.

He was busy with his studies, his religion, and his good works, but there was time for relaxation. As at Eton, wine featured, and at Oxford, as through his life, he was not censorious about reasonable consumption of alcohol. He attended the first Oxford and Cambridge University Boat Race, which was held at Henley-on-Thames in June 1829. Oxford won and five of the winning crew were from Christ Church. At the time of writing this book, Oxford has won eighty races, Cambridge has won eighty-four races, and there has been one dead heat.

During his time at Oxford, Gladstone had friends, but he was not particularly popular or unpopular. He could, though, be rather priggish, which some found irritating. On the night of 24 March 1830, a group came to his room and gave him a beating. It is fair to speculate that they were annoyed by the way that he had monitored their behaviour in the chapel. His diary records his feelings in the following words:

> Here I have great reason to be thankful to that God whose mercies fail not....
> 1) Because this incident must tend to the mortification of my pride, by God's grace.... It is no disgrace to be beaten for Christ was buffeted and smitten....
> 2) Because here I have to some small extent an opportunity of exercising the duty of forgiveness ... and if this hostile and unkind conduct be a sample of their ways, I pray that the grace of God may reveal to them that the end thereof is death. Even this prayer is selfish. I prayed little for them before, when I knew that they were living in sin and had rejected Christ their Saviour ... I ought to have prayed before as much as now.[4]

Roy Jenkins, who was an admirer of Gladstone and thought him a great prime minister, wrote: 'Unfortunately his diary reaction was an orgy of holier-than-thou self-abnegation which had it been available to his assailants would have confirmed them in their worst suspicions'.[5]

Gladstone was studying *literae humaniores* and mathematics. *Literae humaniores* is a course focussed on classics and incorporates ancient Rome, ancient Greece, Latin, ancient Greek, and philosophy. He did not much enjoy mathematics and considered giving it up, but he rejected the idea. He only worked moderately hard in his first two years, but did much more in the last year. His efforts were rewarded with a double first.

While at Oxford, Gladstone was torn between a career in politics and becoming a Church of England priest. His father wanted him to choose politics, and he was influential in his son making that choice. William would probably have followed a parental instruction, but his father shrewdly acted as a sounding board while his son bombarded him with the arguments for and against each option. As we know, he chose politics and, as they say, the rest is history. One of his reasons was that he saw it as an effective way of serving God.

Away from his studies, Gladstone made a considerable mark at the Union Society, which had been formed a few years earlier. It was sometimes called the Debating Society and later the Oxford Union. He was a very powerful speaker and debater, and he honed his skills there. One of his speeches greatly affected his future political career. In the autumn of 1830, he was elected president for a term, and on that night, his motion 'that the Duke of Wellington's government is undeserving of the confidence of the country' was carried by a single vote.

Parliamentary reform was the biggest political issue of the day. Gladstone's speech at the Union vehemently opposing it was a great triumph. Prior to the 1832 Reform Act, approximately 10 per cent of adult males were allowed to vote in Parliamentary elections, and voting eligibility varied from constituency to constituency. The distribution of constituencies was absurd. For example, Manchester did not have separate representation and was treated as part of Lancashire. There were many so-called rotten boroughs where a tiny number of electors chose two MPs. These were often under the control of a single powerful person or a small group of powerful people. The most notorious of all was Old Sarum where just one man controlled the election of two MPs.

Looking back from the twenty-first century, it is hard to see how anyone could oppose reform, but many did, including Gladstone. Perhaps it is fair to say that some of them opposed just some of the reforms and not necessarily all of them. Opponents tended to include Tories, land owners, aristocrats, the rich, the powerful, and MPs who stood to lose their seats when the rotten boroughs were abolished. The issue caused great bitterness in the country and there were riots and deaths. In 1831, the Whig government carried a Reform Bill in the House of Commons, but it was rejected by the House of Lords. A subsequent bill was passed and became the Parliamentary Reform Act 1832.

In May 1831, Gladstone made a devastatingly forceful and effective speech at the Union. It lasted forty-five minutes and was in opposition to the Reform Bill. Afterwards, the resolution opposing reform was carried by ninety-four votes to thirty-eight. Among the listeners impressed by his oration was his Eton friend the earl of Lincoln. This man was the son and heir to the immensely powerful duke of Newcastle.

As well as speaking in the debate, Gladstone vociferously campaigned against the bill elsewhere. This included organising a petition and taking part in a procession. This almost led to violence against his person. He spent no fewer than fifty hours in the House of Lords listening to the debate, which led to the rejection of the 1831 Reform Bill. Although from his point of view they were on the wrong side of the argument, he expressed admiration for the speech of Prime Minister Earl Grey and also of Lords Lansdowne and Brougham. All this activity caused Gladstone to miss three days' chapel and this caused him to write in his diary that he was really ashamed.[6]

Gladstone later regretted his fervent opposition to parliamentary reform, and it was not the only one of his early political opinions on which he subsequently changed his mind. He later supported further reform and was prime minister at the time of the Parliamentary Reform Act 1884. Among other measures, this increased the size of the electorate from around 3 million men to around 5 million men.[7] It still left around 40 per cent of men without the vote, and there were no votes for women. In 1866, Disraeli chided him for his earlier views on parliamentary reform. Gladstone replied: 'My youthful mind and imagination were impressed with some idle and futile fears which still bewilder and distract the mature mind of the right honourable gentleman'.[8]

After graduating from Christ Church, Gladstone spent half of the following year making his grand tour in Europe, much of it spent in Italy. He did it in the company of his elder brother, John Neilson Gladstone, who at the time was a naval officer temporarily without a ship. The tour lasted 179 days and started on 1 February 1832. It ended when, in Geneva, he received an invitation from the duke of Newcastle, which features in the next chapter. He hurried home and arrived in London on 28 July.

5

1832–1837

Following the Whig triumph at the 1831 general election, the House of Commons approved another Reform Bill. Facing the prospect of the mass creation of peers willing to approve the bill, and with the country in turmoil, the House of Lords let this one through on 7 June 1832. This was followed by another general election, which was held in December that year. It was held in accordance with the expanded franchise and the reformed distribution of constituencies, and it was this election that enabled Gladstone to enter the House of Commons.

The earl of Lincoln, Gladstone's friend at Eton and Oxford, recommended him to his father, the duke of Newcastle. Gladstone, Lincoln, and Newcastle held similar views on parliamentary reform and many other matters. They could simplistically be summarised as Ultra Tory. Newcastle wrote to Gladstone's father offering to sponsor William as a Tory candidate for the Newark constituency. This was on the basis that the father, John Gladstone, would split the election expenses with him. These were expected to be about £1,000. Agreement was reached and Lincoln then wrote to William Gladstone, who was in Milan enjoying his European tour. After brief consideration, Gladstone accepted the invitation and hurried home.

The duke of Newcastle was an immensely powerful man and had controlled a number of constituencies. He was still very influential, including in Newark, but Gladstone's election was not a foregone conclusion. The constituency boundaries had not changed, but the number and make-up of the voters had. In the 1831 election, the electorate numbered about 500 and a Whig had topped the poll. This was despite the duke evicting forty tenants for not voting as he instructed.[1] There were now around 1,600 electors and it was estimated that Newcastle controlled 700 of them.[2] There were other men with significant influence, and there were also the independent burghers.

Gladstone campaigned vigorously, and at times, the atmosphere was very boisterous. His diary records that a missile was thrown at him and missed his head by 12 inches. As with so many things, his records and estimates were precise. In the event, his election expenses were around £2,000, a figure that at the time he did not know, and when he did know he did not approve. It created a suspicion of corruption, which was widespread in many constituencies. His father's involvement in slavery presented a problem for him. During the campaign, he prevaricated and said that 'he was unable to see the difficulties of emancipation in so strong a light as my father does.'[3]

The constituency returned two MPs, and there were two Tory candidates (including Gladstone) and a Whig. Gladstone topped the poll with 887 votes and his fellow Tory was elected with 798. The defeated Whig, who was a future lord chancellor, got 726 votes. After the declaration of the result, Gladstone spoke for no less than an hour. Long, passionate speeches were to be a feature of his entire parliamentary career. He took his seat in the House of Commons on 7 February 1833. The Tories were heavily outnumbered by the Whigs, and Earl Grey continued as prime minister.

Gladstone's maiden speech lasted for the seemingly lengthy time of fifty minutes and was well received, though this was probably more due to personal admiration of him than approval of the views that he expressed. This approval contrasts with the disastrous reception of Disraeli's maiden oration, as told in the next chapter. Gladstone's speech was delivered during consideration of the Whig government's successful bill to end slavery throughout the British Empire. Gladstone's father had been accused of ill-treating his slaves in the West Indies. Gladstone defended his father but agreed that the slaves should be set free. However, this was said with the extraordinary proviso that it should only be done when the slaves had become Christians.[4] The bill did not provide for this, so he voted against.

It is astonishing that the man considered by many to have been the greatest of all the Liberal prime ministers voted not to abolish slavery in the British Empire. At the time and a little later, his views on this and other issues can fairly be described as reactionary. Among other things, he asserted that the Anglican monopoly of Oxford and Cambridge Universities should be maintained, and he opposed the abolition of the restriction of Jewish civil liberties.[5] This was not likely to endear him to Disraeli.

In the very early years of Gladstone's parliamentary career, it was clear that he was a man to watch and could have a great future. He was privately congratulated on his maiden speech by his party leader, Sir Robert Peel, and shortly afterwards, he was elected to the Tory Carlton Club.

In late 1834, William IV dismissed Lord Melbourne and his Whig ministers. After a very short period with the duke of Wellington as prime minister, Sir Robert Peel formed an administration. The Tories gained 100 seats in the January 1835 general election, but were still in a minority. Peel's government only lasted from 10 December 1834 to 8 April 1835, when Melbourne resumed office as prime minister. Shortly after taking this position, Peel sent for Gladstone, who inconveniently was in Edinburgh at the time. He hurried back to London, and on Christmas Eve 1834, he took office as a junior lord of the Treasury. He was still short of his twenty-fifth birthday.

Almost immediately afterwards, the under-secretary for war and the colonies lost a by-election and Gladstone was promoted to the position. It was a particularly big promotion because the secretary of state, Lord Aberdeen, sat in the Lords and Gladstone led in the Commons. Gladstone became a privy councillor shortly after his twenty-fifth birthday. Gladstone and Aberdeen got on well, and each man formed a high regard of the other's abilities. This was important because Aberdeen was a future prime minister. Gladstone performed well in his elevated position, but he did not have time to make a significant mark before he and Peel were back in opposition.

Just a few days after Gladstone's appointment as a junior lord of the Treasury, he met Disraeli for the first time. It was at a dinner organised by Lord Lyndhurst. As told in Chapter 2, this was the man who shared the affections (to say the least) with Disraeli of Henrietta Sykes. Lyndhurst regarded Disraeli as his friend and protégé and was trying to promote his political career. The main aim of the dinner was to introduce Disraeli to the influential Winthrop Mackworth Praed, and further aims included introducing him to Gladstone.[7]

Lyndhurst's strategy worked well with Praed, but not with Gladstone. In the view of Richard Aldous, Gladstone and Disraeli loathed each other from the beginning. Afterwards, Disraeli wrote to his sister and reported that he had met young Gladstone at a dinner and found him rather dull.[9] Gladstone did not mention Disraeli in his account of the dinner written in his diary.

Gladstone was returned unopposed at both the 1835 and 1837 general elections, something that we find almost inconceivable now, but which was not uncommon at the time. After the latter of these two elections, he was joined in the House of Commons by Disraeli.

During the 1830s, the Tory Party gradually became known as the Conservative Party. There is not an agreed date for the change, but Peel's issue of the Tamworth Manifesto in 1834 is a contender. So far, this book has called it the Tory Party and referred to Tories. For the remainder, it is the Conservative Party and Conservatives.

PART III

Conservatives under Peel:
1837–1845

6
1837–1841

The 1837 general election was called because of the death of William IV and the accession of eighteen-year-old Victoria. The law at the time required that a general election be held immediately after the start of a new reign. This was the last time it happened because the requirement was abolished in 1867. The previous general election in 1832 had been the first held after the passage of the Reform Act and had given the Whigs a majority of more than 250 over the Conservatives. This time, it was different, though Whig Prime Minister Lord Melbourne, with Irish support, had a majority of thirty-four over the Conservatives led by Sir Robert Peel and continued in office.

Disraeli was one of the two members elected to represent the Maidstone constituency. He joined Gladstone who was unopposed in Newark. Both were Conservatives in the party led by Sir Robert Peel.

There is a long tradition of maiden speeches in the House of Commons being heard indulgently. Some have been very good. An example is the one given by William Pitt the Younger at the age of twenty-one. Afterwards, Edmund Burke said: 'He is not a chip off the old block. He is the old block itself'.[1] The old block was Pitt's father and former Prime Minister William Pitt the Elder. An example of a bad maiden speech was the offering of Robert Maxwell in 1964. Disraeli's maiden speech was most definitely one of the bad ones, though it is remembered with admiration for the final shouted sentence.

The speech was delivered on 7 December 1837. Disraeli, as so often flamboyantly dressed, used it to attack the Irish members and in particular his enemy Daniel O'Connell. An account of their feud is given in Chapter 2. The opportunity was a debate on the validity of Irish returns at the recent election. He spoke in a sarcastic and theatrical manner, and his attack included reference to 'Irish intimidation and corruption which had assumed a deeper and darker hue'.[2] The following day's issue of the *Morning Chronicle* gave an account of the final part of the speech in the following terms:

'When we remember at the same time that, with emancipated Ireland and enslaved England, on the one hand a triumphant Nation, on the other a groaning people, and notwithstanding the noble lord, secure on the pedestal of power, may wield in one hand the keys of St Peter, and'—(Here the Hon. Member was interrupted with such loud and incessant bursts of laughter that it was impossible to know whether he really closed his sentence or not). The Hon. Member concluded in these words: 'Now, Mr Speaker, we see the philosophical prejudices of man.' (Laughter and cheers). 'I respect cheers, even when they come from the lips of political opponents.' (Renewed laughter). 'I think, sir—' (Hear, hear, and repeated cries of 'Question, question.') 'I am not at all surprised, sir, at the reception which I have received.' (Continued laughter). 'I have begun several times many things—' (laughter) 'and I have often succeeded at last.' (Fresh cries of 'Question!') 'Ay, sir, and though I sit down now the time will come when you will hear me!' The Hon. Member delivered the last sentence in a very loud tone, and resumed his seat.[3]

The speech was a disaster, but the last defiant sentence was prescient. They did indeed hear him, and did so for nearly forty years. A few weeks later, Disraeli watched a speech given by Gladstone and possibly learnt from it. He told his sister that he was very impressed.[4] He was willing to listen to advice, and he modified his dress, his behaviour, and his style of speaking. It worked, and after a few months, he was on his way to living down his unfortunate start.

Disraeli's maiden speech in the House of Commons: Though I sit down now the time will come when you will hear me.

Neither Gladstone nor Disraeli made a major impression during the 1837 Parliament, and the two men had little contact with each other. During these years, Disraeli established his reputation, but there was no great breakthrough. Gladstone spent time sitting on no fewer than ten committees, most of them of a religious nature. In August 1838, he commenced a six-month tour of the continent.

According to Philip Magnus, Gladstone's speeches in parliament were consistently reactionary, and he gives as an example his strong opposition in 1839 to a government motion to suspend the constitution of Jamaica. It wanted to do this because of the blocking of humane measures to help former slaves.[5] The government came close to defeat, and Lord Melbourne resigned. However, Peel did not take office because Victoria was unwilling to change the Ladies of her Household and install Conservative ones to replace the Whig ones to whom she had become close. So Melbourne continued in office until 1841. The affair was ridiculous. At the time, Gladstone was out of favour with Peel because of a book that he had written. According to Philip Magnus, Peel's failure to form a government was perhaps fortunate for Gladstone.[6] He might not have been included in it. Although Gladstone's positions were generally reactionary, it should be noted that in 1840 he strongly opposed Palmerston's Opium War against the Chinese.

The book that had incurred Peel's displeasure had the title *The State in its Relations with the Church*. It contained 500 pages and was written in less than two months in the summer of 1838. Throughout his life, Gladstone customarily approached his tasks with frenetic energy and this was a good example. More time and reflection would have been sensible. The book was published by the end of the year and the publisher was John Murray. This was the man who had some years earlier partnered Disraeli in publishing a failed newspaper and who had fallen out with him.

The book was dense, difficult to read, and exceedingly intolerant. One of its themes was advocacy that there should be no public service jobs throughout the British Isles for anyone who was not a communicating member of the Church of England. It expressed Gladstone's belief that doctrines other than those espoused by the established church were in error. Not surprisingly, it upset a lot of people, including his party leader. Peel is said to have thrown the book on the floor and said: 'That young man will ruin a fine career if he writes such books as these'.[7] Not deterred, Gladstone wrote a second book in 1840. This one had the title *Church Principles Considered by their Results*. It pursued the same themes as the first book and was written in the same style, but fortunately for him, it attracted much less attention.

It has been said that the views of many politicians tend to become more conservative as they get older. Gladstone is a very prominent example of one whose views moved the other way. The events described in this chapter occurred when he was in his late twenties and very early thirties. By the time that he retired in his eighties, he had long become the Grand Old Man of Liberalism, and anathema to his Conservative opponents.

Both Disraeli and Gladstone married in the summer of 1839. In Disraeli's case, it was on 28 August at St George's Church in Hanover Square, London. Gladstone married at Hawarden in Flintshire on 25 July. Hawarden was the home of his fiancée, Catherine Glynne, and her home was to feature prominently in Gladstone's life. The motivations of the bridegrooms were very different and so were their financial circumstances. The brides too were very different. In both cases, the marriages were long-lasting and happy. Furthermore, both women in different ways were great helps to their husbands.

Disraeli had enjoyed a number of affairs with older women, but in 1839, the newly elected MP, aged thirty-four, was still unmarried. It was time to put that right and what he most looked for in a prospective wife was money. He was still desperately in debt and feared that this would prevent him standing at the next election.

Mary Anne Lewis was the childless widow of his fellow Conservative MP for Maidstone, who had died in March 1838. She was twelve years older than him and she had money, though not nearly as much as he hoped and at first believed. He did not hide from her that money was a significant part of his motivation. She was infatuated by him and he liked her. This liking developed into something more and the marriage became a genuine love match. Mary Anne was vivacious, outspoken, rather scatty, and completely devoted to her husband and his career. His love for her deepened, and it was a somewhat curious but very successful marriage. Despite Gladstone's dislike of Disraeli, he did like Mary Anne. Much later, he wrote a kind and solicitous letter to his rival when she died at the age of eighty.

In her book *Pride and Prejudice*, Jane Austen memorably wrote: 'It is a truth universally acknowledged that a single man in possession of a good fortune must be in want of a wife'. The words were written in 1813, but they were applicable to William Gladstone in his mid- and late twenties. He was single, came from a very wealthy family, and was an MP who had briefly been a minister. He was on the verge of a glittering future. He wanted a wife, but found it difficult to get one. Two earlier marriage proposals to different women had been turned down.

Part of the problem was that he had an awkward way with women, perhaps influenced by the fact that he was used to overwhelmingly male company. Eton, Oxford, and the House of Commons had not led to him meeting many women, and his family and friends were mainly male. Furthermore, his very strong and rigid religious convictions somewhat narrowed his options. He had a strong sex drive, but was probably a virgin at the time of his marriage.

Eventually, the lucky lady was Catherine Glynne. She did not find his courtship easy and did not immediately accept him, but he must have been encouraged by the fact that she read his controversial, 500-page book. Gladstone proposed by letter in January 1839, and his written proposal contained the following extraordinary sentence containing 141 words and eighteen clauses and sub-clauses:

> I seek much in a wife in gifts better than those of our human pride, and am also sensible that she can find little in me: sensible that, were you to treat this note as the offspring of utter presumption, I must not be surprised: sensible that the lot I invite you to share, even if it be not attended, as I trust it is not, with peculiar disadvantages of an outward kind is one, I do not say unequal to your deserts, for that were saying little, but liable at best to changes and perplexities and pains which, for myself, I contemplate without apprehension, but to which it is perhaps selfishness in the main, with the sense of inward dependence counteracting an opposite sense of my too real unworthiness, which would make me contribute to expose another—and that other![8]

It is not hard to see why he had problems with women. Another prime minister, Clement Attlee, wrote: 'He really was a frightful old prig. Fancy writing a letter proposing marriage including a sentence of 140 words all about the Almighty. He was a dreadful person'.[9] This judgement is unkind and very harsh. Gladstone certainly had faults, but he was very far from being dreadful. What is more, Attlee could not count. The sentence contains 141 words.

Miss Glynne asked for time and then accepted the proposal five months later. It was a successful and happy marriage that lasted until his death nearly fifty-nine years later. She, in her way, was a great support to her husband, and it is interesting to note that she helped him in his rescue work to help prostitutes. According to Richard Aldous, she loathed Disraeli and anti-Semitism was part of the reason.[10]

In the latter years of the 1837 government, the authority of Melbourne and the Whigs drained away. In May 1841, they lost a vote on the budget, and the following month, they lost a vote of confidence. Melbourne resigned and Peel's Conservatives won the consequent general election. Gladstone and Disraeli were both elected and then served the governing party.

7
1841–1845

Sir Robert Peel and the Conservatives regained power in the general election held in the summer of 1841. They had a substantial majority of eighty over all parties. Disraeli returned to the Commons, this time as one of the two members for Shrewsbury, and Gladstone was again elected as a member for Newark. Peel, Disraeli, and Gladstone all fought the election as protectionists, something that would be very significant in the coming years. Disraeli hoped for a position in Peel's government and Gladstone hoped for a cabinet appointment. Both were disappointed.

On 18 August, Gladstone journeyed by train from Chester to London. It was still in the early days of rail travel, and it is interesting to note that he wrote in his diary 'Arrived well thank God'. In modern times, most years pass without a passenger death on Britain's railways, but in 1841, safe arrival was worthy of comment. On 21 August, he was one of ten people who met with Peel to discuss their amendment to Melbourne's final address to parliament, and this reinforced his hope and expectation for a senior position in the new government. However, he was surprised and disappointed to be asked to be vice-president of the Board of Trade.

Gladstone had wanted to be chief secretary for Ireland, but Peel told him that stout Ulster Protestants might resent a chief secretary who was reputed to belong to the Puseyite Party.[1] This meant an association with the views of the Reverend Edward Pusey, who was one of the promoters of the Oxford Movement. Gladstone did not argue with Peel, but he told friends that he was scandalised by the suggestion. He was not a Puseyite and there could not be a 'party' in the church.[2]

Peel endeavoured to conciliate the disappointed Gladstone. He stressed the importance of the Board of Trade position and he expressed his confidence that he would do it well. Gladstone accepted the job, but said that 'he had hoped to concern himself with the affairs of men but found himself set to governing packages'.[3] Nevertheless, Peel's judgment turned out to be sound. Gladstone quickly mastered the post and rapidly revised his views on its importance. An indication of the significance of the Board of Trade is that in 1840, £35m of tax revenue came from Customs and Excise duties. This was out of a total tax revenue of £47m. There was a job to be done—not least because there were 750 separate and mostly illogical duties.

Gladstone's boss, the president of the Board of Trade, was Lord Ripon. As Viscount Goderich, he had briefly been an unsuccessful prime minister for a few months in 1827–28. He was not hard working and not effective in this role either. Gladstone, however, was effective and he was very hard working. Home Secretary James Graham noted that Gladstone could do in four hours what it took any other man sixteen to do. He went on to add that he nonetheless worked sixteen hours a day.[4] Apart from everything else, he spoke in parliament no fewer than 129 times in a single session.

In May 1843, Peel moved Lord Ripon to another position and asked Gladstone to join the cabinet as president of the Board of Trade. He had previously threatened to resign over the issue of the Corn Laws, and in his interview with Peel, the two men agreed that they were no longer defensible.[5] It was another portend of trouble to come.

Gladstone was, of course, pleased with the promotion, but he hesitated to accept because of a problem that now seems ridiculous, and indeed surely seemed ridiculous at the time. The Sees of Bangor and St Asaph had been merged in 1836, and he was committed to trying to reverse the amalgamation. Peel was not willing to commit himself on the issue. After three days of prayer and consultation with his wife and religious friends, he decided to accept the promotion. Catherine Gladstone, like her husband, was very religious and she took pride in his principles. She wrote in her journal: 'How proud I am to be joined to one whose mind is purity and integrity itself'.[6]

Gladstone's many achievements as vice-president of the Board of Trade and then president of it included the Railway Acts of 1842 and 1844, and the Companies Regulation Act of 1844. This is regarded as the founder of the regular succession of Companies Acts that have reached the statute book ever since. The 1844 Railway Act required every railway company to run at least one train each day in each direction, and it had to stop at each station if required to do so. It had to have reasonable seating accommodation for third-class passengers and the maximum charge was a penny a mile. Prior to this, provision for third-class passengers was frequently appalling. Needless to say, this was very popular. However, it is worth noting that due to the restricted franchise, most of the beneficiaries did not have the vote.

During the years covered by this chapter, Gladstone was confronted by a distressing family problem. It concerned his younger sister, Helen, who was unmarried and who led a rather troubled and unhappy life. In 1842, she scandalised her brother by being received into the Roman Catholic Church. Gladstone was horrified and unforgiving. He forbade her from seeing his children and he urged his father to turn her out of his house. John Gladstone too was very upset, but he rejected this horribly intolerant advice. She continued living there but became increasingly addicted to opium.

In 1845, Helen was in a terrible state in Baden-Baden, which is in south-west Germany, and William Gladstone was despatched to bring her back. He found her much worse than he expected and she was not willing to return with him. On one occasion, she took 300 drops of laudanum and became partly paralysed. Gladstone stayed in Baden-Baden for five weeks and eventually, accompanied by a priest and a doctor, got her to travel as far as Cologne. Gladstone had to leave her there, but a few weeks later, she returned to London and her father. His threat to cut off her money was probably the decisive factor in making her return. Sadly, the remainder of her life remained very troubled.

For a long time, Gladstone was prone to considering resignation, though despite only being in his mid-thirties, he sometimes called it 'retirement'. He had problems over a number of issues, but particularly religion. Eventually, he did resign.

Since the Act of Union in 1800, the British government had made an annual payment of £9,000 to the Roman Catholic seminary at Maynooth near Dublin. Gladstone objected to this and he had criticised it in his 1838 book *The State in its Relations with the Church*. Even allowing for more than two centuries of inflation, it was a small sum, and in 1842, he reluctantly voted for the grant's renewal. However, in 1844, Peel proposed making the grant permanent and raising the annual sum to £30,000.

Gladstone fulminated, and in July 1844, he wrote to Peel suggesting that he resign from the cabinet and from parliament, and that he be appointed British Envoy to the Vatican. His letter said that if the prime minister did not like the suggestion, he need not reply. Peel took him at his word and did not do so.

In time, Gladstone realised how absurd his proposal has been. Fifty years later (in 1894), he wrote: 'I have difficulty in conceiving by what obliquity of view I could have come to imagine that this was a rational or in any way excusable proposal ... there existed in my mind a strong element of fanaticism'.[7] He continued to agonise, and on 3 February 1845, he did resign over the Maynooth grant. His reasons were given to the House of Commons in an almost impenetrable hour-long speech. Disraeli, showing no signs of animosity, formed the view that his career was finished.[8] Roy Jenkins, in an example of the glorious phraseology for which he was noted, commented: 'The resignation was not the first but the last departing swallow of Gladstone's theocratic intolerance'.[9] It seems a silly resignation and this feeling is enhanced by the fact that following a two-hour and thirty-minute speech, he voted for the Maynooth Bill. His vote helped secure the measure against which he had resigned in protest.

Most of his colleagues thought that over an extended period, his behaviour was to say the least unwise, and they found it difficult to comprehend his concerns. Nevertheless, there was so much admiration for his work rate, abilities, and contribution on a number of issues that they sincerely regretted his departure. Gladstone was only out of the cabinet until 23 December 1845.

A full account of the Corn Laws and their repeal is given in the next chapter. At the time of the 1841 election, he had supported their retention, but his views had progressively changed. By 1845, he strongly favoured repeal, and Peel had more slowly come to the same conclusion. Stanley (the future 14th earl of Derby and future prime minister) resigned because of his opposition on this issue, and Peel asked Gladstone to return to the cabinet as secretary of state for war and colonies. When he accepted, the delighted prime minister held his hand and said 'God Bless You'.

Gladstone's return to the cabinet precipitated a problem for him, and indeed for Peel and the government. Until the First World War, an MP joining the cabinet was required to leave the Commons and win an election. This was because cabinet members were paid. Re-election was often a formality, but it could be a problem and sometimes the minister concerned was rejected by his constituents. In 1908, Winston Churchill was a prominent example.

The duke of Newcastle who had great influence in Gladstone's Newark constituency strongly disagreed with his views on the Corn Laws and refused to support him. Knowing that he was sure to lose, he did not contest the by-election and looked for another constituency. This turned out to be very difficult and many overtures were unsuccessful. He performed his duties as secretary of state but did so without a seat in parliament. His formidable speaking and debating skills would have been very valuable to Peel at this turbulent time. It was not until August 1847 that he returned to parliament as a member for Oxford University.

Disraeli sat on the back benches throughout the whole of Peel's 1841–46 administration, and it was not until 1852 that he held any government office. This was as chancellor of the Exchequer for just ten months in the first brief government of Lord Derby. His failure to be given office in 1841 was not for want of asking.

After the 1841 election, Disraeli wrote to Peel asking for a position, and his letter included the following:

> I have had to struggle against a storm of political hate and malice which few men ever experienced, from the moment, at the instigation of a member of your Cabinet, I enrolled myself under your banner, and I have only been sustained under these trials by the conviction that the day would come when the foremost man of this country would publicly testify that he had some respect for my ability and my character. I confess to be unrecognised at this moment by you

appears to me to be overwhelming, and I appeal to your own heart—to that justice and that magnanimity which I feel are your characteristics—to save me from an intolerable humiliation.

The letter was preposterous and impertinent, and to make matters worse, his wife, Mary Anne, who was acquainted with Peel's wife, Julia, also wrote asking for office for him. Accounts differ about whether or not this letter was sent with her husband's knowledge and approval. Peel did not offer a position to Disraeli.

It is intriguing to wonder if Peel later regretted not finding a place for Disraeli in his government. Probably not, but he had considerable talents and was a formidable performer in the House of Commons, something that Peel already knew and would later experience to his cost.

It is stretching an analogy to breaking point, but the question puts one in mind of a remark made by Lyndon Johnson, who was president of the United States from 1963 to 1969. He was asked why he did not fire the troublesome J. Edgar Hoover, who had headed the FBI's predecessor organisation and then the FBI since 1924. Johnson is said to have replied that he would rather have Hoover inside the tent pissing out than outside the tent pissing in (sorry about the language, but they are LBJ's words not mine).

Disraeli was left disappointed and resentful by his failure to obtain office in 1841, and it is fair to assume that he was angry too. However, for a time, this was hardly apparent and he supported Peel for the next couple of years or rather longer. He sought to become an expert on international affairs and attacked the foreign policy of the previous Whig government. He had abandoned his excessively flamboyant style of address and behaviour, and his speaking and debating skills had progressed notably. He was most definitely an effective speaker in parliament, and in 1842, he worsted Lord Palmerston in a debate.

In 1842, he became the leader of what became known as the Young England Group. This included three backbench Conservative MPs, George Smythe, Lord John Manners, and Alexander Baillie-Cochrane. They were young, quite a bit younger than Disraeli who was thirty-seven at the time, and unlike Disraeli, they were aristocrats who had progressed to parliament from Eton College and university.

If we are being harsh, we might say that some of the group's views encapsulated a ridiculous, romantic throwback to a bygone age of feudalism. Smythe even wanted to revive the royal practice of touching as a cure for scrofula. To be more kind, we might say that their views stressed the obligations of the landowning classes to look after the interests of the poor. The grouping lasted until 1845. It broke up partly due to the participants' different views on the government's proposed grant to the Maynooth seminary.

During the mid-1840s, Disraeli wrote a trio of novels. They were *Coningsby* (published in 1844), *Sybil* (published in 1845), and *Tancred* (published in 1847). All three were political, and barely disguised politicians of the time featured in them. They were not at all kind to Peel. Disraeli later wrote that *Coningsby* considered the origin and condition of political parties, *Sybil* considered the condition of the people, and *Tancred* considered the condition of that race who had been the founders of Christianity.[11]

The novel *Sybil* was responsible for the introduction of the phrase 'ONE NATION CONSERVATISM' into the English language. It is still used today and is indelibly linked to Disraeli and his policies. The following is a celebrated passage from the book:

> Two nations; between whom there is no intercourse and no sympathy; who are as ignorant of each other's habits, thoughts and feelings, as if they were dwellers in different zones, or inhabitants of different planets; who are formed by a different breeding, are fed by a different food, are ordered by different manners, and are not governed by the same laws.
> 'You speak of—' said Egremont, hesitatingly.
> 'THE RICH AND THE POOR.'

Gladstone read the book and wrote two pages of notes about his views on it. He thought that the characters spent too much time chattering on subjects of which it is impossible that they can know anything, but he thought that the political scenes were 'capital'. He further thought that the book brilliantly exposed 'the two-faced effects of the Peel legislation'.[12]

From 1843, Disraeli became increasingly antagonistic towards Peel. He attacked the government on Ireland and on foreign policy, and he voted against the Canada Corn Bill. He asked for a job for his brother, but Peel turned down the request.

In February 1844, Peel omitted to send him the circular letter sent to all his supporters, summoning them to attend the forthcoming parliamentary session. Disraeli wrote to him protesting in strong terms. Peel's reply said that he had honestly doubted that he could be counted as one of his supporters, but expressed satisfaction that he had been proved wrong. He added: 'I am unconscious on having on any occasion treated you with the want of that Respect or Courtesy which I readily admit was your due. If I did so, the act was wholly unintentional on my part'.[13]

In April 1845, Disraeli landed a significant blow on Gladstone, the man who would be his rival and enemy for the next thirty-six years. It was on the Maynooth Bill and followed Gladstone's contorted speech trying to explain why he would vote for it. This was following his resignation because he opposed it. His position was absurd and he presented a very easy target.

Disraeli was very effective in pointing out the ridiculous contradictions. His speech and vote were of course another slap in the face for Peel.

Why was Disraeli so antagonistic towards Peel? There were certainly policy differences, but Peel's manner grated on him. Douglas Hurd (with Edward Young) says that 'Everything about Peel grated on Disraeli. He disliked his manner, his speeches and his vocabulary. To Disraeli, Peel was like a second-rate schoolmaster, always lecturing and moralising in slow plodding detail'.[14] However, Hurd goes on to say that the overwhelming reason was self-advancement. The destruction of Peel was the key to Disraeli's future political success.

The stage was set for the epic battle over the repeal of the Corn Laws.

PART IV

The Feud:
1846–1881

8
1846–1847

The issue that exacerbated the animosity between Disraeli and Gladstone was the repeal of the Corn Laws in 1846. The feud lasted for thirty-five years, right up to Disraeli's death in 1881. The repeal ended the premiership of Sir Robert Peel and triggered the events leading to the realignment of the political parties. Among other things, it caused a massive division in the country and in parliament, and by no means least it propelled Disraeli from the backbenches to a leading position in the Conservative Party. It is so important that it is appropriate to set the scene of the events.

The Corn Laws were introduced in 1815 by Lord Liverpool's Tory government. They were designed to keep grain prices high to the great benefit of the landowners and, it was claimed, serve the national interest by giving them an incentive to increase production. Keeping imported grain out of the country and consequently keeping bread prices high was, of course, greatly to the disadvantage of the poor, almost all of whom did not have the vote.

The 1815 Act set a price of 80*s* a quart, which was almost eight bushels. Only when the price of domestically produced grain reached this figure was the import of foreign grain permitted. In fact, it was not until 1848 that this amount was reached. Initially, there was an outright ban, but later taxes were imposed that had much the same effect. The figure of 80*s* was reduced in 1822 and again in 1828, both times by Tory governments. On the latter occasion, a sliding scale was introduced, but the barrier was prohibitively high. In 1842, Peel's Conservative government enacted a further reduction.

By 1845, most Whig MPs favoured a repeal of the Corn Laws, but the party had not done it when in government. Whig Prime Minister Lord Melbourne once said to his cabinet: 'Now is it to lower the price of corn or isn't it? It is not much matter which we say, but mind, we must all say the same'.[1]

The times since 1815 had been turbulent, and the Corn Laws had caused great discontent. Periodic bad harvests had exacerbated the situation and the last straw in late 1845 was the start of the terrible Irish famine.

Gladstone's twenty months outside parliament were intensely frustrating, mainly for him of course, but also for Peel. This was not least because his highly regarded oratorical and debating skills would have been invaluable for pressing the case for repeal and rebuffing Disraeli's onslaught. Instead, Gladstone was forced to watch from the gallery and give support and advice from outside. For the first six of these months, he was, although not an MP, secretary of state for war and colonies.

Gladstone did not enjoy a happy or particularly successful period in this office, and he was not able to look back on it with much satisfaction. He put out feelers for a number of parliamentary seats but was not successful. He came closest at Wigan and his failure was a considerable tribute to his abilities in parliament. The Whigs had petitioned for the by-election, but when they learnt that Gladstone was the likely Conservative candidate, they withdrew the petition. This was to protect themselves from his firepower at a critical time.

By late 1845, Peel had come to the conclusion that the national interest, as he saw it, had to come before the interests of himself and his party. He knew that getting the support of his cabinet and party would be very difficult, but he thought that it could be done. When he told the cabinet of his intention to repeal the Corn Laws, the news leaked and the reception within his party was hostile. Peel then thought it right to resign in order to allow the Whigs, led by Lord John Russell, to push the measure through. He did try to resign, but party difficulties prevented Russell from forming an administration. Party difficulties prevented Russell forming an administration. Palmerston would only serve as foreign secretary, and this was not acceptable to all Russell's intended cabinet. So the poisoned chalice returned to Peel. He picked it up and pressed on.

Temporary suspension of the Corn Laws for the duration of the Irish famine and difficulties in Britain would have had a better chance of getting through, but Peel did not take this route. It was to be repeal, whole repeal, and nothing but repeal. Nevertheless, cliff edge termination was not proposed. The bill provided for phased reduction over three years, but leading to total abolition. This did nothing to appease the critics.

Peel managed to get the somewhat reluctant support of most of his cabinet, but Stanley (the future Lord Derby) was a prominent exception. This was the man who would lead the Conservative Party for twenty-two years, all but for three brief periods as prime minister with Disraeli as chancellor of the Exchequer, as leader of the opposition. Peel woefully failed to get the support of most of his MPs who were not holding a government position. Many of his ministers were in the Lords, and the burden of getting the bill through the Commons would weigh heavily on his shoulders. He badly missed Gladstone.

Peel's Conservative opponents in the Commons had a problem. They had the numbers but were short of talent. To put it bluntly, they were not an impressive group. The two men who stepped forward to fill the void were Disraeli and Lord George Bentinck. Disraeli had a great deal of talent, especially of a certain kind. He was determined, organised, and had become a very effective debater, particularly when he was out to destroy someone or something. He supplied what was needed. However, he was something of an outsider, slippery, and not always to be trusted.

Bentinck brought an aristocratic background, an impeccable pedigree, and a faultless position as a representative of the landowning class that was about to be disadvantaged. He was the second son of the 4th duke of Portland. He had been an MP for many years, but, like many of his colleagues, he had made little contribution to parliament. What he had contributed to was horse racing and gambling. His achievements included the exposure of a fraud connected to the running of the 1844 Derby. It is a race for three-year-old horses, but the purported winner was actually four years old. He was passionate in his opposition to repeal and surprisingly effective. Irreverent wits dubbed the Disraeli–Bentinck duo 'The Jew and the Jockey'.

What was Disraeli's motivation in so vehemently opposing repeal? Three theories have been advanced. One is that he genuinely believed that retaining the Corn Laws was in the public interest. Very few people think this, and it is pertinent to point out that when, much later, he might have been able to bring them back, he did not do so.

The second theory, quite widely believed, is that he did not have strong views one way or the other. Stanley, the future Conservative prime minister, later told Queen Victoria that he did not think that Mr Disraeli had ever had a strong feeling one way or the other about protection.[2] However, Disraeli did believe that political parties should be true to their principles and the class that they represented, which in the case of the Conservatives was the landowning class. If the Corn Laws were to be repealed, it should be done by the Whigs.

The third theory is that principles had nothing to do with it. He hated Peel and he hated the fact that he had not held office. He once said of the prime minister: 'The Right Honourable Gentleman's smile is like the silver fittings on a coffin', and on another occasion, 'The Right Honourable Gentleman is reminiscent of a poker. The only difference is that a poker gives off occasional signs of warmth'. Disraeli wanted revenge and he wanted to advance his career. For what it is worth, this is closest to my own view.

Peel presented his bill to the House of Commons on the evening of 24 January 1846. His speeches were generally worthy but uninspiring, and this one was no exception. It was full of facts and figures, but dull. He sat down to a silent reception. Replying for the Whig opposition, Russell spoke in much the same way. He was boring. He did, of course, have a dilemma sometimes faced by leaders of the opposition. He wanted to embarrass the government but support the measure.

Shortly after this, Disraeli seized the initiative and electrified the House. He grabbed attention. He was funny. He was wounding, sarcastic, and inspiring. In short, his speech was a masterpiece. Just one example of his sarcastic wit must suffice. He compared Peel with the admiral of the Ottoman fleet, who, on taking command, had steered the Sultan's entire navy into the enemy's port. He quoted the admiral as saying: 'I have an objection to war'.[3] His oration finished with: 'Above all maintain the line of demarcation between the parties; for it is only by maintaining the independence of party that you can maintain the integrity of public men, and the power and influence of Parliament itself'.[4] He sat down to roars of approval from the Conservative benches. 'The skies are black enough,' commented Gladstone.[5]

Peel's motion to take the bill into committee was backed by only 112 Conservatives. Disraeli, Bentinck, and 240 other Conservatives voted against or abstained, so Peel was backed by just less than a third of his party. However, the votes of the Whigs and the radicals gave him a majority of ninety-seven. On 6 May, Gladstone gave his first cabinet dinner and it was a sombre evening. Afterwards, he gloomily wrote: 'We were thirteen'.[6] This was an obvious reference to the last supper, just before the arrest and crucifixion of Jesus.

On 15 May, the debate on the third reading of the bill was Disraeli's greatest triumph, surpassing his earlier contribution. He spoke for just over three hours and lacerated the prime minister. It was bitter, personal, excoriating, and devastatingly effective. There was a final twist to come. Peel, for reasons still debated, did not take an opportunity to expose Disraeli as a liar. As Mr Profumo discovered to his cost 117 years later, the House takes a firm line when it is lied to.

Speaking after Disraeli, Peel commented that taking into account his views, it was surprising that he had asked for a job in his government. He said: 'Surely this desire to unite his fortunes with mine in office [implies] the strongest proof which any public man can give of confidence in the honour and integrity of a Minister of the Crown'. This was a reference to Disraeli's 1841 letter in which he had asked for office. Peel quite possibly had the letter with him, but at the least could almost certainly have produced it later. Some MPs thought that he fingered a piece of paper in his pocket.[7]

Disraeli could and should have ignored this taunt, but instead he leapt to his feet and denied that he had ever done any such thing. It was an appalling risk, but he got away with it. Peel, ever the gentleman, did not produce the letter. He just made a dismissive remark. Peel got his bill through, but the victory came at a terrible cost. Only 106 of the 328 Conservatives who voted gave him their support. He needed the votes of the Whigs and the radicals.

Peel was defeated and exhausted, and his time as prime minister did not have long to run. A month later, Disraeli and the protectionists had their revenge. Combining with many of the Whigs, they defeated his Irish Coercion

Bill. This time, a majority of the Conservatives supported the prime minister, but there were not enough of them.

The beaten and demoralised Peel then had a choice. He could resign or he could ask the queen for dissolution and a general election. His strong inclination was to resign and most of his battered cabinet accepted this. Two who urged him to choose an election were Gladstone and the duke of Wellington. Gladstone was particularly strong in urging this, but his advice was rejected. Peel chose resignation.

Gladstone disliked Disraeli and was contemptuous of his tactics, but he had no hesitation in acknowledging his achievement. He wrote that 'Dizzy's parliamentary brains had brought down the government' and that 'His performances in the House were quite as wonderful as the report makes them'.[8] Forty-five years later, Gladstone told John Morley that Disraeli's performances against Peel were 'quite as wonderful as report makes them. Peel altogether helpless in reply'.[9]

It was time for the Whigs to take over, and Lord John Russell accepted the queen's invitation to form a government. The ubiquitous Palmerston was foreign secretary, and this time his appointment was not an insuperable problem. The Conservatives informally split. Some of them stayed loyal to Peel, and their number included Gladstone from outside parliament. They became known as the 'Peelites'. The remainder were under the informal leadership of Bentinck and Disraeli. The duke of Argyll shrewdly commented that Disraeli was 'like a subaltern in a great battle where every superior officer was killed or wounded'.[10]

Gladstone's unsatisfactory six months as a cabinet minister without a seat in parliament came to an end. In another example of his peerless way with words, Roy Jenkins commented that his position was like 'putting Napoleon in charge of army supply while forbidding him to fight any campaigns, except that Napoleon would have been better at intendance than Gladstone was at exercising calm judgement on delicate colonial issues'.[11] For anyone, like myself, not familiar with the word 'intendance', it means 'an administrative department, especially one in the government system introduced by the French statesman Richelieu in the 17th century'. Gladstone, with some qualifications, felt that the Russell government made a good start. However, he was dispirited and considered withdrawing from public life. Fortunately for his country, you may think, and fortunately for the sales of this book, he did not do so.

The next general election was held a year later in July–August 1847. Disraeli had no difficulty in being re-elected, this time as one of the two members for Buckinghamshire. He held this constituency, sometimes unopposed, until going to the House of Lords in 1876.

Gladstone managed to secure a seat, this time as one of the two members for Oxford University. It was a very unusual seat, not least because there were a large number of electors and they were very widely scattered. This made campaigning extremely difficult. Religion played a very large part and this caused the high church Gladstone some problems. Apart from anything else, his brother, Tom, said that he would not vote for him. This was either because of his low church inclinations or just possibly because of brotherly jealousy. Their mutual father firmly instructed Tom that he had to vote for his brother, and he duly did so.

9
1847–1851

Their wives were very different, but Disraeli enjoyed a happy marriage with Mary Anne, and Gladstone enjoyed a happy marriage with Catherine. It is important to make this point because Gladstone's sexual urges, his reading of pornography, his work trying to rescue prostitutes, and his friendships with courtesans attract great interest and are relevant to understanding the man.

Gladstone's work trying to rescue prostitutes lasted forty years and so could be considered through much of this book. However, his activities were most intense during the period covered by this chapter, and although they are mentioned from time to time, the whole story is told here.

What was his motivation in helping prostitutes, which he called his rescue work? How much was Christian charity and a wish to help distressed women? How much was to gratify his sexual feelings? Let us consider the evidence.

A strong case can be made for Christian charity. Inevitably, the number of his failures greatly exceeded the number of his successes, but he tried hard to help and occasionally he succeeded. Furthermore, he provided very considerable sums of money to provide refuges for prostitutes trying to lead a different life. He also helped found the St Barnabas refuge in Soho.

Also in support of Christian charity is the fact that he took no steps to keep what he was doing secret. His wife knew and supported him. His colleagues knew, and although they were often uneasy, they generally accepted his motives. Numerous prostitutes knew and many of them resented it. Brothel madams knew and were sometimes angry because his presence outside was bad for trade. There was an attempt to blackmail him and he reported the blackmailer to the police. In certain quarters, it was no secret. At one time, a scurrilous rhyme circulated. It ran 'Eight little whores, with no hope of heaven, Gladstone might save one, and then there'll be seven'.[1]

Two things in particular point to satisfaction of his sexual needs being part of his motivation. The first is that, in London, his rescue work was conducted exclusively in the West End. He did nothing for the desperate harlots of the

East End. The women and girls of the more prosperous West End were much more physically attractive. Henry Labouchère, a Liberal MP, commented:

> Gladstone manages to combine his missionary meddling with a keen appreciation of a pretty face. He has never been known to rescue any of our East End whores, nor for that matter is it easy to contemplate his rescuing any ugly woman and I am quite sure his conception of the Magdalen is of incomparable example of pulchritude with a superb figure and carriage.[2]

The second and more compelling pointer to Gladstone's sexual needs being at least part of the motivation is the evidence of his diaries, which only started being made available to the public in the 1960s. He meticulously recorded his activities and sometimes commented at length on a particular woman. He also recorded his pornographic reading and that he was ashamed of it. He would usually put these remarks in a foreign language, often Italian.

At times, he felt that he should be punished, and for some years in middle age, he would physically chastise himself with what seems to have been a scourge or a very small whip. When he did this, he put a small diagram of a scourge at the appropriate place in his diary. No one else was involved and no marks were visible on his clothed body. We are left wondering how hard and on what part of his anatomy the scourge struck. We also wonder if marks were left and if his wife saw them.

Earlier in this chapter, the question was posed whether his rescue work was Christian charity or because of his sexual feelings. It seems clear that it was both.

The attempted blackmail took place in 1853 when Gladstone was chancellor of the Exchequer. A rather pathetic young man, who was unemployed, saw him talking to two prostitutes and threatened to expose him unless he was given a government job. Gladstone told the police and the blackmailer was convicted and sentenced to twelve months' hard labour. The merciful Gladstone asked the home secretary, Lord Palmerston, to intervene, and he was released after just two months.

In July 1859, Gladstone started a friendship with a courtesan by the name of Marian Summerhayes. He described her as 'full in the highest sense of interest and beauty'.[3] He met her almost daily, and shortly after their friendship started, he commissioned her portrait. It was reportedly an excellent painting and showed her to be very attractive. The friendship continued at an intense level and they corresponded when he was away from London. In September, perhaps realising that his infatuation was dangerous, he wrote: 'My thoughts of Summerhayes need to be limited and purged'.[4] Nevertheless, he spent four and a half hours with her shortly afterwards. In December of the same year, the lady married a Mr Dale, or at least came under his protection. After this,

Gladstone only met her or wrote to her infrequently. In 1867, her rehabilitation lapsed and she returned to her old ways. Gladstone later destroyed her letters.

Ten years after his infatuation with Marian Summerhayes, he embarked on another close relationship with a courtesan, this time a retired one. Her name was Laura Thistlethwayte and she was aged forty at the time. Gladstone was nineteen years older and was in his first year as prime minister. As with Marian Summerhayes, he later destroyed her letters. Laura came from a respectable family in Northern Ireland. Reports may not be entirely reliable, but it appears that she was a teenage prostitute in Belfast and Dublin. On coming to London, her fortunes improved enormously and the term courtesan became appropriate. One of her associations was with the king of Nepal who was spending an extended period in London. He was fabulously wealthy and he was extremely generous with the gifts that he showered upon her. When she was aged twenty-four, she married the wealthy and respectable Captain Frederick Thistlethwayte. It was not a happy marriage.

Around the time of her marriage, she became a reformed courtesan. Not only that, she became religious and started giving religious lectures. This, of course, pleased Gladstone, but her religious views were by no means the same as his. Roy Jenkins describes them as 'half-baked theosophical ideas'.[5] For several months, Gladstone's relationship was intense and it took a lot of his time. They met very frequently and corresponded extensively. Gladstone started his letters 'Dear Spirit', and she gave him an engraved ring, which he wore.

One gains the impression that she enjoyed leading him on. After the relationship cooled, they stayed in touch, though much less frequently. Captain Thistlethwayte was tolerant of his wife's close friendship. However, in 1887, he shot himself. It is not clear whether it was suicide or an accident. Had details of Gladstone's closeness to Laura Thistlethwayte been generally known, it might have been more damaging to his reputation than his rescue work with prostitutes. She was an attractive woman who had already rescued herself.

Gladstone did not stop his rescue walks until his late seventies, when he promised his private secretary that he would do so. Even then, he made it a condition that he would continue to be available to anyone who approached him for help and that he would continue working with existing cases. He was eighty before he stopped completely.

Eighteen months before he died, Gladstone wrote a letter to his son, the Reverend Stephen Gladstone. It was in a sealed enveloped marked to be opened only after his death. In fact, Stephen waited two years after his father's demise before doing so. The letter read:

> With reference to rumours which I believe were one time afloat, though I know not with what degree of currency: and also with reference to the times when I shall not be here to answer for myself; I desire to record my solemn declaration

and assurance, as in the sight of God and before His judgement seat, that at no period of my life have I been guilty of the act which is known as that of infidelity to the marriage bed. I limit myself to this negation, and I record it with my dear son Stephen, both as the eldest surviving of our sons, and as my pastor. It will be for him to retain or use it, confidentially unless necessity should require more, which is unlikely: and in any case making it known to his brothers.

I believe him, but the denial of 'the act which is known as that of infidelity to the marriage bed' is rather curiously phrased. It invites speculation about behaviour that may have taken place outside the terms of it. The men and circumstances are very different, but it puts one in mind of President Clinton saying 'I did not have sexual relations with that woman, Miss Lewinsky'. It might depend on what is meant by the term sexual relations. Under some interpretations, Clinton may have been telling the truth. It is also pertinent to mention that the legal interpretation of it varies in some states in America.

The story of Gladstone's rescue work, his other behaviour, and his motivations has a postscript set in 1927, nearly thirty years after his death. William Gladstone's sons, Herbert Gladstone (1st Viscount Gladstone) and Henry Gladstone (1st Baron Gladstone of Hawarden), managed to clear their father's name and circumvent the obstacle that normally prevents a legal action clearing a dead person's reputation.

Captain Peter Wright had written a book with the title *Portraits and Criticisms*, and it contained many allegations about the former prime minister. They included that he had fathered an illegitimate child and had enjoyed a string of liaisons with prostitutes, ex-courtesans (including Lillie Langtree), and even a female Russian spy.

The Gladstone brothers vehemently insulted Wright in an open letter to the press with the result that Wright sued them for defamation. The case was *Wright v. Gladstone*, and it hinged on whether or not Wright's allegations were true. The jury decided that they were not and found for the Gladstones. Furthermore, they added the rider that the evidence placed before them had completely vindicated the reputation of the late Mr W. E. Gladstone. The verdict was greeted with enthusiasm in the court, outside the court, in the press, and in the country generally.

The verdict not only cleared the reputation of William Gladstone, it did the same for the various women named. Most of them were dead, but the blameless Lillie Langtree was still alive. The jury were not aware of William Gladstone's diary and its contents. It is fair to speculate what, if any, difference such knowledge might have made.

The 1847 general election returned 325 Conservatives, 292 Whigs, thirty-six Irish Repeal, and three others. The Conservatives were in the majority, but they were split. The Free Traders, led by Sir Robert Peel, were in the minority.

The Protectionists, led by Lord George Bentinck, were in the majority. Disraeli held a leading position under Bentinck, and Gladstone was firmly with the Free Traders, who became known as the Peelites. The two factions of the Conservative Party were not able to unite and form a government, so Russell and the Whigs continued in office. Stanley led the Protectionists in the Lords.

As detailed in the last chapter, Disraeli had taken a major part in bringing down the Peel government, and now had a very senior role in the Protectionist part of the Conservative Party. However, his party was split and his followers were distinctly unimpressive. There would not be a majority Conservative government until he formed one in 1874. In the intervening twenty-seven years, there would be three minority Conservative governments. They lasted a total of only three years and 280 days. Disraeli was chancellor of the Exchequer in each of them, and Stanley (Lord Derby from 1851) was prime minister in all three. During the same period, Gladstone was twice chancellor of the Exchequer and his periods in this office totalled seven and a half years.

There is considerable scope for confusion in the use of the names Stanley and Derby. Edward Stanley was the heir to the 13th earl of Derby and sat in the Commons with the courtesy title Lord Stanley. He went to the Lords in 1844 with the title Lord Stanley. In 1851, his father died and he became the 14th earl of Derby. He was prime minister in 1852, 1858–59, and 1866–68. It gets worse. His son was also called Edward Stanley, and like his father, he also used the courtesy title Lord Stanley. On the death of his father in 1869, he became the 15th earl of Derby. Before this, he sat in the Commons from 1848 until 1869. He was secretary of state for foreign affairs in 1866–68 and again in 1874–78. The son was a friend of Disraeli but eventually they fell out.

Following the fall of Peel and the succession of Russell, Disraeli spent many years manoeuvring to try and gain power by means of alliances with the Peelites, the Whigs, the Radicals, and even the Irish. This did no favours to his reputation as a man lacking in principles, but on one issue, he acted out of principle and to his disadvantage. This was his support for the Jewish Disabilities Bill.

In the 1847 general election, the Jewish Lionel de Rothschild was elected as one of the Whig candidates for the City of London constituency. As a practising Jew, his conscience did not allow him to take the required Christian oath and he was not able to take his seat. Following this, Lord John Russell's Bill was introduced to allow Jews (but not atheists or the followers of other religions) to sit in parliament.

The bill was opposed by many of Disraeli's colleagues, and as a baptised member of the Church of England, he could easily have opposed it. However, he thought that it was right in principle and he was always proud of his Jewish heritage. He therefore spoke in favour of the bill and voted for it. However, his stated reasons for doing so were highly obscure and he sat down to total silence.

The fiercely Anglican Gladstone might also have been expected to oppose the bill, particularly as his Oxford University constituents were Anglican Protestants and many did not want it. However, he too spoke in favour of the bill and voted for it. His speech, like Disraeli's, put forward convoluted arguments and was far from being his best. One of his points was that there would only be a very few Jewish MPs so it did not matter very much. This was true, but it was hardly a principled contention. The Jewish Disabilities Bill passed the Commons but was defeated in the Lords. Jews were not permitted to sit in parliament until 1858.

Bentinck was the leader of the Protectionist element of the Conservative Party in the Commons, and like Disraeli, he supported the Jewish Disabilities Bill. This so annoyed his colleagues that in December 1847 he gave up the leadership. As there were no viable alternatives with the drive and talent of Bentinck and Disraeli, the two men led informally in the 1848 session.

Bentinck and Disraeli were close personally, as well as close politically, and in an act of extraordinary generosity, Bentinck gave him massive financial assistance. On 6 September 1848, Disraeli completed the purchase of Hughenden Manor, which is on the edge of High Wycombe and in his Buckinghamshire constituency. The estate was 750 acres (later increased to 1,400 by enclosures and purchases). The price was £35,000 and Disraeli was still heavily in debt. Much of the money was loaned by Bentinck and his two brothers.

It could have gone horribly wrong. Bentinck died suddenly just two weeks after completion, leaving Disraeli owing £25,000 to his two brothers and to him. Fortunately, the two brothers were magnificent and did not call for the repayment of the loans.

Hughenden had a beneficial and major impact on the rest of his life. It made him a country gentleman. He loved it and, henceforth, he split his time between living there and living in central London. Trees became one of his passions, and he supervised the planting of a vast number. This provides an interesting contrast with Gladstone who enjoyed chopping them down, though it is often overlooked that he replaced them with saplings. Hughenden Manor is now owned by the National Trust and open to the public.

There is an interesting footnote to the purchase of Hughenden, and it is revealing of Disraeli's character. In 1880, Disraeli asked the then head of the Bentinck family to visit him at Hughenden. This was the twenty-two-year-old duke of Portland, who was serving in the Coldstream Guards. The young man was understandably nervous. Disraeli came down for dinner resplendent in the blue riband of the garter. The two men, plus Disraeli's secretary, ate the meal in almost total silence. When the meal was over, Disraeli, who was in the last year of his life, rose and said: 'My Lord Duke I come from a race that never forgets an injury, nor forgets a benefit'.[6]

Lord Stanley, sitting in the Lords, was the undisputed leader of the Protectionist part of the Conservative Party, and Disraeli's career was very closely linked to his for the next twenty years. Stanley did not much like him, and it was a partnership of convenience. The two men's approach to politics differed. Stanley had many other interests, including and especially horse racing. In his spare time, he translated the whole of *The Iliad* into blank verse.[7] One suspects that no modern prime minister would do that for fun. Enoch Powell was never prime minister, but he just might have been an exception.

Stanley's antipathy dated back to 1831. His younger brother had accompanied Disraeli from Falmouth to London on the last part of his Middle East tour. On arriving in the capital, his brother had gone missing. After an extensive search, he was found at what Douglas Hurd and Edward Young describe as the home of the notorious money-lender Effie Bond. Furthermore, he said that Disraeli had introduced him there.[8] Richard Aldous says the same but indicates that it was a notorious house of ill-repute and that he had taken rooms there.[9] Whatever the exact circumstances, Stanley held Disraeli partly responsible.

The truth was that regardless of their feelings, Stanley and Disraeli needed each other. It is stretching the comparison to breaking point, but there is some similarity to two show-business performers who do not get on but are in a successful and long-running double act. Jimmy Jewel and Hylda Baker are said to be examples.

Disraeli was clearly in many ways the ablest of the Protectionist Conservatives in the Commons, but he did not have the trust of many of his colleagues. William Beresford, a Party Whip, was just one of many who held these views. He said that he would sooner trust a convicted felon than Disraeli.[10] Partly because of these attitudes and partly because of his own inclinations, Stanley did not want Disraeli to lead in the Commons. On 21 December 1848, he wrote to him and, while praising his abilities highly and saying that he would have a commanding position, said that he should not be leader.

This was not acceptable to Disraeli, and he refused to serve under another leader. His letter of reply said: '… in the present distracted state of parties, it is my opinion that I could do more to uphold the cause to which I am attached … by acting alone and unshackled, than if I fell into the party disciple, which you intimate'.[11] Stanley needed him and a compromise was arranged. Disraeli would be part of a triumvirate of leaders alongside Lord Granby and J. C. Herries.

This was never going to work because the other two men were nonentities. Within a few days, Disraeli was the undisputed leader. Lord Aberdeen noted that the triumvirate was like the one that had briefly ruled France in the 1790s, comprising Napoleon Bonaparte, Sièyes, and Ducos. There was never any doubt that Napoleon Bonaparte would soon become the sole leader.[12]

In June 1850, Sir Robert Peel, one of the country's greatest prime ministers, was thrown from his horse, and after eighty agonised hours, he died. He was sixty-two. Gladstone seconded the motion for the House of Commons to adjourn, but according to Roy Jenkins, his reaction was surprisingly cool.[13] Less surprisingly, Disraeli was also cool. He immediately discerned a possible political opportunity and speculated on the possibility of enticing Gladstone and Graham back from the Peelites. He thought that this might be done if there was a definitive abandonment of protection.

A few months later, Lord John Russell's Whig administration collapsed and the queen asked Stanley to form a government. According to Stanley's son—who was a friend of Disraeli and an MP—Disraeli, surprisingly, was willing to serve under Gladstone if he would join the government. Stanley asked Gladstone to join his proposed cabinet, and with only minor qualifications said that he could choose his position. Gladstone might or might not have agreed, but Stanley went on to say that he planned to restore a duty on corn. This was not acceptable and Gladstone declined the offer.

Stanley realised that his attempt to form a government would not succeed and is said to have remarked: 'These are not names that I can present to the Queen'. Disraeli was very despondent and Russell and the Whigs struggled on a bit longer. The Peelites remained intact without the presence of their former leader. Sir James Graham, Lord Aberdeen, and Gladstone were prominent among them.

The years 1847–51 were not Gladstone's happiest. He was back in parliament but not in government, and he was in the minority part of the opposition party. A comment that he made to his father in 1849 about Disraeli is telling. He said: 'It is a very unsatisfactory state of things to have to deal with a man whose objects appear to be those of personal ambition and who is not thought to have any strong convictions of any kind upon public matters'.[14] Gladstone's personal life was not at its best and this was perhaps a factor in the high volume of his rescue work with prostitutes at this time. His melancholy mood was reflected in his diary entry for his fortieth birthday on 29 December 1849:

> And this day I am forty years old. Forty years long hath God been grieved with me—hath with much long suffering endured me! Alas I cannot say better of myself. The retrospect of my inward life is dark.... In some things I may seem to improve a little: but the flesh and the devil if not the world still have fearful hold upon me.[15]

Five months earlier, a fruitless and rather ridiculous wild goose chase had probably contributed to his sombre mood. He travelled round Italy to try to persuade Lady Lincoln to return to the path of righteousness and the arms of her husband.

Lord Lincoln was his Eton and Oxford friend and heir to the duke of Newcastle. It was his recommendation to his father that had been instrumental in launching Gladstone's parliamentary career as MP for Newark. After five children and seventeen years of marriage, the possibly pregnant, though not by her husband, Lady Lincoln had decamped to Naples in the company of Lord Walpole. Lord Lincoln was, not surprisingly, upset, and Gladstone was more upset still and decided to intervene. His wife shared his concern and, had she not been heavily pregnant herself, would probably have gone with him. Instead, she wrote a letter to 'Dear Suzie' for her husband to take and give to Lady Lincoln.

On arriving at Naples, he found that 'Dear Suzie' had moved northwards because she did not want to see him. Furthermore, and worse, he learnt that she was indeed pregnant. After a number of stops, he did finally catch up with her, but she refused his entreaties. With nothing more to be done, he returned home. Meticulous record keeper that he was, he recorded that he had travelled 3,010 miles and been away for twenty-seven days. His sanctimonious diary entry recorded his feelings:

> Oh that poor miserable Lady L.—once the dream of dreams, the image that to my young age combined everything that earth could offer of beauty and of joy. What is she now! But may that Spotless Sacrifice whereof I partook, unworthy as I am, today avail for her, to the washing away of sin and the renewal of the image of God.[16]

Lord Lincoln subsequently obtained a divorce by an Act of Parliament. His father died in 1851 and his former wife was denied the title of duchess of Newcastle.

In these difficult few years, one thing that must have cheered him was the rapid and seemingly miraculous recovery in the health of his sister, Helen. In the autumn of 1848, Cardinal Wiseman touched her with a holy relic and conducted a makeshift religious service. Helen improved dramatically and almost instantaneously, and what is more, the recovery lasted. Gladstone thought that his sister had been the subject of an illusion typical of the trickery of the Church of Rome, but he must have been thankful for the result.

Gladstone would have enjoyed two very well-received parliamentary speeches in 1850 and 1851, though both times he was on the losing side. The first of these was in the Don Pacifico debate in June 1850.

Don Pacifico was a Portuguese Jew who happened to have been born in Gibraltar. Crucially, this enabled him to claim British protection. He was a controversial and, many would say unscrupulous, man, who had been the Portuguese consul general to Greece. In 1847, an anti-Semitic mob had attacked his house in Athens. The son of a government minister was part of the mob, and the police did nothing to prevent the attack. Pacifico's house was badly damaged and much of its contents were destroyed or stolen. Pacifico justifiably claimed compensation from the Greek government, but in the government's view (and the view of many others), the amount asked for was wildly excessive.

The claim made no progress and he appealed to the British government for help. The foreign secretary, Lord Palmerston, was noted for gunboat diplomacy, and the affair ended with the British Navy blockading Greek ports for eight weeks. The Greek government then agreed to compensate Pacifico.

A splendid victory for Palmerston one might say, but many in Britain thought that his action had been seriously disproportionate to the underlying grievance. A vote of censure on Palmerston was passed in the Lords, and this was followed by a similar debate and vote in the Commons.

It was one of the most famous parliamentary occasions of all time. Gladstone supported the censure motion, and he spoke for nearly three hours. It was an exceptionally fine speech, but it was overshadowed by an incredible oration by Palmerston. The foreign secretary spoke for nearly five hours. Its most memorable assertion was 'As the Roman, in days of old, held himself free from indignity when he could say, Civis Romanus sum, so also a British subject, in whatever land he may be, shall feel confident that the watchful eye and strong arm of England will protect him from injustice and wrong'. The censure vote failed by forty-six votes. Gladstone recorded that Disraeli's speech was 'below the mark, though he seemed in earnest'.

Gladstone's second oratorical triumph was on the second reading of the Ecclesiastical Titles Bill. Looking back from the twenty-first century, it is clear that this was an extreme piece of anti-Catholic nonsense. Quite a few of Lord John Russell's ministers thought so at the time, but the great libertarian had convinced himself that it was necessary. The Roman Catholic Church had set up a hierarchy of dioceses in England and Wales, and the bill sought to ban this. The bill was passed and became the Ecclesiastical Titles Act 1851. However, it was never properly implemented, and Gladstone's first government repealed it twenty years later. Gladstone opposed the 1851 Bill and voted against. Disraeli sided with Russell and voted in favour.

Gladstone's speech lasted just under two and a half hours. Lord Morley in the first great Gladstone biography published in 1903 wrote that 'it was in all its elements and aspects one of the great orator's three or four most conspicuous masterpieces'.[17] Morley served in Gladstone's last two governments and in the Liberal governments from 1905 to 1914. At the age of seventy-five, he was one of two cabinet members to resign because they opposed Britain's declaration of war on Germany.

At the time of the Ecclesiastical Titles Act and afterwards, Russell's government was in a poor state and it had not long to run. As described in the next chapter, 1852 was a turbulent year at Westminster. There were three prime ministers (Russell, Derby, and Aberdeen), three chancellors of the Exchequer (Wood, Disraeli, and Gladstone), and there was a general election. It was the year in which the poor relationship between Disraeli and Gladstone exploded into something more toxic.

10
1852

Disraeli had been very disappointed by Derby's failure to form a government, and he believed that the commitment to protection had played a significant part. It was not popular in the country and free trade was proving to be a success. He noted that 'every public man of experience and influence, however slight, had declined to act unless the principle of Protection were unequivocally renounced'.[1] He was determined to drop the policy on which he had defeated Peel. Derby was very reluctantly coming round to the same conclusion.

The end of Russell's Whig government and its replacement by Derby's Conservative administration came in February 1852. The catalyst was the action of the foreign secretary, Lord Palmerston, concerning events in France. Louis Napoleon had dissolved the National Assembly, made strategic arrests, and pronounced himself emperor. The foreign secretary was in the habit of acting unilaterally and not properly involving the cabinet and the queen.

The queen and, through her, Prince Albert, expected to be consulted and up to a point have the right to contribute and influence, and they certainly expected to be kept informed. Palmerston had not always done this and the queen had previously complained to the prime minister. Her rebuke had been communicated to Palmerston, with whom Russell did not enjoy good relations. Notwithstanding this, Palmerston had without consultation congratulated Louis Napoleon on his action. The queen, Prince Albert, and the cabinet were significantly displeased and in December 1851, under pressure from the queen, Russell fired him.

Palmerston was popular and had a lot of support in the country. He felt hard done by and, in his words, decided that he would have his tit for tat with Johnnie Russell. He did not have long to wait. A few weeks later, he joined forces with Disraeli and they defeated the Militia Bill. Russell and the government promptly resigned, and the queen once again turned to Lord Derby.

The manpower at Derby's disposal was no stronger than before, but this time he decided that he would put the names to the queen. Needless to say, Disraeli was very pleased. Derby's first administration is sometimes known as the 'Who? Who?' government. Sitting on the benches in the House of Lords,

Derby communicated the names to the duke of Wellington. The duke was eighty-two, very deaf, and only had six months left to live. As the names were given to him, he repeatedly shouted 'Who? Who?' This was partly because he did not recognise many of the names.

Only Derby himself and two of his cabinet had previously held office, which meant that the rest had to be sworn in as Privy councillors. The only comparable situation was the first Labour government of Ramsay MacDonald in 1924. Neither MacDonald nor any of his cabinet had held office before.

Disraeli was leader of the House of Commons, and to his surprise, Derby asked him to be chancellor of the Exchequer. He was not obviously qualified for this because he had no particular preparation for it and, what is more, he had made a spectacular mess of his own finances. He demurred and put to Derby the first of these points, but not the second. Derby was not concerned. 'You know as much as Mr Canning did. They give you the figures,' he replied. This was true. In 1827, after just four months as prime minister and chancellor of the Exchequer, Canning had died in office. He came to the office with minimal experience of finance. Gladstone and the Peelites were very unimpressed with the quality of Derby's appointments. In a letter to his wife, Gladstone told her that Disraeli could not be worse placed.[2]

So, on 27 February 1852, Disraeli took office. He was forty-seven years old, and it was his first government position. He had longed for office and now he had it. In the remaining twenty-nine years of his life, he would be three times chancellor of the Exchequer and twice prime minister. Only in his second spell as prime minister would he serve in a government with a majority in the House of Commons. Gladstone, who was four years younger, did have government experience. Together with the rest of the Peelites, he had no position in Derby's administration. The Peelites were exhibiting differences. Some were showing signs of closeness to the Whigs. Gladstone and the others were not.

Gladstone was not in government, but it should not be thought that he was idle. He was never that. As an indication, he had recently finished the first two of the four volumes of his translation of Farini's *History of the Papal States from 1850–51*. In an article in the *Edinburgh Review*, he described the Pope's government as 'a foul blot upon the face of creation, an offence to Christendom and to mankind'.[3] Gladstone was a sincere and devout Christian, but most definitely not a pillar of the ecumenical movement.

The Peelites had the votes to quickly bring down Derby's government, but they decided that they should give it a chance. This was provided that there was an early general election, which was duly held in July. Disraeli and Derby decided that in the circumstances there would be an interim budget in April then, provided that they were still in office, a full budget towards the end of the year.

Disraeli had only a short time to prepare his interim budget, but, as Derby had promised, they give you the figures. Surprisingly, Disraeli followed the line of the 1851 budget delivered by Sir Charles Wood, his Whig predecessor. Wood was strong for free trade and Disraeli's performance was consistent with this.

It made him look unprincipled and inconsistent, but it was welcomed in many quarters. It did not, though, please many of the Protectionists sitting behind him, and it did not please the prime minister, Lord Derby, in the House of Lords. In a letter of complaint to Disraeli, he wrote: '... it was one of the strongest free trade speeches I have ever heard'.[4] Prince Albert commented: 'The Protectionists themselves (if one can any longer call them so) are a great deal startled and don't know what to make of the triumph of Peel which the very man gives him who hunted him down'.[5]

The general election was held during July. Derby decided to defer, issuing a definitive statement about his party's policy on protection until afterwards. Candidates stated their own positions and Disraeli's was clearly on the side of free trade. Gladstone and the other Peelites, although nominally Conservative, were of course free traders. Since the formation of Derby's government, they had, after considerable heart searching, elected to sit on the opposition benches with the Whigs.

The result of the election was an improvement for the Conservatives, but nevertheless a disappointment for them. At the time, party labels were sometimes fluid, so it is impossible to be precise, but the Conservatives secured around 330 seats. However, about forty of them were Peelites. The Whigs and their allies got about 324. As the Peelites were likely to side with the Whigs on many issues, the Conservatives were forced to continue as a minority government. Gladstone was re-elected for Oxford University and Disraeli was re-elected for Buckinghamshire, with Gladstone's result being gratifyingly better than the last time.

After the election, Disraeli wrote: 'We built up an opposition on Protection and Protestantism'. In a vulgar phrase, he continued: 'The first the country has positively pissed on'.[6] So it had, and Derby performed the last rites. His words were 'Free trade is now established and working more advantageously for the working classes than we anticipated ... on the part of myself and my colleagues I bow to the decision of the country'.[7]

The next parliamentary session opened in November, and it did so for the first time in the new House of Commons building constructed after the disastrous fire in 1834. Disraeli's budget was a keenly awaited and very important item of business. Before that, he did something that then and now seems incomprehensible, and which did his reputation no good at all.

The duke of Wellington had died in September. This was the very great military hero who had been twice prime minister, and who had inadvertently dubbed Derby's government the 'Who? Who?' ministry. It fell to Disraeli as leader of the House to pay tribute to the great man. In doing so, he very extensively and exactly copied the words used by the French writer Adolphe

Thiers, in an obituary of Maréchal St Cyr in 1829. The plagiarism was noticed. It seemed inexplicable and it still does.

The title of this book includes the word 'feud'. It is most certainly justified, but there are different views about when it started and how and when the mutual dislike built up. What cannot be doubted is that the feud went toxic in the early morning of 17 December 1852, and that it lasted until Disraeli's death in 1881. The catalyst was Gladstone's vituperative reply to Disraeli's budget speech.

This book dates the feud from the Corn Laws controversy in 1845–46, but the dislike had been building up progressively before that. Douglas Hurd and Edward Young say: 'As the years went on Gladstone's disapproval of Disraeli deepened into detestation. Politics brought the two men into unavoidable contact and increasingly they lined up on opposite sides'.[8] Despite this, Gladstone liked Mary Anne, Disraeli's wife, and felt no animosity towards her. He felt sorry that she had the misfortune to be married to such a dreadful man. Mary Anne did not see it that way at all. She was happy with her husband and happy with her marriage.

Looking back in later years, Gladstone admitted that 'a strong sentiment of revulsion for Disraeli personally, a sentiment quite distinct from that of dislike alone sufficient to deter me absolutely from a merely personal and separate reunion.'[9] Disraeli had similar feelings about Gladstone. Hurd and Young put it in these words: 'Disraeli, for his part, thought Gladstone was a hypocrite who could summon up reserves of bogus indignation to further his political purposes. He did not credit Gladstone with any genuine feeling. He was merely a self-righteous, but more negligible reincarnation of Robert Peel. More specifically Disraeli thought that Gladstone was a prig'.[10] Former Chancellor of the Exchequer Kenneth Clarke put it well in a television programme about the two men. He said that Gladstone thought that Disraeli was a charlatan and Disraeli thought that Gladstone was mad.

The mutual dislike between Disraeli and Gladstone had consequences. Shortly before Disraeli's budget, Derby met Gladstone on a social occasion and sounded him out about the possibility of him joining the government. Gladstone declined, and although he put it diplomatically, the difficulty, or indeed impossibility, of him working with Disraeli was one of his reasons. He told Derby that the Peelites were going to review their position after the budget. At this point, some of them were showing signs of wanting to move to the Whigs.

Disraeli suffered considerable misfortune in preparing and delivering his budget. He was very short of time, and he was suffering from a severe bout of influenza. Some people think that influenza is like a bad cold, but this is not the case. It is a significant illness, and it often leaves the unfortunate sufferer feeling weak for an appreciable time afterwards. 'They give you the figures,' Lord Derby had told him, and so they do, but the main person doing it was the chancellor's private secretary. He was suffering from influenza at exactly the same time.

To make matters worse, just before the budget, Disraeli had to sit through a very difficult debate. In order to embarrass the Conservatives and Disraeli in particular, a motion had been tabled stating that repeal of the Corn Laws had been a wise, just, and beneficial measure. This was amended to a compromise motion, but it was not easy for Disraeli who now espoused free trade but had brought down Peel on the issue. The debate lasted three nights and the ill chancellor had to sit through it.

A really serious problem was a war scare at precisely the wrong time. There was a fear that the newly enthroned Louis Napoleon planned a war between France and Britain. There was nothing in this and, indeed, in less than two years' time, France and Britain were allies in a war against Russia. Derby, who was under pressure from the queen, demanded that more money be found for the forces, especially the Royal Navy. With only three days left before he had to present the budget, Disraeli had to oblige, with the effect that the budget had a hole in it. He woefully told Derby: 'I fear we are in a great scrape and I hardly see how the budget can live in such a stormy sea'.[11]

Disraeli was one of many chancellors who over the years have suffered from a clamour for more military spending. Lloyd George, who needed money for pensions and other things, was a notable example. Prior to the First World War, he had to listen to shouts of 'We want eight and we won't wait'. This was a demand for additional dreadnought warships. Afterwards, Winston Churchill commented: 'The Admiralty wanted six ships, the economists offered four, and we finally compromised on eight'. It was perhaps fortunate that Britain did have the eight extra warships. During the war, Britannia ruled the waves, or at least she ruled the top of them. German submarines under the waves caused a lot of damage.

An irony was that, in the event, Britain's financial performance was quite a bit better than the budget assumptions. It was too late for Disraeli. By the time that this was known, Gladstone was the chancellor and he got the credit and the extra spending opportunity.

Nearly all budgets can be classed as political, and Disraeli's was most definitely no exception. It was rather a forlorn hope, but he wanted to get support in the House for the minority government in which he served. He wanted to continue free trade, which was proving successful. He wanted to appease traditional Conservative supporters who had suffered from free trade, or at least thought that they had, and he wanted to attract broad support in the country. In short, he wanted to square the circle and it was a very tall order.

He proposed to continue the income tax. This had been introduced by Pitt the Younger in 1799 in order to help pay for the Napoleonic Wars, and it had been repealed in 1816. Peel's Conservative government reintroduced it in 1842, but it was intended to be a temporary measure requiring annual renewal. In fact, it has never been repealed and is with us to this day. Not only did Disraeli propose to renew it, he proposed to adjust the schedules to make it yield more revenue. Furthermore, he proposed to differentiate between earned and unearned income. This created all sorts of practical difficulties. In another revenue raising measure, householders had to pay more because he proposed lowering the threshold for house tax and doubling the rate of it.

He proposed to halve the duty on malt, which pleased many land owners and all the beer drinkers. Other duties were to be reduced, and these mainly benefitted land owners, agricultural interests, sugar, and shipping interests. Many people thought that the package was unfair and Macauley said that the net effect was 'nothing but taking money out of the pockets of people in towns and putting it into the pockets of growers of malt'.[12]

Disraeli presented his budget to the House on 3 December. He was still suffering from the late stages of influenza, but his speech lasted the extraordinary period of just under five hours. Its length matched Palmerston's oration in the Don Pacifico debate. The general view was that the budget speech was very good, but that it was too long. This relates to the quality of the speech, not the quality of the budget's contents. It is interesting to contrast the length of this speech with the length of modern budgets. They normally last about fifty minutes. Gladstone strongly disliked Disraeli, and he expected to strongly dislike his budget. His expectation came to pass.

After a seven-day interval, the budget was debated in the House over four nights. During the four nights, Gladstone spoke twice. The full House sat as a committee of ways and means, which had the consequence that members could speak more than once. Gladstone spoke twice. He told his wife that it was 'the least conservative budget I have known'.[13] During the four nights of debate, the budget unravelled. Speaker after speaker picked holes in it.

It was the custom, but not the rule, that the chancellor spoke last and wound up the debate. Afterwards, the House would move to the division. Disraeli commenced his winding-up speech at 10.20 p.m. on 16 December and finished at 1 a.m. the following morning. The sense of drama was heightened by a violent and extremely unusual mid-winter thunderstorm that rocked the Palace of Westminster during his speech. He had suffered through four days of hostile debate and some of it had come from the Peelites, who seemed to be moving towards the Whigs. He expected to lose the vote.

Apart from one aspect, Disraeli's speech was compelling and excellent. Roy Jenkins says that Gladstone thought that it was brilliant.[14] The aspect that let the speech down was the vicious and personal way that he attacked his critics. For example, he said that his predecessor as chancellor, Sir Charles Wood, 'had yet to learn that petulance is not sarcasm, and insolence is not invective'. In the famous twentieth-century words of Dale Carnegie, it was not the way to win friends and influence people—not those people anyway.

The Feud: 1846–1881

Disraeli's remarkable speech ended with an assertion that claims a place in books of quotations: 'I know what I have to face. I have to face a coalition! The combination may be successful. A coalition has before been successful. But coalitions, although successful, have always found this, that their triumph has been brief. This too I know, that England does not love coalitions'. In saying this, he was acknowledging that he faced the combined votes of the Peelites, the Whigs, and the Radicals. It is debatable, but he had a point. Consider: in a referendum held in 2011, citizens of the UK were asked to vote on the question 'At present the UK uses the "first past the post" system to elect MPs to the House of Commons. Should the "alternative vote" system be used instead?' A 'yes' vote would very probably have resulted in almost continuous coalitions and minority governments—67.9 per cent voted 'no'.[15]

As the exhausted Disraeli sat down and the House prepared to divide, Gladstone sprang to his feet. Despite having already spoken at length twice during the four days of debate, he was demanding to make a full, detailed reply to Disraeli's speech. This caused dissention from the Conservatives and general uproar. The chairman initially tried to stop him, but he then relented and allowed him to do so.

It is sometimes said that Gladstone's decision to speak was spontaneous, but this is not correct. He had planned to do so, and he had prepared his speech carefully and at length. As he started to speak, it was clear that he was blazing with anger—at the budget, at the speech that he had just heard, and at his enemy the Right Honourable Benjamin Disraeli PC, MP. The feud already existed, but at that point, it moved up a gear and lasted until Disraeli's death twenty-eight years later. Edward Stanley MP, friend of Disraeli and son of the prime minister, commented: 'Gladstone's look when he rose to reply will never be forgotten by me. His usually calm features were livid and distorted with passion. His voice shook, and those who watched him feared an outbreak incompatible with parliamentary rules'.[16]

Over a cacophony of noise from the Conservative benches, Gladstone started by rebuking Disraeli for his vicious personal attacks on individual MPs who disagreed with him. After a while, the House calmed down and he then delivered a devastating critique of the budget and Disraeli's budget speech. Among other things, he established—to his side's satisfaction at least—that the claimed budget surplus was not real. The phrase was not in use at the time, but he showed that it was all smoke and mirrors. He said that the budget was 'the most subversive in its tendency and ultimate effects which I have ever known submitted to this House'.

During Gladstone's two-hour speech, the most apparently calm person in the house was Disraeli. He relaxed on the government front bench, frequently with his eyes closed feigning sleep. At one point when Gladstone was berating him vociferously, he leant forward, ostentatiously took out his eyeglass, and stared at the clock. After a few seconds, he put the eyeglass away and resumed his apparent slumber.

At 3 a.m., Gladstone sat down and the House proceeded to vote. As expected, Gladstone and the Peelites joined the Whigs and the government was defeated by 305 votes to 286. Gladstone left at 4 a.m. and insensitively went into the Conservatives' Carlton Club, of which he was still a member. Three days later, when he went into the Carlton Club again, he was harassed by some young members who threatened to throw him across the road into the Liberals' Reform Club where they thought he belonged. They may or may not have done this, but he made a dignified exit of his own accord.

The game was up, and Derby knew that he had to resign. This he duly and immediately did, and the queen was graciously pleased to accept his resignation. He informed his colleagues in the House of Lords with a rather sour countenance. Disraeli made the corresponding announcement in the House of Commons, and in contrast, he managed to do so with considerable good humour. He was desperately disappointed and probably very angry, but he managed not to show it. Once again, using a perhaps inappropriate modern expression, he earnt himself some brownie points.

The next government was a coalition of Whigs and Peelites, with the Whigs having by far the most MPs. It might have seemed logical for the Whigs to provide the next prime minister, but this was very difficult because the two most senior candidates were Palmerston and Russell. The two men did not get on and each would have had a problem serving under the other. The queen and Prince Albert did not like Palmerston, and their memories were very fresh concerning his precipitate approval of Louis Napoleon's coup in France. Russell's reputation was low following his calamitous handling of the Ecclesiastical Titles Bill and recent collapse of his previous government.

The queen's solution was to appoint a Peelite as prime minister. Gladstone was not a contender for the top position, although at this stage of his career, he was liked by both the queen and Prince Albert. He later became Victoria's least favourite prime minister. Instead, the honour fell to Lord Aberdeen, who for some time had been the Peelites' informal leader. Gladstone liked and respected him and was pleased with the appointment. Russell was foreign secretary because the very experienced Palmerston was not acceptable in this role. Palmerston was home secretary. Each of them would have been better suited to the other position.

The Peelites provided little more than 10 per cent of the coalition's MPs, but they held a disproportionate number of cabinet positions. Unsurprisingly, Gladstone was chancellor of the Exchequer, and they also headed the War Office, the Admiralty, and the Colonial Office. Gladstone was one day short of his forty-third birthday, and he was delighted with his appointment.

11
1852–1855

Gladstone became chancellor of the Exchequer on 28 December 1852 and moved into Downing Street five weeks later. He was just past his forty-third birthday and this house and/or the prime minister's house next door would be available to him for more than twenty-one of the remaining forty-five years of his life. He would be prime minister four times, and his periods in this office would exceed twelve years. He would be chancellor of the Exchequer four times, the two shortest of these, unwisely many think, while he was also prime minister. He would present thirteen budgets.

Disraeli was just past his forty-eighth birthday, and he had just been chancellor of the Exchequer for less than a year. In the remaining twenty-eight years of his life, he would hold this position twice more, once for fourteen months and once for twenty months. He would be prime minister twice, once for just nine months, then with real power for slightly more than six years starting in 1874. Until Disraeli's death in 1881, the two men were opponents and enemies.

Gladstone threw himself into his position as chancellor of the Exchequer with great enthusiasm and prodigious work. However, there was an irritating hurdle to overcome. He was required to resign his position as an MP for Oxford University and have himself re-elected. This turned out to be not just a formality. He was out of favour with the low church faction in his constituency and some of the electors were annoyed by his support for the Jewish Disabilities Bill. This had passed the Commons but been defeated in the Lords. It would have allowed Jews to sit as MPs, but this did not become possible until 1858. Gladstone was opposed by the son of the assassinated former Prime Minister Spencer Perceval. In the event, Gladstone won by the unimpressive margin of 124 votes. It was 1,022 to 898. His relationship with the constituency would continue to be uneasy and it would end twelve years later.

At this time, Disraeli was sore about the defeat of his budget and his loss of office, but he was no doubt cheered by three developments. In 1853, his waxwork was installed in Madam Tussauds. It was not until 1870 that Gladstone was accorded this honour. Furthermore, in the same year, a new shilling edition of his novels sold 300,000 copies and he was awarded an honorary degree by Oxford University.

After Gladstone had viciously demolished Disraeli's 1852 budget, Gladstone wrote to his wife: 'I am very sorry it fell to me to say it. God knows I had no wish to give him pain, and really with my deep sense of his gifts, I would only pray they might be well used'.[1] Despite this, the two men strongly disliked each other, and the personal bitterness grew more intense with two silly feuds over the chancellor's furniture and the chancellor's robes. Disraeli was in the right over the furniture, but in the wrong over the robes.

The furniture was in the chancellor's residence in 12 (now No. 11) Downing Street, and it had long been the custom for an incoming chancellor to take it over at a valuation fixed by the outgoing one. Disraeli had only occupied the building for less than a year, and he reasonably proposed that Gladstone pay him the amount that he had given his predecessor, Sir Charles Wood. Gladstone refused to pay because, he maintained, the Office of Works would run the chancellor's house and he should apply to them. Disraeli angrily suggested that he should talk to Wood, who 'is a man of the world'. Gladstone's reply stated: 'I am afraid that I did not make it sufficiently clear in my last letter that there was no longer any question as to the furniture to be settled between an outgoing and incoming Chancellor of the Exchequer'.[2] The money was not paid.

Disraeli took his revenge by refusing to pass on the chancellor's robes of office. These had been worn by Pitt the Younger who, as well as being prime minister, had been chancellor of the Exchequer for long periods in the late eighteenth and early nineteenth centuries. Since then, they had passed through eleven chancellors and had reached Disraeli from Sir Charles Wood. The robes had symbolic significance, which, to some of the chancellors at least, was of considerable importance. Gladstone had good reason to expect that they would come to him.

In his letter in which he refused to pay for the furniture, Gladstone insensitively added: 'I adverted at the close of my letter to the Official Robe, but the allusion to it has perhaps escaped your attention'. Disraeli's reply ignored the point and he kept the robes. They are now at Hughenden. Gladstone had a new set made and they passed to successive chancellors until 1886. Then the departing Sir William Harcourt took them with him. Lord Randolph Churchill had a new set made for his very brief spell in the office, but his successor, George Goschen, preferred to have a new set made. Sir Winston Churchill worshipped his father's memory, and in 1924–29, when he was chancellor of the Exchequer, he wore Lord Randolph's robes with great pride.

The correspondence between Disraeli and Gladstone lasted a month, and the tone of the letters deteriorated during this time. Disraeli's first letter ended with the customary, for the time, 'I have the honour to remain, Dear Sir, your obedient servant.' After Gladstone had refused to pay for the furniture, he moved to styling his letter in the third person. He wrote: 'Mr Disraeli regrets very much that he is obliged to say that Mr Gladstone's letter ... is not satisfactory'.

Gladstone replied in the same way and also switched to the third person:

> Mr W. E. Gladstone has read with regret and pain the note which he received last night from Mr Disraeli. He has endeavoured in this correspondence to observe towards Mr Disraeli the courtesy which was his due, and he is not aware of having said or done anything to justify the tone Mr Disraeli has thought proper to adopt.... It is unpleasant to Mr W. E. Gladstone to address Mr Disraeli without the usual terms of courtesy; but he abstains from them only because he perceives that they would be unwelcome.

Gladstone presented his first budget three and a half months after taking office. It was an important event and eagerly awaited by all the factions in the House of Commons. The Whig–Peelite coalition hoped that it would head the country's finances in the right direction, and looked forward to him building on his recent demolition of Disraeli and the Conservatives. The latter, of course, hoped that he would fail, though they probably suspected that he would not. As mentioned in the previous chapter, he was very fortunate that Disraeli's predictions had been much too pessimistic. The credit was not his, but he had been handed a windfall surplus of £2.5 million.[3] This was almost 5 per cent of the budget's revenue.

Before delivering the budget, Gladstone had to clear it with the cabinet, and although he succeeded on all points, this was by no means a formality. It took four meetings and several of his colleagues were left unhappy. However, he stood his ground, argued persuasively, had clearly mastered the details, and, most importantly, had a clear vision of the path that he wanted the government to take. Roy Jenkins commented: 'The second Disraeli budget particularly had been a conjuror's rather than a philosopher's or even a political economist's budget. That at least had been the grounds on which Gladstone had destroyed it. This left him, as the incoming Chancellor, with a heavy obligation to coherence, as well as an heir's desire to revive the Peel tradition of probity and courage. His need was not so much a budget for a year as a system of finance for the third quarter of the century'.[4]

Gladstone was a Peelite, and his 1853 budget would in some respects be regarded as a tribute to his late leader, Sir Robert Peel. It was a big step towards free trade. A total 123 duties were abolished and a further 133 were reduced. Believers in the benefits of free trade regard this as a factor in the mid-nineteenth-century Victorian prosperity. However, the government still had to pay its bills. Gladstone, like many chancellors, planned to cut government expenditure, but unlike some of them, he believed in it and set about doing it. Nevertheless, revenue had to be found. His solution was income tax.

Income tax had been introduced to help finance the Napoleonic Wars. It had been abolished in 1816, but reintroduced by Sir Robert Peel's government in 1842. This was, of course, unpopular, and many politicians (including Gladstone) wanted to phase it out. Not only did Gladstone not end it, he increased it and extended it for a further seven years. He proposed making the rate 7 pence in the pound for the next two years, 6 pence in the pound for the two years after that, then 5 pence in the pound for a final three years. The law, unless subsequently changed, would require it to end on 5 April 1860. The tax would be extended to Ireland and the threshold at which it started would be lowered from £150 to £100.

Disraeli hoped that, at best, he would be able to humiliate Gladstone in the way that he had suffered, or at least be able to show up flaws and contradictions in his budget. He had prepared himself and said: 'If our men are true, we must win, and triumphantly. Every sinew must be strained'.[5] He was to be disappointed. The budget was a great triumph for his rival.

Gladstone spoke for the extraordinarily long time of just under five hours. During his career, he made a number of very long speeches to the House of Commons, and this was the longest of them, though not by very much. The incredibly long speech ended with an incredibly long sentence of 344 words. It almost beggars belief, but it may be recalled (see Chapter 6) that his letter proposing marriage to Catherine contained a hard-to-follow sentence of 141 words. This was a man who sometimes did not hesitate to express himself at great length and with great complexity. To put it into context, the whole of Lincoln's Gettysburg Address contained just 272 words.

Despite the speech's great length, Gladstone secured the attention of the House and the enthusiastic approval of his supporters. This was coupled with the disappointment and grudging respect of his opponents. Disraeli knew that his hopes had come to nothing, and that in relation to budgets, he had been outclassed a second time.

A wave of congratulations poured over the triumphant Gladstone, not least from the royal family. Prince Albert said that he would 'certainly have cheered had he sat in the House'. Prime Minister Lord Aberdeen passed on the queen's expression of delight 'at the great success of Mr Gladstone's speech last night'. It seems hardly the strict impartiality of the monarch that we expect today. Gladstone later became Victoria's least favourite prime minister, but while Prince Albert was alive, he was highly regarded by both of them. Aberdeen wrote 'if the existence of my government shall be prolonged it will be your work.'

Disraeli fully understood what had happened. He said 'the general feeling on our side was opposed to any attempt at a contest'.[6] He abandoned the possibility of a frontal attack and instead opted for criticism of some of the details. He had some success, and, in particular, he damaged an attempt to reduce the rate of interest on part of the national debt. Disraeli's endeavours were not the only reason that the result of this was disappointing, but Gladstone thought that his actions were improper.

After the budget, Disraeli entered a period of depression, not medically so—just a period of low spirits. In a letter to Lord Derby, he wrote: 'I am voiceless'. A few weeks after the budget, he told his friend Stanley, Lord Derby's son and heir, that he was thinking of giving up politics. He talked about returning to literature and perhaps writing an epic poem and the life of Christ from a national point of view.[7] It is hard to understand exactly what he meant by that. Regardless, it did not happen. He soldiered on.

Following his 1853 triumph, Gladstone probably expected that when he framed his 1854 budget, the financial outlook would be benign, but it was not to be. It is not known if he was familiar with the poetry of Robert Burns, but, like all of us, he should have kept in mind 'The best-laid schemes o' Mice and Men Gang aft agley. An lea'e us nought but grief an' pain'. Much later, Harold Macmillan is said to have replied 'Events, dear boy, events' when asked by a journalist what is most likely to blow governments off course. Gladstone and his government were about to suffer a bad case of events. It was the Crimean War. Disraeli did not foresee it either.

War broke out between Russia and Turkey in October 1853, and Britain entered the conflict on the side of Turkey on 28 March 1854. As well as Turkey, Britain was allied with France and later Sardinia. In time, and not very much time, Gladstone became ill at ease with the war, but he supported Britain's entry. Indeed, he bolstered the prime minister, Lord Aberdeen, who was reluctant to do it. Gladstone's diary entry for 22 February 1854 records: 'He [Aberdeen] said how could he bring himself to fight for the Turks? I replied we were not fighting for the Turks, but we were warning Russia off the forbidden ground'.[8] Aberdeen vacillated and was very unhappy, and the decision eventually led to the end of his premiership. There are similarities with Herbert Asquith who was prime minister from 1908 to 1916. Both were decent men who were good peacetime prime ministers, but poor wartime ones.

The country was on the very brink of war when Gladstone presented his second budget. Wars are expensive and are apt to upset the fiscal intentions of chancellors of the Exchequer. This one was no exception, and he needed to raise money. He budgeted for a deficit of £2,840,000 and refused an intention to borrow. Instead, he raised income tax from its 1853 level of 7 pence in the pound to 10 pence–halfpenny in the pound. In a comment that is instructive

WHAT IT HAS COME TO.
Aberdeen. "I MUST LET HIM GO!"

George Hamilton Gordon, 4th Earl of Aberdeen reluctantly took Britain into Crimean War. A John Tenniel *Punch* cartoon of February 1854 shows him unable to restrain the British lion from chasing after the Russian bear.

about his religious beliefs and his feelings about war, he said: 'The expenses of a war are the moral check which it has pleased the Almighty to impose on the ambition and the lust of conquest that are inherent in so many nations'. It is an interesting concept.

The cost of the war and his intention to avoid borrowing caused Gladstone considerable trouble. He became involved in a dispute with the Bank of England, and a couple of weeks after the budget, Disraeli mounted an effective attack on him. Gladstone felt that his criticism was both damaging and unfair.

He was forced to introduce a further budget, an emergency one, a couple of months later. Income tax was raised again, this time from 10 pence–halfpenny in the pound to 14 pence in the pound. This made the rate double the one announced in his 1853 budget. As we know, despite his earlier intention to abolish income tax in 1860, it is still very much with us. In addition, spirits, malt, and sugar were taxed. Despite his support for entering the war, he was troubled. Three weeks after his first budget, he wrote to his wife: 'War! War! War! I fear it will swallow up everything good and useful'.[9] The next day, he told her: 'We do not yet know the meaning of the word'.[10]

Gladstone and Disraeli.

Gladstone was right to be despondent. The war went badly for his country and his government. Britain was not prepared and its troops suffered from military and administrative incompetence, the lack of the best equipment, the very harsh weather, and from disease. Florence Nightingale's magnificent efforts notwithstanding, the lack of good medical facilities extracted a terrible toll. Unlike in previous wars, these matters were reported to the public in the press by war correspondents. During the war, Disraeli resisted the jingoistic patriotism displayed by some of his compatriots, and after the fall of Sebastopol in 1855, he demanded a swift peace.

Aberdeen's government became increasingly unpopular, and in January 1855, the Commons voted by a large majority to appoint a select committee to examine the conduct of the war. Aberdeen took this as a vote of no confidence, and to the dismay of Gladstone, he resigned.

There was not an obvious successor to Aberdeen, and the queen was left with a dilemma. Her first attempted solution was to send for Derby. Palmerston visited Gladstone and said that they would both serve under Derby, with himself as leader in the Commons and Gladstone as chancellor of the Exchequer. Surprisingly, Disraeli had accepted that he would hold neither position. Presumably, he thought it a price worth paying in order to get back into government.

Derby vacillated then decided that he did not have the support necessary to proceed. Disraeli was furious. His leader had once again turned down the chance of holding the top job, and thus turned down his own chance of a leading position. He was already very disappointed with Derby's leadership, believing that he spent far too much time on his other interests, including horse racing.

The queen's next move was to ask Russell to form a government. He rather hesitantly asked Gladstone to continue as chancellor, but he said no. That effectively ended Russell's chances.

This only left the course that was the least favourite of both the queen and Gladstone. She sent for Palmerston and he succeeded. Victoria did not like him and took the step reluctantly. Gladstone did not have an easy relationship with him, and had held out in the unrealistic hope that Aberdeen, whom he greatly admired, would continue. Gladstone reluctantly agreed to continue as chancellor under Palmerston and four other Peelites took cabinet positions. Palmerston was aged seventy, and he was and is the oldest person to have become prime minister for the first time. The cross and disappointed Disraeli continued in opposition.

The public was pleased. The outspoken and energetic Palmerston was, they thought, the man to win the war. He did win the war, or at least he was in office when the war was won. It is not necessarily the same thing.

Gladstone served under Palmerston for just thirteen days. Then, together with two of the other four Peelites, he resigned. He had been unhappy from the start and he had endured three, from his point of view, unsatisfactory cabinet meetings. The issue on which he resigned was the decision of Palmerston and the majority of the cabinet to accept the appointment of a select committee to examine the conduct of the war. He felt that this was a slur on the Aberdeen government, in which he had been proud to serve, and was an admission that the new government did not have the confidence of the House.

Gladstone and Disraeli were destined to sit on the back benches for rather more than four years. After that, one of them was prime minister, chancellor of the Exchequer, or both for the following twenty-six years until 1885. Gladstone would be prime minister twice more after that. It is not hard to see that they dominated politics for the next quarter of a century.

12
1855–59

If you can fill the unforgiving minute
With sixty seconds' worth of distance run

From *If* by Rudyard Kipling

What is this life, if full of care,
We have no time to stand and stare?

From *Leisure* by W. H. Auden

Both of the poems were written after Gladstone's death, but there can be no doubt that he would have subscribed to Kipling's words rather than those of Auden. His energy and use of time were extraordinary, and for almost all of his life, his diary chronicled what he did and the time that he allocated to each activity. It was both physical and mental, and it was when he was in office and when he was not. The period out of office covered in this chapter was no exception, and there are numerous examples.

In September 1855, while staying in North Wales, he walked 40 miles in a single day, and on another he walked 15 miles in addition to ascending and descending Snowdon.[1] In 1858, he started felling trees, an activity that he enjoyed for most of the rest of his life, though it is often forgotten that he planted them as well. Many years later, Lord Randolph Churchill commented: 'The forest laments, in order that Mr Gladstone may perspire'.[2]

In 1855, Gladstone commenced a three-volume work entitled *Studies on Homer and the Homeric Age*, and this was published in 1858. During the rest of his life, he added to it with many books and articles. Lord Randolph Churchill's son, Winston, wittily remarked that 'Gladstone read Homer for fun, and that it served him right'.[3]

The product of his writing was very controversial. In it, Gladstone attempted to examine his believed revelation of God to the Greeks, and to relate it to the more commonly accepted revelation to the Jews as told in the Bible.[4] He claimed that God had used the Jews to teach man how he should behave towards God, and that He had used the Greeks to teach him how he should behave towards his fellow-men.[5]

This was at odds with a view that had been expressed a few years earlier by Disraeli, a man proud of his Jewish heritage. He had indicated that Judaism was not just the source of Christianity, but the inspiration for modern culture. He had written: 'We hesitate not to say that there is no race ... that so much delights, and fascinates, and elevates, and ennobles Europe as the Jewish'.[6] He had added: 'The Jews were the inspiration for the creative, moral, intellectual and spiritual foundations of the modern world'.[7]

Gladstone's effort of work and scholarship received an almost universally hostile reception. Nearly everyone who studied it thought that his theories and conclusions were mistaken, and some went as far as thinking that they were daft. Despite the attention that he was giving to his writing, Gladstone missed being in government, or even holding a front bench in the opposition. In 1856, he drew up a great programme of measures that he planned to introduce if and when he had the chance to do so. He had the opportunity after 1859 when he again became chancellor of the Exchequer. In 1857, he told Samuel Wilberforce: 'I greatly felt being turned out of office, I saw great things to do. I longed to do them. I am losing the best years of my life out of my natural service'.[8] Both the Conservatives and the Whigs would have welcomed him. Despite the Peelite break in 1846, Gladstone was still a Conservative, and they had modified the policies to which he had taken exception. It is probably true to say that he was instinctively closer to them than the Whigs. He was on good terms with the Conservative leader, Lord Derby, but had had no affinity whatsoever with their leader in the Commons, Disraeli. He had some sympathies with the Whigs and some of his Peelite colleagues were serving in Palmerston's government. The main difficulty was with the prime minister, Lord Palmerston, who presented a problem to Gladstone almost as big as Disraeli.

Disraeli had been very disappointed that Derby had not pursued the possibility of forming a government in 1853, and that as a consequence, he was doomed to spend more frustrating years in opposition. The Conservative leader, Derby, sat in the Lords and took his responsibilities lightly. Disraeli led the party in the Commons and it was a wearing role. Reports say that he was physically and mentally exhausted, and when Palmerston took office, he was showing his age. The American consul in Liverpool wrote:

> By and by there came a rather tall, slender person, in a black frock [coat], buttoned up, and black pantaloons, taking long steps, but I thought rather feebly or listlessly. His shoulders were round; or else he had a habitual stoop in them.

He had a prominent nose, a thin face, and a sallow, very sallow complexion, and was a very unwholesome looking person; and had I seen him in America, I should have taken him for a hard-worked editor of a newspaper, weary and worn with night-work and want of exercise; shrivelled, and withered, before his time. It was Disraeli, and I never saw any other Englishman look in the least like him.[9]

During the first Palmerston government, Disraeli came close to losing the confidence of his MPs, but he survived because they, like the party leader Lord Derby, needed his skills. Part of the problem was that he took every opportunity to oppose, even when opposition did not seem merited. He took every chance to challenge something in the legislation and to wear down the government. Apart from anything else, this meant that his supporters had to attend the House more frequently than they would otherwise be inclined to do.

Despite their opposition, in 1857, Disraeli joined forces with Gladstone to strongly oppose Palmerston's gunboat diplomacy in relation to a dispute with China. They both made powerful speeches in a vote of censure and the motion was passed. Disraeli's speech ended with a challenge for Palmerston to call a general election. This turned out to be a mistake, because the prime minister obliged and increased his majority.

BENJ. DISRAELI, EARL OF BEACONSFIELD.

Disraeli.

Shortly after this, Gladstone exercised his considerable energy and skill in unsuccessfully opposing the new Divorce Bill. His tactics included obstruction and parliament was in session for much of August. Prior to the successful passage of the bill, divorce could only be obtained by means of an Act of Parliament, which inevitably meant that, in practice, it was only possible for the rich and powerful. In 1769, the 3rd duke of Grafton had obtained a divorce in this way while serving as prime minister. Gladstone argued passionately that marriage was indissoluble, but suffered the embarrassment of his action in the affair of the duke of Newcastle's divorce being held against him. This is recounted in Chapter 9.

The last chapter made the point that it is frequently events that blow governments off course, and it was an unforeseeable event that prematurely ended the government of Lord Palmerston soon after he had increased his majority. The catalyst was the failed attempt in January 1858 by Felice Orsini and three accomplices to assassinate Napoleon III in Paris. The plot had been hatched in England and the bombs had been made in Birmingham. The French ambassador protested in terms violent and impertinent, and demanded that something be done to stop future outrages. At the time, British law classed conspiracy as a misdemeanour rather than a felony, and so there was no possibility of extradition.

Palmerston obliged and introduced into parliament a Conspiracy to Murder Bill, which made conspiracy a felony. The mood of the country and of MPs was that this was unnecessary and subservient to the insolent French. Both Gladstone and Disraeli spoke and voted against the bill and it was defeated. Palmerston promptly resigned, which was ironic because he was known as a man most likely to stand up to foreign pressure.

The queen asked Lord Derby to form a government, and to Disraeli's delight, this time he agreed. Disraeli was again chancellor of the Exchequer and leader of the House of Commons. Like Derby's previous 1852 administration, it was a minority Conservative government and, also like its predecessor, it was reasonable to expect that it would not have a long life. Derby needed to bolster its support. He wanted Gladstone, who, to use a modern expression, was a big beast and would strengthen the government, and perhaps bring others with him. So he offered him a cabinet position. However, after a brief period of reflection, the offer was refused.

Three months later, Derby asked again, and this time the offer was bolstered by an unexpected letter from Disraeli. Richard Aldous said that it was perhaps the most extraordinary and unlikely communication of Gladstone's political life. With what was surely hyperbole, he added that US President James Buchanan was probably not more surprised when, in the same year, he received the first ever transatlantic telegram. It was from Queen Victoria, and Buchanan thought that it was a hoax.[10] Disraeli's letter read as follows:

Napoleon III who survived an assassination attempt.

> I think it of such paramount importance to the public interest, that you should assume at this time a commanding position in the administration of affairs, that I feel it a solemn duty to lay before you some facts, that you may not decide under a misapprehension.
>
> Our mutual relations have formed the greatest difficulty in accomplishing a result which I have always anxiously desired.... For more than eight years, instead of thrusting myself into the foremost place, I have been, at all times, actively prepared to make every sacrifice of self for the public good, which I have ever thought identical with your accepting office in a Conservative Government.
>
> Don't you think the time has come when you might deign to be magnanimous?... I may be removed from the scene, or I may wish to be removed from the scene.
>
> Every man performs his office, and there is a Power, greater than ourselves, that disposes of all this.
>
> The conjuncture is very critical, and, if prudently yet boldly managed, may rally the country. To be inactive now is, on your part, a great responsibility. If you join Lord Derby's Cabinet, you will meet there some warm personal friends; all its members are your admirers. You may place me in neither category, but in that, I assure you, you have ever been sadly mistaken.[11]

The letter did not achieve the desired result. Despite its warm tones, it is safe to assume that 'Don't you think the time has come when you might deign to be magnanimous?' was not well received. Also, reference to 'a Power greater than ourselves' may well have been resented. Gladstone regarded himself an authority on the Almighty and he would not have appreciated an appeal based on this. As noted by Jenkins in his book *Gladstone* (p. 189, 1995), he replied:

> My Dear Sir—The letter you have been so kind as to address to me will enable me, I trust, to remove from your mind some impressions with which you will not be sorry to part.... You consider that the relations between yourself and me have proved the main difficulty in the way of certain political arrangements. Will you allow me to assure you that I have never in my life taken a decision which turned upon those relations.
>
> You assure me that I have ever been mistaken in failing to place you among my friends or admirers. Again I pray you to let me say that I have never known you penurious in admiration towards any one who had the slightest claim to it, and that at no period of my life, not even during the limited one when we were in sharp political conflict, have I either felt any enmity towards you, or believed that you felt any towards me.
>
> At the present moment I am awaiting counsel [with Aberdeen] which at Lord Derby's wish I have sought. But the difficulties which he wishes me to find means of overcoming, are broader than you may have supposed. Were I at this time to join any government I could not do it in virtue of party connections. I must consider then what are the conditions which make harmonious and effective co-operation in cabinet possible—how largely old habits enter into them—what connections can be formed with public approval—and what change would be requisite in the constitution of the present government, in order to make any change worth a trial.
>
> I state these points fearlessly and without reserve, for you have yourself well reminded me that there is a Power beyond us that disposes of what we are and do, and I find the limits of choice in public life to be very narrow.—I remain, etc.

There was no repeat of the use of the third party in phrasing the letters, which had featured in the exchange over the chancellor's robes and furniture. The rejection was clear, and it was the last possibility that the two men might serve together.

Out of office, Gladstone accepted a short-lived role in the governing of the Ionian Islands. Roy Jenkins called it a preposterous undertaking and it did his reputation no good at all.[12] The colonial secretary and friend of Disraeli, Edward Bulwer Lytton, persuaded him to do it. Richard Aldous asserts that he acted in concert with Disraeli, and that the motive was to set up Gladstone for failure.[13] Gladstone's friends strongly advised him to have nothing to do with it, but he disregarded the advice.

The Ionian Islands had been made a British Protectorate at the end of the Napoleonic Wars, but by 1858, many of the inhabitants wanted union with

Greece. Sir John Young was the high commissioner, but Gladstone was sent as commissioner extraordinary with the task of reporting on the situation to the government and making recommendations. He greatly enjoyed the travel, the sightseeing, and the culture, but his mission went badly.

His actions led to the recall of Young and, with the consent of the government and the queen, the appointment of himself as the replacement. This caused resentment and a feeling that Young had been harshly treated. Furthermore, Gladstone had overlooked the fact that holding the position precluded him from sitting as an MP, and, in addition, he would not be allowed to stand at the consequent by-election. He promptly resigned, stood in the by-election, and was returned unopposed. His failure was ignominious and, to make matters worse, most of his recommendations were rejected by the government. Word reached him that Disraeli had expressed satisfaction in his embarrassment, which greatly annoyed him, but he tried hard to put the fiasco behind him and he largely succeeded.

Perhaps predictably, the Derby–Disraeli government only lasted less than sixteen months, from February 1858 to June 1859. It did rather well and Disraeli's management of the country's finances was more successful than it had been in 1852. His only budget was praised by Gladstone, and he strongly resisted Derby's attempts to get more money for the Royal Navy's ships. The government's measures included the Government of India Act, which transferred power from the East India Company to the State. There was also the Oaths Act, which allowed Jews to sit in the House of Commons. This had the very strong support of Disraeli and remedied the failure of a similar bill in 1847. It still did not allow persons with no religious faith to sit in the Commons, something that would cause Gladstone great problems in his 1880–85 government.

There had been a number of unsuccessful attempts to extend the franchise beyond the limits set in the 1832 Reform Act. Palmerston was opposed to this, though both Gladstone and Disraeli were cautiously in favour. The word cautiously is important, because both of them were a very long way from supporting votes for all men, let alone votes for women. Perhaps naturally, and like nearly all politicians, they were concerned about the details and the probable consequences for their parties. In later years, Disraeli would be largely responsible for the Second Reform Act in 1867, and Gladstone would largely be responsible for the Third Reform Act in 1884. The Derby–Disraeli government tried and failed in 1859.

The failed bill, introduced by Disraeli, extended the number of people allowed to vote based on their ownership or rental of property, and there was a redistribution of seats, mainly from the boroughs to the counties. This was manifestly fair and likely to favour the Conservatives. The bill featured so-called 'fancy franchises' (a term coined by John Bright), and Disraeli had

Disraeli addressing the House of Commons.

great influence in this. The fancy franchises gave the vote to persons who had £60 in a savings bank, ministers of religion, graduates, members of the learned professions, and persons who had £20 pensions in the naval, military, or civil services. These votes were, if applicable, additional to their votes due to their ownership or rental of property.

The bill was defeated in the House of Commons by 330 votes to 291. Derby called a general election, which resulted in Conservative gains, but they still did not have enough seats to form a majority. When the Commons assembled, Derby's government was defeated on an amendment to the address from the throne and the prime minister resigned. Gladstone had voted with the government in the crucial vote. Disraeli was disappointed but probably took some satisfaction from his short time in office. The political commentator, Walter Bagehot, said that Disraeli alone had kept the government in power for sixteen months, and that he had learnt to lead with dignity and fail with dignity.[14]

Shortly before the fall of the government, the Whig factions and the radicals had coalesced, and it is normal to date the birth of the Liberal Party at that time. They were a formidable force and Gladstone would be their chancellor of the Exchequer or prime minister for most of the following fifteen years. Disraeli would be chancellor and then prime minister for two and a half years starting in 1866.

13
1859–1866

Following Derby's resignation, the queen wanted forty-four-year-old Lord Granville to be her next prime minister, but this rather foolish idea was blocked by Palmerston and Russell. Palmerston would not accept being the effective number two and Russell would not accept being the effective number three. So the dismayed Victoria once again sent for Palmerston, and at the age of seventy-four, he returned to 10 Downing Street. Like Derby sixteen months earlier, he was keen to have Gladstone in his cabinet, so keen in fact that he was willing to let him have any position that he chose.

In accepting the offer, Gladstone was influenced by his frustration at being out of office, and the fact that there was so much that he wanted to do. He might well have said that he wanted to do them for his lord and for his country. He was extremely confident of his abilities, and like nearly all politicians, he was personally ambitious

Gladstone had disapproved and still did disapprove of Palmerston personally, and in the past, he had disagreed with him on a range of issues, but at this time, they were in agreement on two very important ones. Despite his later views, Gladstone like Palmerston was cool on the idea of extending the franchise. Also, and very importantly, Gladstone favoured Italian unification and independence. Roy Jenkins said that it was the prominence of these two issues that made Palmerston temporarily less repugnant to him than was Disraeli and led him to make a choice of direction, which had the most momentous permanent effects.[1]

Gladstone chose his previous position as chancellor of the Exchequer, and this was not universally welcomed. Lady Clarendon asked: 'Why he who voted in the last division with the Derby ministry should not only be asked to join this one but be allowed to choose his office. I cannot conceive or rather, I can conceive, for I know that it is in his power of speaking. They want his tongue and they dread it in opposition'.[2] Her assessment of Palmerston's motivation was spot on.

Not everyone understood Gladstone's reasons, and this included his niece by marriage, seventeen-year-old Lucy Lyttleton. She wrote in her diary:

> Uncle William has taken office under Ld. Palmerston as Ch. of the Exchequer, thereby raising an uproar in the midst of which we are simmering, [in] view [of] his well-known antipathy to the Premier. What seems clear is that he feels it right to swallow personal feelings for the sake of the country; besides he agrees at present with Lord P's foreign policy, also he joins several Peelites.... There is this question, however, why, if he can swallow Palmn. Couldn't he swallow Dizzy, and in spite of him go in under Lord Derby? I don't pretend to be able to answer this, but one can enough understand things to be much excited and interested...[3]

Gladstone was now divided from Disraeli by what he termed 'longer and longer differences than perhaps ever separated two persons brought into constant contact in the transaction of public business'.[4] Although he had chosen Palmerston over his nemesis Disraeli, he continued to have frequent policy and personal differences with the prime minister, and they continued for the rest of Palmerston's life. It was not literally true, but Gladstone sometimes joked that he never attended a cabinet meeting between 1859 and 1865 without carrying a letter of resignation in his wallet. He came close to resignation many times but never did so. For most of the time, they managed to conduct their disputes in a civil way.

The mandatory by-election in his Oxford University constituency did not go well for Gladstone. He was re-elected by 1,050 votes to 859. The once-again chancellor was disappointed and offended, so much so that he visited Oxford only three times in the six years to the next general election. What happened then is told later in this chapter.

History is inclined to recall Gladstone as a cheeseparing but successful chancellor. Many say that he was a very successful or even an exceptional one. He inherited a run of annual deficits and, seven years later, he handed Disraeli a run of annual surpluses. It would be tedious to dwell on the detail of his financial measures, but it would be remiss not to mention how he handled three controversies.

He was often at odds with Palmerston over expenditure on the military, and on the navy in particular. The prime minister and several other ministers wanted much more money spent, especially on fortifications for the Plymouth and Portsmouth dockyards. In 1860, the country was engaged in a small colonial war with China, and there were fears of an invasion by France. Gladstone thought that the French invasion scare was much ado about nothing, and subsequent events (or perhaps we should say non-events) proved him right. However, it caused a major split with Palmerston and part of the cabinet, and it almost led to his resignation. Palmerston told the queen that Gladstone's resignation would be a serious blow to the government, but that it would be better to lose Gladstone than risk losing Portsmouth or Plymouth.[5]

His 1860 budget speech lasted four hours and was his third-longest speech in parliament. It was acclaimed as a great success, including by the prince consort and by Napoleon III of France.[6] Nevertheless, a really major problem followed it. One of his budget proposals was to repeal the excise duty on paper. From the vantage point of the twenty-first century, it seems incredible that such a tax existed, but it did. Among other things, it made books and newspapers more expensive, and it was justly attacked as a tax on knowledge. However, parts of the upper classes thought that helping the masses have access to books and newspapers was a dangerous thing to do.

At the time, every budget proposal was the subject of a separate bill. The Paper Bill scraped through the Commons, but it was rejected by the House of Lords. This had the makings of a constitutional crisis. Palmerston did not favour the bill, and, incredibly, he had written to the queen expressing the hope that the Lords would reject it.[7] The queen agreed with him and told the king of the Belgians that the rejection was a very good thing and that it would save a great deal of revenue.

The Commons passed three resolutions asserting the exclusive right of the Commons to decide questions of finance and taxation, and the resolutions were proposed by Palmerston. While doing this, he said that the argument over the Paper Bill was closed. Shortly afterwards, Gladstone said that it was not. The argument between the prime minister and the chancellor delighted the Conservatives, who were almost unanimous in wanting the tax retained. Derby and Disraeli twice told the prime minister that they would support any provisional administration that he might form if Gladstone's behaviour broke up the government. The outcome was that the bill was dropped in 1860, but that Gladstone succeeded in getting it through in the following year.

Nearly everyone would now concede that Gladstone was right in the two budget controversies detailed so far. Although he had some interesting and, up to a point, valid arguments, not many would think that about the third one. Few people did at the time either, and it did some damage to his reputation. In 1863, he tried to remove the tax exemption that the income of registered charities enjoyed. His proposal was nodded through by the cabinet prior to his budget speech. Roy Jenkins said that it is impossible to avoid the thought that there must have been some colleagues who were quite willing to see him take a tumble.[9]

He had two main arguments to justify what he wanted to do. He said that most charities were inefficiently or even corruptly run. There must have been an element of truth in this, as is the case today, but the word most was surely an unjustified insult. Secondly, he said that legacies were less morally laudable than charitable giving during the donor's own lifetime. In the latter case, the givers were depriving themselves of something, whereas legacies deprived other people of something. Again, he had a point, but a very unpopular one.

He made a brilliant budget speech, which among many other things tried to justify this proposal, but it was a lost cause and he withdrew the relevant clauses. The debacle puts one in mind of Margaret Thatcher who, in 1971, while minister of education, tried to stop free milk for children in schools. As a result, she acquired the sobriquet 'Thatcher the Milk Snatcher'. Gladstone's endeavour was on a similar scale, though they both went on to be long-serving and great prime ministers. It is worth noting that, during his lifetime, he personally gave the very large sum of £114,000 to charities, and what is more, he did it more or less evenly over the decades.[10]

Gladstone's great speeches were not only made in parliament, they were made in great tours and speaking engagements, often to vast audiences. Sometimes he was heard by thousands, most of whom did not have the vote. It was one of the reasons that he acquired the nickname 'The People's William'. In 1862, he began a new series of speeches and tours. They attracted massive and generally impressed audiences. He started in Manchester, and then, in October of that year, it was the turn of the Northeast. Roy Jenkins commented that he became hooked on crowds.[11] It is reported that during this October tour, he had the honour of a swimming escort as the boat in which he was travelling progressed down the River Tyne and that crowds lined the banks. His speech to 500 in Newcastle Town Hall contained a very controversial section that caused him a great deal of embarrassment. It was eighteen months after the start of the American Civil War and he said:

> We know quite well that the people of the Northern States have not yet drunk of the cup and they are still trying to hold it far from their lips—which all the rest of the world see they nevertheless must drink of. We may have our own opinions about slavery; we may be for or against the South, but there is no doubt that Jefferson Davis and other leaders of the South have made an army; they are making, it appears, a navy; and they have made what is more difficult than either, they have made a nation.

It is hard to understand why he said it. Despite slavery being the source of much of his family's wealth, he certainly had no love for what was sometimes euphemistically termed the 'peculiar institution'. It was probably a frank recognition of the success of the Confederate States in frustrating the efforts of the Union forces. However, some listeners and others took it as a hint that the country would soon recognise the Confederacy.

The American ambassador was understandably very upset. The foreign secretary, Russell, publicly defended Gladstone, but privately rebuked him. The prime minister, Palmerston, was more pro-South, and probably did not much mind. Towards the end of his life, Gladstone acknowledged that he had made a bad mistake. As always, Disraeli and the Conservatives were pleased by an embarrassment for Gladstone and the government, but they did not make a big fuss. Some of Disraeli's supporters are believed to have had pro-South sympathies.

It is not strictly relevant, but to this day, a minority of Americans use different terms for the Civil War. I was recently trying to be polite to a lady from South Carolina, and I mentioned that her state was the first to secede at the start of the Civil War. She fixed me with a steely stare and said: 'You are quite right, but where I come from we call it the War of Northern Aggression'.

This chapter has not so far included much about Disraeli. One reason for this is that, for a number of years following the fall of the Conservative government in 1859, he went through a rather listless and depressed period in his life. He was feeling his age (fifty-four when he left the Exchequer) and he was looking it too. His black hair had developed into a single curl, and he often felt tired. Derby was also feeling his age (fifty-nine at the same time), and his health was not good. He too was going through an extended listless phase. In 1863, Disraeli only voted in eight out of 188 divisions in the Commons. In the following year, it was seventeen out of 156.[12]

During the period in question, Disraeli was affected by the deaths of several people close to him. They included his early mentor, Lord Lyndhurst, and his sister, Sarah, to whom he had been devoted. He started to plan his life after politics, and his ideas included sponsoring a literary competition with a prize of £1,000, which he would provide. The theme of the competition would be 'The position of the Hebrew race in universal history viewed with reference to their influence on Man'. He envisaged the judges being Canon Stanley (of Christ Church Oxford), himself, and, very surprisingly, Gladstone.[13]

In 1861, Disraeli found an issue that appealed to his Conservative supporters and on which the government could be defeated. This was the intention of Palmerston's governing party to abolish church rates. He led the opposition to this and the government was defeated in 1861, 1862, and 1863. His motives were probably not based on his Christian beliefs, but a manoeuvre for political advantage. It was partly an attempt to appeal to Irish, Catholic MPs. He involved himself in other church matters too.

In 1864, the great and the good of Oxford gathered in the Sheldonian Theatre in that city, though a notable absentee was one of the university's MPs, William Gladstone. His diary rather feebly records that he stayed at home because of a cough. The purpose of the gathering, chaired by the bishop of Oxford, Samuel Wilberforce, was to consider Darwin's theory of evolution. Disraeli made a great speech, and it included one of his most memorable remarks, which can be found in numerous books of quotations: 'The question is this—is man an ape or an angel? My Lord, I am on the side of the angels'.[14]

Gladstone was close to the mark when he said that Disraeli was simultaneously 'Derby's necessity and his curse'.[15] He was extremely effective at harrying the government in the Commons, but his activities sometimes alienated his own (and Derby's) supporters. A particularly influential, alienated MP was Robert Cecil (aged twenty-nine when Gladstone returned to the Treasury). In 1867, he led a cabinet revolt and was one of three ministers who resigned in protest at the Derby–Disraeli proposals that became the 1867 Reform Act. However, as the 3rd marquess of Salisbury, he served in Disraeli's 1874–80 cabinet and was foreign secretary at the time of Disraeli's triumph at the Congress of Berlin. He went on to be prime minister three times.

It was mentioned earlier in this chapter that, in the early 1860s, Disraeli had been saddened by the deaths of a number of people close to him. Mrs Sarah Brydges Williams was one of them, but her passing brought an enormous benefit to his financial problems. She was an elderly widow without children, and she had for some time been an admirer of his. Like Disraeli, she was an Anglican of Jewish heritage.

In 1851, she had written to Disraeli to ask if he would be her executor and the main beneficiary of her estate. Not surprisingly, he had agreed. Despite the financial inducement, it was a genuine friendship. They corresponded regularly, and Disraeli expressed his frank views on people and events. He and his wife visited her once a year in Torquay, but she never visited them in Hughenden. She died in 1863, and he really did miss her. On her death, he inherited the sum of £30,000. Sarah was buried at Hughenden Parish Church in a common vault with, in due course, Mary Anne Disraeli and Benjamin Disraeli.

Disraeli's finances had also benefitted from the generosity of another admirer, a Yorkshire landowner by the name of Andrew Montagu. He had bought up Disraeli's debts, totalling £57,000, and only charged a very low rate of interest.[16]

In November 1861, Albert, the prince consort, died, and to say that the queen was grief-stricken is a great understatement. The death had a profound effect on the careers of both Gladstone and Disraeli, and it affected Victoria for the rest of her life. Albert was only forty-two and had never been popular with the British people, probably because of his German origin. He gave the name Saxe-Coburg and Gotha to the royal family, and this continued until 1917 when George V changed it to Windsor. The German Kaiser, a man not noted for his sense of humour, responded by saying that he would take an early opportunity of attending a performance of Shakespeare's play *The Merry Wives of Saxe-Coburg*.

Despite his relative unpopularity, the country had much for which to thank Albert. He had worked himself to the limit of his endurance, achieved much, and generally given wise counsel to the queen. She had come to depend on him a great deal, and she generally followed his advice. Albert had a favourable opinion of Gladstone, and while he was alive, so did Victoria. This was to change.

Gladstone visited the queen three months after Albert's death. It was a long interview and he stood throughout. He had been rather nervous in advance, but he spoke well when addressing her in her role as queen. However, he did not do so well when doing so to a grieving widow. He tried, but his language was too formal. Just a month later, Victoria wrote a letter of thanks to him following a speech that he had made paying tribute to her husband. The letter ended:

> Her *only* wish is to get soon to her own darling again. Every day seems to increase the intensity of a sorrow which *nothing, nothing* can alleviate, as there never was *love* and devotion like hers! Every source of interest or pleasure causes now the acutest pain. *Mrs* Gladstone, who the Queen knows is a *most* tender wife may, in a faint manner, picture to herself what the Queen suffers.[17]

Gladstone's reply was not ideal, as expressed in Magnus's *Gladstone* (p. 159, 1954):

> It is impossible for human hands to carry to Your Majesty the consolation that such a bereavement requires.... One who, as is Your Majesty's sorrow, sorrowed and suffered more, can in His own time and way, either lighten the burden, or give strength to bear it, or bring the conflict gently to an end. Unable to see into the future, we believe, Madam, that He can choose for You the best of these; and that He will.

Disraeli, on the other hand, got it exactly right and continued to do so. This is part of a letter that he sent in April 1863:

> The Prince is the only person, whom Mr Disraeli has ever known, who realized the Ideal. None, with whom he is acquainted, have ever approached it. There was in him an union of the manly grace and sublime simplicity of chivalry, with the intellectual splendour of the Attic Academe.... As time advances, the thought and sentiment of a progressive age will ... cluster round the Prince; his plans will become systems, his suggestions dogmas, and the name of Albert will be accepted as the master type of a generation of profounder feeling, and vaster range, than that which he formed and guided with benignant power.[19]

From then on, things got worse and worse for Gladstone, and better and better for Disraeli. Gladstone became Victoria's least favourite prime minister, and there are many examples of her scorn. A particularly well-known one is her comment that 'He speaks to me as though I was a public meeting'. Disraeli on the other hand, became her clear favourite, not least because he flattered her outrageously. Addressing Matthew Arnold, he said: 'Everyone likes flattery; and when you come to royalty you should lay it on with a trowel'.

Disraeli disreputably stoked the queen's antipathy towards Gladstone. He did, though, perform a public service. Following Albert's death, Victoria retreated into an extraordinarily extended period of public mourning. She neglected her duties as monarch and became almost invisible to her subjects. This stoked the fires of republicanism and even put the future of the monarchy in doubt. Disraeli flattered her, engaged her interest, and persuaded her to think of the present and the future. The queen's mourning for Albert was, to a limited extent, a problem for the rest of her life, but Disraeli managed to greatly reduce it. The country was the better for it.

Many deaths are mentioned in this chapter, but until 1865, one old man (at least old for his time) had sailed serenely on. This was the prime minister, Lord Palmerston. He was born in 1784 and had been in government for most of his adult life. At the age of twenty-five, he had been appointed secretary at war, and he had served in this position for twenty years. He was three times foreign secretary and his tenure in this office had lasted a total of sixteen years. He was home secretary for just over two years, and with a gap of eight months, he had been prime minister for more than ten years. He had been popular with the public, though not with Gladstone and not with Queen Victoria.

Palmerston had become prime minister at the age of seventy and is still the oldest person to have become prime minister for the first time. He died in office two days before his eighty-first birthday, and he was active and effective almost until the day that he died. He is the last prime minister to have died in office. In 1908, Sir Henry Campbell-Bannerman died while still living in 10 Downing Street. It was just nineteen days after ill health compelled him to resign. Gladstone in 1892–94 is the only older person to have been prime minister. He was eighty-four when he finally stepped down.

Many of the stories about Palmerston are untrue or exaggerated, but it is true to say that he did not lead a celibate life and it is true to say that his wife was not the only recipient of his affections. At the age of seventy-nine, he was named as co-respondent in a divorce case brought by a Mr Kane. Palmerston denied the accusation and his denial was accepted. Mr Kane was a scurrilous journalist, and it was probably an attempt to blackmail him. Disraeli is believed to have said that it was a pity that news of the divorce petition had got out and that Palmerston would sweep the country at the next election. If he did say this, his forecast was prescient. The general election was held three months before Palmerston died. He did not sweep the country, but the ruling Liberal Party did increase its majority. A rather good joke did the rounds at the time of the divorce petition. People asked: 'She was Kane but was he able?'[20]

It is generally believed that Palmerston died in bed while working on a treaty, and that his last words were 'That's article 98, now let's go on to the next'. However, some people believe that he had a seizure while in a compromising position on a billiard table with a maid. They further believe that his last words were 'Die my dear doctor, that's the last thing I shall do'.[21]

Palmerston was buried at Westminster Abbey, and Disraeli delivered a touching tribute in the Commons. It was probably sincere. They had been opponents for nearly thirty years, but he probably recognised and admired quite a bit of himself in him. He was realistic enough to see that the prime minister's passing would increase the chances of him and his party gaining office, and it was one of the factors that lifted his spirits out of the gloom of the early 1860s.

The recent general election had been a great disappointment for Gladstone because the Oxford University electors rejected him. Religion was once again an issue, and his views differed from those of many of his constituents. They were fed up with him and he was fed up with them. He had also stood as a candidate for South Lancashire, and he was elected there. At the time, it was common for leading politicians to stand in more than one constituency at the same election.

Gladstone might have been a candidate for prime minister, but within hours of hearing of Palmerston's death, he ruled himself out. He wrote to Russell and told him that he would have his support. This left Gladstone as heir presumptive to be the leader of the Liberal Party, and he would only have eight months to wait.

Russell was duly appointed. He was the third son of the duke of Bedford and this had entitled him to use the courtesy title of lord. He had sat in the Commons and indeed been prime minister using the name 'Lord John Russell', but in 1861, he had taken the title Earl Russell and moved to the House of Lords. He was seventy-three, and it was more than thirteen years since the end of his first spell as premier. It is the longest spell between two periods as prime minister by the same person. Gladstone continued as chancellor of the Exchequer, and with Russell in the Lords, he became Leader of the Commons. In this role, he directly faced Disraeli who led the Conservatives in the lower House.

It was immediately clear that the Russell government would try to secure a further measure of parliamentary reform. It was Russell who, in 1830, had introduced the first Reform Bill into a raucous and incredulous House of Commons.[22] It failed and so did another one, but Russell played a major role in getting the 1832 Reform Act onto the Statute Book. Over the years, he had tried more than once to widen the franchise and push through other reforms. Gladstone was on good terms with Russell and he had come to share his views on the matter. Just three and a half months after Russell had become prime minister, Gladstone introduced into the Commons the Representation of the People Bill.

The bill was a cautious one, which Russell and Gladstone thought would increase their chances of getting it through. The net effect of the proposed increase in the franchise was to enlarge the number of voters from around 1,050,000 to around 1,450,000.[23] This was an increase of 40 per cent, which sounds a lot, but it was from a low base. The vote would still have been denied to all women and about 70 per cent of men. There would also have been a minor redistribution of seats.

It was an epic battle, but the hopes of Russell and Gladstone were frustrated. Nearly all the Conservatives opposed the bill and so did a group of about forty Liberals. The latter acquired the intriguing name of the Adullamites. The term originated with John Bright, who had a memorable turn of phrase. In describing them, he brought in a biblical reference to the cave of Adullam, where David and his allies sought refuge from Saul. Adullam's cave was said to be a refuge for the discontented, and the name stuck.[24]

The Adullamites were brilliantly led by Robert Lowe, an albino Liberal MP. Showing a remarkable absence of rancour, Gladstone made him chancellor of the Exchequer and then home secretary in his 1868–74 government. Furthermore, when he moved to the House of Lords, he secured for him the rank of viscount. This was despite the reservations of the queen, who favoured the more usual rank of baron.

After eight nights of debate and just a week before presenting his budget, Gladstone made another of his truly memorable speeches to the Commons. In doing so, he secured an amendment to the Representation of the People Bill. He started at 1 a.m. and spoke for rather more than two hours. It is interesting to dwell on his use of untranslated Latin. He was acknowledging his late conversion to the cause that he was now espousing. Among other things, he said:

> I came among you an outcast from those with whom I associated driven from them, I admit, by no arbitrary act, but by the slow and restless forces of conviction. I came among you, to make use of the legal phraseology in pauperis formá. I had nothing to offer you but faithful and honourable service. You received me, as Dido received the shipwrecked Aeneas—
>
> *Ejectum littore egentum*
> *Excepi* [an exile on my shore I sheltered].
>
> And I only trust you may not hereafter at any time say
> *Et regni demens in parte locavi* [and, fool as I was, I shared with you my realm].
>
> You received me with kindness, indulgence, generosity, and I may even say with some measure of confidence. And the relation between us has assumed such a form that you can never be my debtors, but that I must for ever be in your debt.[25]

Above left: Sir Robert Peel, 2nd Baronet (1788–1850), portrait by Henry William Pickersgill (1782–1875). (*National Portrait Gallery*)

Above right: Lord John Russell, 1st Earl Russell (1792–1878), portrait by Sir Francis Grant (1803–1878). (*National Portrait Gallery*)

Left: The Earl of Derby by an unknown photographer, *c.* 1855.

Below: George Hamilton-Gordon, 4th Earl of Aberdeen (1784–1860), a portrait by John Partridge (d. 1872) *c.* 1847. (*National Portrait Gallery*)

Above left: Henry John Temple, 3rd Viscount Palmerston (1784–1865), a portrait by John Partridge (d. 1872) *c.* 1845, (*National Portrait Gallery*)

Above right: Lord Palmerston, a studio portrait photograph by Pierre Louis Pierson (1822–1913), *c.* 1865.

Above left: Benjamin Disraeli, Earl of Beaconsfield (1804–1881), a portrait by Sir John Everett Millais (1829–1896), 1881. (*National Portrait Gallery*)

Above right: Portrait photograph of Benjamin Disraeli by W. & D. Downey, *c.* 1878.

Above left: William Ewart Gladstone (1809-98), a portrait by Franz von Lenbach (1836–1904). 1886. (*Art in Parliament*)

Above right: An informal photograph of Gladstone by Elliott & Fry *c.* 1887.

Above left: Robert Arthur Talbot Gascoyne-Cecil, 3rd Marquess of Salisbury (1830–1903), portrait by George Frederic Watts (1817–1904). (*National Portrait Gallery*)

Above right: Memorial to Disraeli erected by Queen Victoria in the Church of St Michael and All Angels in Hughenden. (*Photograph by Dorothy Mason*)

Burial vault at Hughenden Parish Church. It contains the bodies of Benjamin Disraeli, Mary-Anne Disraeli, Sarah Brydges Williams and five members of Benjamin Disraeli's family. (*Photograph by Dorothy Mason*)

Above left: Rear of Disraeli's home in Hughenden. (*Photograph by Roger Mason*)

Above right: Monument to the memory of Isaac Disraeli at Tinkers Hill near Hughenden. It was erected as a surprise gift by Mary-Anne Disraeli for her husband. (*Photograph by Roger Mason*)

Left: Statue of Gladstone at Aldwych, London. (*Photograph by Roger Mason*)

Below: New Hawarden Castle, Gladstone's home in Flintshire. The house and estate passed to him on the death of his wife's brother.

Christ College, Oxford. Gladstone was the ninth of the thirteen Prime Ministers to have been educated there.

Above left: Lord Lyndhurst: Disraeli's early patron.

Above right: Queen Victoria and her husband Prince Albert.

Above left: Queen Victoria.

Above right: Albert the Prince Consort, he admired Gladstone and while he was alive Victoria generally accepted his view.

Above left: Mary-Anne Disraeli, who was twelve years older than her husband. It was a happy marriage. (Politics as an aphrodisiac: the secret of the Disraelis' happy ———. *The Spectator*).

Above right: Catherine Gladstone, who contributed to a happy marriage. (*Wikipedia*)

Above left: Benjamin Disraeli. (*Wikipedia*)

Above right: Benjamin Disraeli.

Right: William Gladstone.

Above left: Lord George Bentinck: He helped Disraeli buy Hughenden and he collaborated with him in bringing down Peel. (*Wikipedia*)

Above right: Lillie Langtree: known as the Jersey Lillie she was an actress and one of the many mistresses of the Prince of Wales. She was a friend of Gladstone, but despite claims to the contrary not his mistress.

Left: Edward Henry Stanley 15th Earl of Derby: he was for a long time a friend of Disraeli and served as his Foreign Secretary. Their friendship declined, he resigned and moved to Gladstone and the Liberals.

Above left: Daniel O'Connell, in an 1836 watercolour by Bernard Mulrenin. He was an Irish nationalist and a bitter enemy of Disraeli. (*National Portrait Gallery*)

Above right: The Prince of Wales (later King Edward VII): he admired Gladstone who tried to persuade his mother to give him a meaningful role. He was a pall bearer at Gladstone's funeral.

Above left: George Leveson-Gower 2nd Earl Granville: he was a friend and admirer of Gladstone and twice served as his Foreign Secretary.

Above right: Montagu Corry (later 1st Baron Rowton): he was a philanthropist and Disraeli's faithful secretary from 1866 until Disraeli died in 1881. (*Wikipedia*)

Right: W. H. Smith: the ubiquitous bookseller and newsagent served Disraeli as First Lord of the Admiralty. Some think, probably wrongly, that W. S. Gilbert based Sir Joseph Porter KCB in the comic opera 'H.M.S. Pinafore' on him. (*Wikipedia*)

Below left: Sir Stafford Northcote (later 1st Earl of Iddlesleigh): among other things he served Disraeli as Chancellor of the Exchequer from 1874 to 1880.

Below right: Otto von Bismarck: he presided over the Congress of Berlin in 1878 and was impressed by Disraeli. He famously said 'Der alte Jude, das ist der Mann'.

Above left: Major General Charles Gordon CB: he disregarded his orders and was killed at Khartoum. His death enraged Queen Victoria and she was furious with Gladstone.

Above right: John Spencer 5th Earl Spencer: he was Gladstone's choice to succeed him. The Queen had other ideas. (*Wikipedia Commons*)

Left: Archibald Philip Primrose 5th Earl of Rosebery: he was a supporter and helper of Gladstone, but not his choice to succeed him. He was, though, the choice of the Queen. (*Wikipedia*)

Gladstone addressing the House of Commons.

He did not offer the translations because, at that time and in that place, it was not necessary to do so. Sir Winston Churchill once used Latin with great humour. In a speech in the Commons, he used the phrase '*primus inter pares*' and said that he would translate it 'for the benefit of'. At this point, socialist members hooted because they thought that they were being patronised. Churchill, who had been educated at Harrow, continued 'for the benefit of any old Etonians who may be present'.[26]

Disraeli had taunted Gladstone with the memory of his speech to the Oxford Union in 1831. This is recounted in Chapter 4 of this book, and in it, he had vehemently opposed the failed Reform Bill that preceded the 1832 Reform Act. Gladstone's reply and put down was magnificent:

> As the Right Honourable gentleman has exhibited me, let me exhibit myself. What he has stated is true. I deeply regret it. But I was bred under the shadow of the great name of Canning. Every influence connected with that name governed the politics of my childhood and my youth. With Canning I rejoiced at the removal of religious disabilities and at the character which he gave to our policy abroad; with Canning I rejoiced at the opening which he made towards the establishment of free commercial interchanges between nations. With Canning, and under the shadow of the yet more venerable name of Burke, I grant that my youthful mind and imagination were impressed with the same idle and futile

fears which still bewilder and distract the mature mind of the Right Honourable gentleman. I had received that fear and alarm of the first Reform Bill in the days of my undergraduate youth at Oxford which the Right Honourable gentleman now feels; and the only difference between us is this—I thank him for bringing it out—that having those views I moved the Oxford Union Debating Society to express them clearly, plainly, forcibly, in downright English while the Right Honourable gentleman does not dare to tell the nation what it is that he really thinks, and is content to skulk under the shelter of the meaningless amendment of the Noble Lord...[27]

Before sitting down, he ended with the peroration 'You cannot fight against the future. Time is on our side'. How true then and how true now, though I sometimes wish that we could. This is listed in the *Oxford Library Book of Quotations* and is one of three under Gladstone's name. Disraeli on the other hand has twenty-two. He surpassed his rival with memorable phrases. They are very good and worth looking up. Two are in this chapter.

According to Roy Jenkins, Gladstone's opinion of Disraeli was never lower than at this time.[28] Disraeli had long been ambivalent about parliamentary reform and extending the franchise, and he now led the opposition to Russell and Gladstone's modest measures. Yet a year later, he brilliantly manoeuvred parliament into passing the Second Reform Act. This greatly extended the franchise and went much further than the bill that he now opposed. What did he really think? It is hard to know, but he did believe in furthering the success of the Conservative Party and its leader in the Commons, one Benjamin Disraeli. It was another example of his tendency to play fast and loose with his principles in order to gain an advantage.

Gladstone and his party (without the support of the Adullamites) won a vote on an amendment by a margin of just eleven votes. Gladstone had chosen to make it a vote of confidence and the low majority led to the end of the government. There were two possibilities. One was a general election, but it had been less than a year since the last one and this was not favoured. The other was resignation, but this was not favoured by the queen who wanted the government to accept the defeat and carry on. The cabinet chose resignation. Victoria deliberately arrived slowly from Balmoral in order to try and get the result that she wanted. However, this tactic was not successful. Russell and Gladstone went to Windsor together and tendered the government's resignation. Gladstone's diary recorded that they got a warm reception at both railway stations.

14
1866–1868

In June 1866, Derby took office as prime minister, and he promptly appointed Disraeli as chancellor of the Exchequer and leader of the Commons. It was the third and last time that the pair held these positions together. The appointments were not a foregone conclusion. Many MPs had assumed that around forty Adullamites would join the Conservatives in an anti-reform coalition. They did consider it, but they wanted Disraeli excluded and Stanley, who was Derby's heir, as leader of the Commons. It would have been difficult because Derby and Stanley did not get on well together. The Adullamites also favoured the option of the Whig, Lord Clarendon, as head of an anti-reform administration. This had the support of the marquess of Bath and some ultra-Tories.

When Derby became aware of the Adullamites' plans concerning Lord Clarendon, he consulted Disraeli, who was worried and angry. Derby had a history of declining to lead minority Conservative governments and Disraeli was afraid that he might do so again. He furiously told him that his honour required him to accept the position of prime minister of a Conservative government. He wrote: 'The question is not Adullamite it is national. You must take the government; the honour of your house and the necessity of the country require it'.[1]

The 14th earl of Derby was a man who took seriously his honour and the honour of his house. He called a meeting of senior Tories who, with exception of the marquess of Bath, agreed that he should form a government. He should try to do it with the Adullamites, but if it was not possible, the Conservatives should do it alone. It was not possible, and the Conservatives did it alone. Stanley was foreign secretary and Viscount Cranborne was the youthful secretary of state for India. As told later in this chapter, he would resign from the cabinet over parliamentary reform, and, as told later in this book, he would go on to be Disraeli's foreign secretary at the time of the Congress of Berlin, and after that he would be three times prime minister.

On 6 July, Derby, Disraeli, and the entire cabinet travelled to Windsor on a special train. Derby was already prime minister and the purpose was to swear in the rest of the cabinet. Shortly after their arrival at Windsor Castle, a violent thunderstorm broke and water seeped into the room where they were due to meet the queen, and for this reason, the meeting was moved upstairs. As they climbed the stairs, there was an unplanned and rather awkward meeting with Russell, Gladstone, and the departing cabinet coming down. Desultory good wishes were exchanged, though it is not recorded what Gladstone and Disraeli said to each other.

The new president of the Board of Trade, Sir Stafford Northcote, later disclosed that afterwards, Disraeli sat down thinking that it would be on a seat, but instead found himself sitting on the floor. It was an inauspicious beginning to his renewed time in government and could possibly have been interpreted as a bad omen, but he would shortly enjoy a great triumph and then go on to be prime minister.

Less than three weeks after these events, Gladstone annoyed the queen and Disraeli pleased her—a sequence of events that would be repeated many times in the years to come. Through the medium of her secretary, Victoria asked Gladstone to support a motion in the Commons to purchase a small amount of gun metal to be used in the construction of the Albert Memorial. The sum involved was small and it was of great significance to the queen who was still in deep mourning for her late husband. For Gladstone, refusing the request was a matter of principle, and he replied to her majesty's secretary, General Grey, in the following terms:

> It is contrary to the rules of good administration to ask money from Parliament for a particular work without intimating that more will be required, and then to ask for more for the same purpose. And in the rules of good administration none has so deep an interest as the Crown.... Nothing should ever be put into Supplemental Estimates except that which could neither have gone into the original Estimates, nor be postponed to next year. This satisfies neither condition.... You will see after what I have said that I can give no pledge to support the proposal.[2]

The new chancellor of the Exchequer, Disraeli, took a different view and was willing to accommodate the queen's wish, and he secured parliamentary approval for the expenditure. Victoria was very grateful and wrote to him to say so.

At this time, Gladstone was feeling physically and mentally exhausted, and he decided to take an extended holiday in Rome. It might be considered somewhat risky because he had recently led his party through a disappointing session in the Commons, and it was probable but not certain that he would soon succeed Russell as party leader. He might have considered it prudent to remain and cultivate his colleagues. Nevertheless, he needed a break from politics and he took it. He left London on 28 September and did not return until 29 January. He was accompanied by his wife and daughters, and over Christmas, they were joined by three of their sons.

Gladstone's idea of a rest was not the same as that of most people. For him, it meant doing different things. One of them was listening to a great number of sermons and absorbing the different viewpoints expressed in them. He was fluent in Italian and the language was not a problem. No fewer than three of his former cabinet colleagues, the duke of Argyll, Lord Clarendon, and Edward Cardwell were also in Rome for part of his visit. Clarendon described Gladstone's activities as follows in a letter to Lady Salisbury:

> Italian art, archaeology and literature are G's sole occupations. Every morning at 8 he lectures his wife and daughters upon Dante, and requires them to parse and give the root of every verb. He runs about all day to shops, galleries and persons, and only last night he told me that he hadn't time for the reading room, and hadn't seen an English newspaper for three or four days.[3]

It was a somewhat mocking account and Clarendon was known for this. For some reason, his nickname for Gladstone was 'Merrypebble', and for the queen it was 'the Missus'. Victoria was aware of it and was not best pleased.

On 22 October, Gladstone had an audience lasting nearly an hour with the Pope. Archbishop Manning had prepared the Pontiff for the meeting, and told him that Gladstone could be a friend, but if wrongly handled could be a dangerous enemy. The Pope respected him, his position, and his likely future eminence, and wanted him to be a friend. He therefore treated him with great courtesy, even commanding him to sit. Gladstone recorded:

> ... I repaired to the Vatican in household uniform. I found the Pope dressed with great simplicity in white.... When I had bowed and kissed his hand, dropping on one knee as before the Queen (an operation in which he took my hand himself) he motioned, and asked me to sit down on a chair placed over against him. Mr Russell had told me that it was his wont notwithstanding this invitation to stand. I therefore begged permission to do so as I should if before the Queen. But he said if the Queen ordered you to sit, you would sit. *Allora*, I said, *Santo Padre non mi resta altro che di ubbidare: Roma locuta est*, quoting the famous words of St Augustine.... The Pope smiled and finished the sentence, *causa finite est*.[4]

Gladstone brought his family for a formal blessing a few days later, and while in Rome, he saw a total of twelve cardinals. The Pope also gave audiences to Argyll, Clarendon, and Cardwell. He later summarised the meetings by saying

2nd Earl Granville.

'Mr Gladstone I like but don't understand, Mr Cardwell I understand but don't like. I like and understand Lord Clarendon. The Duke of Argyll I neither like nor understand'.[5] News of what he had said reached Gladstone, who was amused.

Since the 1832 Reform Act, public enthusiasm for further parliamentary reform had periodically waxed and waned, and at times, the waxing had been intense. The flood tide of the Chartist movement comes into this category. Following the defeat of the Russell–Gladstone Bill, it waxed again heavily. In the famous words of Edward VIII, when talking about unemployment in the Welsh coalfields, 'Something must be done'. He said it just twenty-one days before he abdicated so that he could marry Mrs Simpson.

Two events in particular deserve a mention. In June, just three months before Gladstone departed for his Roman holiday, a large crowd gathered outside his house in Carlton House Terrace. This was to show their support and to demonstrate their appreciation of his efforts to get the failed Reform Bill on to the Statute Book. Gladstone was out, but his wife came on to the balcony and waved to the crowd. The gesture was greeted with cheering. Some accounts said that she did it at the request of the police. The press criticised her husband, who had not been there, for pandering to the mob.

Events a month later, still before Gladstone's departure, were much more worrying. A great meeting was to be held in Hyde Park, but it was declared illegal by the home secretary and a large contingent of police barred the entrances. The demonstrators tore down the rather flimsy railings along much of Park Lane and went ahead with the meeting. A police constable later died from injuries that he had received. The mayhem was close to Disraeli's house. He was very concerned about the safety of his wife and sent someone to check that she was unharmed. She was. Gladstone privately condemned the rioters, but he neither used his influence with the reform leaders to dampen popular discontent nor did he join them to champion their cause. The result was that he looked weak and irresolute.[6]

The public mood was shown by the generally peaceful meetings called by the Reform League. This had been founded in the autumn and winter of 1864–65 with the aim of campaigning for manhood suffrage and the secret ballot. Support grew very rapidly, and a couple of years later, there were 100 branches in London alone. The radical MP John Bright was a prominent supporter. The demonstrations continued after the events in Hyde Park. Some were very big and another mass demonstration in Hyde Park led to the resignation of Spencer Walpole, the home secretary. He had banned the meeting, then been forced to retract and let it go ahead.

On both sides of the House, there was a hardcore of MPs opposed to any reform, or at least opposed to any major reform. However, it is probably correct to say that the personal convictions of the majority on both sides now favoured some degree of reform. Unsurprisingly, they did not agree on the desired amount of it, nor on the particular measures that they wanted. A further factor was that, like nearly all politicians, then as now, they wanted outcomes that were favourable to them and their parties. This goes some way to explaining why a House with a majority of members favouring reform voted down the moderate Russell–Gladstone Bill. Many believed that extending the franchise would benefit the Liberal Party, but Disraeli came to believe that the extended electorate would reward the party that gave them the vote.

Derby and Disraeli agreed that some degree of reform was inevitable and they wanted it to come from their government. The 1867 Reform Act was a great personal triumph for Disraeli and is indelibly associated with his name, but the early cautious moves came from Derby. The two of them planned to submit a number of resolutions to parliament concerning the setting up of a royal commission. This would probably take a year to report and enable legislation to wait until 1868, and they thought that Gladstone could not reasonably object to this. The cabinet somewhat reluctantly agreed the wording of the resolutions.

Shortly before Christmas, Derby wrote to Disraeli: 'Of all possible hares to start I do not know a better than the extension of household suffrage, coupled with plurality of voting'. Plurality of voting was what had become known as 'fancy franchises'. It meant that some men had more than one vote. As well as the vote for owning or renting a property of a certain value, votes would be given for such things as being a university graduate, being a clergyman, and having savings of a certain amount in a bank. So, for example, a wealthy Church of England clergyman who was a graduate and owned a house in Windsor would have four votes, all of them in the Windsor constituency.

This was clever, but in the phrase used in 1961 by Lord Salisbury about Iain Macleod, many thought that it was too clever by half. Derby was nervous about giving poorer people the right to vote and thought that many of them would not do so responsibly. To counter this, giving extra votes to people who he considered would be more likely to vote responsibly would diminish or eliminate the effect.

From this point onwards, it was Disraeli who was very much in charge. On 12 February 1867, without involving the cabinet, he committed the government to an immediate bill, and on 25 February, he produced it. This became known as the 'Ten-minutes Bill'. It was called this because it had been agreed by the cabinet just ten minutes before Derby presented it to a Conservative Party meeting. It was a modest measure that provided for a £6 franchise in the boroughs, a £20 franchise in the counties and fancy franchises. It was widely criticised, including by Conservative MPs, for not being sufficiently radical, and because of this, Disraeli withdrew it and announced a more far-reaching one.

The withdrawn bill was too much for three cabinet ministers and they had been teetering on the brink of resignation. The new one pushed them over the edge and they did resign. The three were Lord Cranborne (heir to the marquess of Salisbury and sitting in the Commons), the earl of Carnarvon, and General Peel (younger brother of the late Sir Robert Peel and owner of the 1844 Derby winner). Cranborne, who at that stage in his life violently disapproved of Disraeli, was the dominant character of the three and he led the others.

The resignations bear a strong resemblance to the resignation of the three Treasury ministers from Harold Macmillan's government in 1958. In this case, an implacable Enoch Powell strengthened the resolve of Nigel Birch and the Chancellor of the Exchequer Peter Thorneycroft. As in 1867, the resignations did not have much effect, Macmillan referred to 'little local difficulties' and departed on an extensive Commonwealth tour.

The new bill that sealed the resignations gave the vote in the boroughs to any man who had occupied a house for two years, had been rated to the relief of the poor, and had paid his rates. Also to be enfranchised were men who paid 20s (£1) annually in direct taxes, and if they were householders as well, they had a double vote. The bill was primarily about the boroughs, but as introduced, the county rental qualification was put at £15 a year. This high figure was intended to preserve propertied interests and stop them being swamped by new voters. The bill included the fancy franchises and the county boundaries were to be redrawn with the effect of putting more voters into borough constituencies.

No voting rights were given to the large number of compound householders who did not pay their own rates. These were men who paid a sum to their landlords that was inclusive of both rent and rates, the landlord then being responsible for paying the rates. There were, of course, no votes for women. That would not come for another fifty-one years.

The bill was introduced into the House of Commons by Disraeli on 18 March, and his performance in doing so was brilliant. While he did it, Gladstone did himself no favours at all. He fidgeted and he glowered, and he several times rose to ask difficult questions of a technical nature. Over the next few days, he led a bad-tempered onslaught from the opposition benches.

Disraeli, as was his wont, remained calm and his demeanour was very effective. Gladstone's demeanour, on the other hand, worried his supporters and annoyed the Conservatives. At one point, Disraeli said that listening to Gladstone made him concerned for his safety. To laughter, he added: 'His manner is sometimes so very excited and so alarming that one might also be thankful that [we] are divided by a good broad piece of furniture'.[7] Disraeli's one concession was to drop the fancy franchises.

At this time, Disraeli was exceptionally busy, and apart from everything else, he presented his budget on 4 April. He was still conscious of the mauling that he had received from Gladstone following his first budget in 1852, and he knew that it must not happen again. With this in mind, and of course to do a good job for the sake of the country, he spent a lot of time preparing it. He succeeded. His budget speech lasted only forty-five minutes and was the shortest ever at that time. He projected a budget surplus of £1.2 million, and disregarding various calls to spend it, he planned to use it to help pay down the national debt.

Gladstone was generally curt, dismissive, and ill-tempered before and afterwards, but he smiled benignly on the budget, which accorded with his preferred approach. In his reply to the budget speech, he said: 'I think the right hon. Gentleman deserves credit for having resisted the temptations to which he must have been subjected; and I believe the course he has taken a wise one, and one well adapted to the promotion of the national wealth'.[8]

Gladstone's ill humour was directed towards his supporters as well as Disraeli and his opponents. On 21 March, with very short notice, he summoned his MPs to his house, and from a position on the staircase, he lectured them for an hour on the need for discipline and loyalty. They thought that they were going to be consulted, but they were instructed and did not like it.

On 25 March, the second reading of the bill went through without a division. According to Roy Jenkins, Gladstone's two-hour speech was reported as losing the attention of the House.[9] There was now everything to play for with the forthcoming amendments leading to the third reading.

Disraeli had been in charge of the bill and presenting the case for it, but from this point on, his command was near total. Derby was ill, missed cabinet meetings, and made little contribution. Disraeli dominated the cabinet and frequently made key decisions without consulting his colleagues. On the face of it, his task was near impossible because the opposition had a majority of around eighty. But he was on top form, he had a good case, and quite a few Liberals wanted at least parts of the bill, especially as he was willing to consider amendments from them. Furthermore, he could (via Derby) ask the queen to dissolve parliament and call an election. This was not wanted by the Liberals.

There was an early triumph for Disraeli and a serious setback for Gladstone. The latter moved a major amendment and there was a large defection from his own party. Forty-three Liberals voted with the government and a further twenty were absent unpaired. The result was a majority of twenty-one for the government. Gladstone was mortified. Afterwards, Disraeli dined at the Carlton Club, where he was acclaimed by his supporters, then he returned home at 3 a.m. There he found Mary Anne waiting with a bottle of champagne and a Fortnum and Mason pie. 'Why my dear, you are more like a mistress than a wife,' he told her.[10]

Disraeli wanted a more radical bill and he got it. His tactic was to benignly preside over a series of amendments that drove it in this direction, and he was prepared to take them from all quarters of the House, Liberal as well as Conservative. There was, though, a major exception. He would not take them from Gladstone. It had to be seen to be a Conservative bill, not a Liberal one, and it had to be seen to be a Disraeli triumph, not a Gladstone one. The country had to know that it should thank him for what was being done for them, not Gladstone. This led to some curious outcomes. On more than one occasion, he rejected a Gladstone amendment, then later accepted one that was more extreme from another person on the same topic. Arguably, this sometimes caused him to go further than he really wished.

The effect of one amendment dwarfed all the others, and it became known as the 'Hodgkinson Amendment', named after the rather obscure Liberal MP who moved it. Gladstone unattractively called him 'a local solicitor little known in the House'.[11] The effect was that it made it a legal requirement that tenants in the boroughs pay their rates directly and not compound them by paying them to the landlords with their rent, leaving the landlords to make the payment. This, provided that the tenants were otherwise qualified, gave them the vote, and increased the size of the electorate by nearly half a million. Disraeli accepted the amendment, but it had been badly drafted and was withdrawn with a government replacement put in its place. Gladstone wrote: 'Never have I undergone a stronger element of surprise than when, as was entering the House, our Whip met me and stated that Disraeli was about to support Hodgkinson's motion'.[12]

Throughout his parliamentary career, Disraeli was master of the art of wittily deflecting personal attacks on him, and he did so to great effect during these debates. On one occasion, he was the victim of a vicious racist attack by Alexander Beresford Hope, a Conservative backbencher of Dutch descent who was opposed to the bill. Hope finished his remarks with the words 'I for one, with my whole heart and conscience will vote against the Asian mystery'.[13] This was a reference to Disraeli's Jewish origin. Disraeli replied: 'When he talks of Asian mysteries ... there is a Batavian grace about his exhibition which takes the sting out of what he said'.[14]

The reference to Batavian grace was well understood at the time, but will probably need an explanation now. The *Batavia* was the flagship of the Dutch East India Company, and in 1628, it made its maiden voyage to the Dutch East Indies. There were 341 people on board. On the journey, a high-ranking female passenger was molested and there was an attempted mutiny. The ship struck a reef off the west coast of Australia and forty people drowned. To cut a long story short, there was then a water shortage, a mutiny, and more than 100 murders. After a rescue, several crew members were hanged, flogged, keelhauled, or dropped from the yard arm. The second in command was broken on the wheel. Only 141 of the original 341 survived the voyage and what happened afterwards.

The third reading of the bill was on 15 July, and it took place without a division. A disconsolate Gladstone wrote: 'A remarkable night. Determined at the last moment not to take part in the debate for fear of doing mischief on our own side'.[15] The ill Derby managed a last great speech in the Lords and there was little dissent in the Upper House. Royal Assent was on 15 August.

A *Punch* cartoon from August 1867 portraying the Reform Bill as a leap in the dark.

The Reform Act (England and Wales) 1867, better known as the Second Reform Act, passed into law less than two years after the death in office of Lord Palmerston. The great statesman and opponent of reform would have been horrified. Many others were too, or they were at least worried. Lord Derby called it a leap in the dark, and so it was. The effects of the act went way beyond anything realistically envisaged when Palmerston was alive and in a position to discourage or prevent them. The main provisions were as follows:

Voting in the Boroughs

The vote was given to all householders who had been resident for a year, and to all lodgers who paid rent of at least £10 a year and who had been resident for at least a year.

In seats that returned three MPs, each elector only had two votes. In seats that returned four MPs, each elector only had three votes. Electors with more than one vote had to cast them for different candidates.

Voting in the Counties

In addition to persons already entitled to vote, the franchise was given to owners (or lessees on sixty-year leases or longer) of property worth £5 a year, and occupiers of lands with a rateable value of £12 a year, who had paid poor rates on the property.

Size of the Electorate

The overall electorate of England and Wales increased by about 90 per cent to 2 million or very slightly less. The greatest increase was in the boroughs where the number of electors more than doubled. According to the 1861 census, the population of England and Wales, including women and children, was 20,066,224. The 1871 census puts it at 22,712,266.

Redistribution of Seats

The redistribution of seats was relatively modest. The two main themes were the transfer of seats from the boroughs to the counties, and the transfer of seats from boroughs with low population to areas with high population. Major discrepancies remained.

Other

It was no longer necessary to hold a general election following a change of monarch.

Gladstone left London before Royal Assent and spent a holiday in North Wales lasting almost a month, then he spent ten weeks at his home in Hawarden. During that autumn, he visited Scotland, and during a speech, he made the claim that the Reform Act was a triumph of the Liberal Party. This was because the Conservatives were doing their bidding and following Liberal principles. This must have been hard for the listeners to accept because he had just led the unsuccessful opposition to it. However, it should not be overlooked that Gladstone was more popular in the country than he was with his colleagues in parliament. Perhaps his listeners were willing to give him the benefit of the doubt.

Disraeli also went to Scotland that autumn, and he made two very influential speeches. Speaking at a Conservative Party function in Edinburgh, he spoke about the inevitability and management of change, and the need to educate his party on this. In an often-quoted passage, he said:

> In a progressive country change is constant; and the great question is not whether you should resist change which is inevitable, but whether that change should be carried out in deference to the manners, the customs and the traditions of a people or whether it should be carried out in deference to abstract principles, and arbitrary and general doctrines. The one is a national system; the other, to give it an epithet, a noble epithet—which it may perhaps deserve—is a philosophic system.[16]

In 2007, David Cameron, the future prime minister, was asked about his favourite political quotation. He said that it was this one.

A few days later, Disraeli addressed a Conservative working men's meeting. He made the case that the Conservative Party was the natural champion of the poor. These two speeches go some way to promoting the idea that the Conservative Party was (and is) the party of 'one nation Conservatives'. It is a claim that resonates today and it is often linked with Disraeli's name. Disraeli never used the expression and many think that linking him with it is not justified.

Shortly after their return from Edinburgh, the seventy-five-year-old Mary Anne, Disraeli's wife, fell gravely ill. It was a terrible time for Disraeli. Prime Minister Derby was again ill and out of action, and a tremendous amount of work fell upon him. To make matters worse, there was a rare autumn session of the Commons made necessary by a crisis in Abyssinia. During the sitting, Gladstone made a friendly and considerate reference to the very ill Mary Anne, who he liked. It brought tears to Disraeli's eyes.

At the end of November, Disraeli collapsed and both he and his wife were seriously ill. Fortunately, he recovered by the end of the year. It was just as well because both the Liberals and the Conservatives were shortly to change their leaders.

The first to go was the Liberal. Russell stepped down at Christmas. Gladstone was ready, willing, and able to step into his place, and he did so.

His diary entry on 29 December 1867, his fifty-ninth birthday, included: 'Another year of mercies unworthily received is added to the sum of my days of wanderings and backslidings: of much varied experience in the world and in private life. I long for the day of rest'.[17] It does not seem an upbeat, buoyant launch of his new responsibilities.

Derby's health and his absence from cabinet and government business had become a serious problem. He was sixty-eight, five years younger than Russell, when he stepped down and twelve years younger than Palmerston when he died in office. He was suffering from a disabling form of gout and his doctors told him that he had to give up the premiership. Despite his past reluctance to take office, he did not want to go, but he had to. He wrote to the queen and, in a break with protocol, without being asked, he advised her to send for Disraeli.

On 27 February 1868, Disraeli travelled to Osborne on the Isle of Wight and kissed hands with his monarch. Afterwards, she wrote to her daughter, the crown princess of Prussia: 'Mr Disraeli is Prime Minister! A proud thing for a Man "risen from the people" to have obtained! And I must say—really most loyally; it is his real talent, his good temper and the way in wh. he managed the Reform Bill last year—wh. have brought this about'.[18] Afterwards. in a much-remembered phrase. Disraeli told friends: 'I have climbed to the top of the greasy pole'.

Derby died twenty months later. His last words were sad. Asked how he was, he replied: 'Bored to utter distraction'. When unveiling his statue in Parliament Square, Disraeli said: 'He abolished slavery, he educated Ireland, he reformed Parliament'. He did not mention that the abolition of slavery and the education of Ireland had been achieved when he was a Whig serving a Whig prime minister.

Palmerston had famously said that Gladstone was terrible on the rebound. So he was, and from late 1867, it happened again. He had had a bad time, but his spirits and his fortunes greatly improved. What is more, he took up an issue that had a unifying effect on the Liberal Party. This was Ireland, and it was something that would feature very prominently during the rest of his political career. Remarkably, neither he nor Disraeli had ever visited what was sometimes known as 'John Bull's Other Island'.

Gladstone chose a time shortly after an armed gang had rescued two prisoners in Manchester, and in doing so killed a police officer. It was also shortly after part of the wall of Clerkenwell Prison was blown up and twelve people were killed. In both cases, Irish 'terrorists' were responsible. Gladstone advocated Irish land reform and Irish church reform. His church views were a total volte face from the ones expressed in his 1838 book *The State in its Relations with the Church*. In this, he had said that anyone who was not a communicating Anglican should not be permitted to hold any public service job in Ireland.

The Feud: 1846–1881

Disraeli decided to celebrate his elevation to the position of prime minister with a great party and it was held in the reception rooms at the new Foreign Office. Mary Anne set about organising it, and it was going to be a grand affair. Unfortunately, the weather was very inclement and kept some people away. Nevertheless, those present included the prince and princess of Wales and many others of note. Gladstone was one of the guests and he circulated politely. Disraeli was not quite as joyous as might have been expected. He was leading a minority government and there were many difficulties. A resurgent Gladstone would not make things easy.

Disraeli was, of course, very aware of the discontent in Ireland, but solutions did not come easily to him. He had little sympathy with the Irish and a history of speaking harshly of them. One of many such comments was that 'their fair ideal of human happiness was an alternation of clannish broils and course idolatry'.[19] Another was that 'Daniel O'Connell was a more dangerous enemy than Napoleon'.[20] He was flat footed by Gladstone.

On 18 March 1868, Gladstone announced that he wanted to disestablish the Irish church, and a little later, he initiated a debate on his intentions to bring in three resolutions on the subject. Disraeli told the queen that the situation was serious, but that he thought 'Mr Gladstone had mistaken the spirit of the times and the temper of the country'.[21]

During the debate, Disraeli made a floundering speech in reply to Gladstone, and he gave the impression of being intoxicated. Gladstone wittily said that the speech 'had been delivered under the influence of ... a heated imagination'. A Conservative amendment to delay consideration until the next parliament was comfortably defeated, and a month later, the Commons moved to the substantive votes. Two of the resolutions were unopposed and the third was passed with a substantial majority. It was a Gladstone triumph and a Disraeli failure.

Although it had been a Gladstone success, it had come at the price of annoying the queen. She told Derby that she was upset by Gladstone's actions and she was especially annoyed that he had not told her in advance of his intention that the crown should give up its Church of Ireland land and revenue. When Derby told her that he did not think that the government should resign if it was defeated, she had replied: 'Quite right'.

The loss of the resolutions on Ireland made Disraeli's position untenable and he faced the same choice as Russell two years previously, namely resignation or dissolution. Unlike Russell, he chose dissolution. However, he had only been prime minister for three months and he did not want his period of office to perhaps (or probably) end so quickly. So he planned to stay on and hold the election in the autumn. He had the support of the queen and a very good excuse. This was that the new electoral register would not be ready until then, and it did not seem right that voting should exclude nearly a million people newly enfranchised by the recent Reform Act. Gladstone had been advised that the new register would marginally favour the Liberals and he did not object.

There were, however, objections to the delay, and they came from within his cabinet. Hardy and the dukes of Marlborough and Richmond were strongly in favour of an early election and might have resigned. Disraeli cynically defused Marlborough's opposition in a time-honoured way, though perhaps we should say a time-dishonoured way. On 8 May, he wrote to the queen: 'The Duke of Marlborough seemed a little bilious when Mr Disraeli returned from Osborne so ultimately, acting on Yr Majesty's sanction, Mr Disraeli announced to his Grace that Yr Majesty had been pleased to confer on him the blue ribbon [of the Garter]'.[22]

During the remainder of the parliamentary session, Gladstone illustrated his dominance in the Commons and that he was the prime minister in waiting. He spoke frequently on a variety of subjects and generally exhibited his confidence. He introduced a bill to suspend any new beneficial appointments in the Church of Ireland, and comfortably carried it through its second reading. The bill was decisively rejected by the Lords, but its progress illustrated the strength of Gladstone's position.

The recent Reform Act had split Gladstone's constituency, and in the autumn election, he stood as a candidate for South Lancashire. The tide was running for the Liberals but he faced problems in his constituency. Derby, who lived at Knowsley, had considerable influence, and many of his constituents were Protestants with anti-Catholic and anti-Irish inclinations. Gladstone hoped to win there and he campaigned furiously, but he hedged his bets by also being nominated for Greenwich. He made fifteen major speeches in South Lancashire and his passion and speaking style can be gauged by this extract from one of them made in Wigan. He compared the Protestant ascendancy in Ireland with:

> Some tall tree of noxious growth, lifting its head to Heaven and poisoning the atmosphere of the land so far as its shadow can extend. It is still there, gentlemen, but now at last the day had come when, as we hope, the axe has been laid to the root (Loud cheers). It is deeply cut and round. It nods and quivers from top to base (Cheers). There lacks, gentlemen, but one stroke more—the stroke of these Elections (Loud cheers). It will then, once for all, topple to its fall, and on that day the heart of Ireland will leap for joy, and the mind and conscience of England and Scotland will repose with thankful satisfaction upon the thought that something has been done towards the discharge of the national duty; and towards deepening and widening the foundations of public strength, security, and peace (Loud and prolonged applause).[23]

His efforts were in vain and he was in third place (with only two elected). He was 500 votes ahead of his Liberal running mate and 300 votes behind each of the two Conservatives. He was, however, comfortably elected as a member for Greenwich. Gladstone was one of the small number of party leaders who were rejected by their constituencies. The others were Balfour in 1906, Asquith in 1918, and MacDonald in 1935. In these three cases, the reverses were due to exceptional circumstances or when their parties had become very unpopular. This was not true of Gladstone in 1868.

Disraeli was privately pessimistic about the poll, but in public exuded confidence. Just before the voting, he spoke at the annual lord mayor's banquet at the Guildhall in the City of London. To laughter and shouts of Gladstone, his speech included:

> I think I have read somewhere that it is the custom of undisciplined hosts on the eve of a great battle to anticipate and celebrate their triumph by horrid sounds and hideous yells, the sounding of cymbals, the beating of terrible drums, the shrieks and screams of barbaric horns. But when the struggle comes, and the fight takes place, it is sometimes found that the victory is not to them, but to those who are calm and collected.[24]

The results of the election showed that Disraeli's pessimism had been justified. The Liberals increased their majority and the distribution of votes and seats were as follows:

England	Conservative	803,637 votes	211 seats
	Liberal	1,192,098	244 seats
Wales	Conservative	29,866 votes	10 seats
	Liberal	52,256 votes	23 seats
Scotland	Conservative	23,985 votes	7 seats
	Liberal	125,356 votes	51 seats
Ireland	Conservatives	38,767 votes	37 seats
	Liberal	54,461 votes	66 seats
	Others	188 votes	0 seats
Universities	Conservative	7,063 votes	6 seats
	Liberal	4,605 votes	3 seats
Total	Conservative	903,318 votes	271 seats
	Liberal	1,428,776 votes	387 seats
	Other	188 votes	0 seats

Disraeli had hoped that the newly enfranchised voters would thank the Conservatives for the vote. They obviously did not, or if they did, their gratitude was outweighed by other factors. The boroughs were a catastrophe for the Conservatives, but they took 60 per cent of the county seats. The transfer of voters from the boroughs to the counties meant that the counties now had 42 per cent of both the voters and the seats. The Conservatives did rather well in London and its suburbs, and also in Lancashire. As can be seen from the figures, they did better in England than in Wales, Scotland, and Ireland. Their performance in Scotland was particularly bad—in fact, the use of the word dreadful would be justified.

Disraeli's resignation broke with tradition. It was normal for a defeated prime minister to wait until parliament met before resigning, but he did not do this. He wrote to the queen, offering his resignation straight away.

Gladstone was busy felling a tree at Hawarden when the queen's private secretary arrived to deliver a letter confirming that he was to be the next prime minister. Gladstone opened it, read the contents, and then said: 'Very significant'. He aimed a few more blows at the tree, then said: 'My mission is to pacify Ireland'. He then resumed felling the tree.

The next day, the two men travelled by rail from Hawarden to Windsor, and by special arrangement, the through train was stopped at Slough. Gladstone alighted and walked across the fields to Windsor Castle. Before going to meet the queen, he stopped at Eton and spent a short time with his son. His time with Victoria went extremely well and he officially became prime minister, or first lord of the Treasury to give the job its formal title.

On leaving office, the customary offer of a seat in the House of Lords for a former prime minister was available to Disraeli. He did not accept because he wanted to continue his career in the Commons and to regain the position of prime minister while serving there. He waited until 1876 before moving to the Upper House.

When he declined the offer, he caused considerable consternation by requesting that his wife be made Viscountess Beaconsfield. This was unprecedented and risked causing anger and derision, but despite having reservations, the queen granted the request. She wrote: 'The Queen can truly sympathise with his devotion to Mrs Disraeli, who in her turn is so deeply attached to him, and she hoped they may yet enjoy many years of happiness together'.[25] Victoria may well have had in mind her struggle to have Prince Albert named prince consort. Disraeli's reply included 'Mr Disraeli at your Majesty's feet'.[26]

Fears about anger and derision turned out to be misplaced, and it did not become a precedent. Many people were touched by the gesture and the love that lay behind it. They included Gladstone, who wrote to Disraeli and asked him 'to present my best compliments on her coming patent to (I suppose I must still say, and never can use the name for the last time without regret (Mrs Disraeli).'[27]

Mary Anne, who was aged seventy-five and in poor health, was ecstatic. For some reason, she insisted that the first part of her title be pronounced to rhyme with 'deacon' rather than the more usual 'beckon'. Lord Rosebery said that it would take more courage than he had to address her using any other pronunciation. She had various things embossed with the letter 'B', including furniture and book covers. Notepaper was embossed with a coronet and the letter 'B', and she ended letters to her husband with 'Your devoted Beaconsfield'. Sadly, she only had four more years of life to enjoy the honour.

15
1868–1870

The spirits and attitudes of Disraeli and Gladstone on becoming prime minister for the first time were markedly different.

The jubilant Disraeli told friends that he had climbed to the top of the greasy pole. The remark was all about him and with no reference to what he wanted to do for his party, his country, mankind, and his God. This puts it very baldly and possibly unfairly. Maybe he did have thoughts on these matters, but it is perhaps fair comment. He had spent more than a quarter of a century trying to climb the greasy pole, and apart from three very short periods, he had been in opposition all the time. For him, the pole had been very greasy indeed. He probably believed that he would not stay at the top of it for very long, and if he did think this, he was quite correct. His tenure in 10 Downing Street only lasted nine months, then he was very decisively rejected by the voters, including those that he had played a very large part in giving the vote. He was destined to later have another spell as prime minister, this time lasting for more than six years and with a solid majority.

Gladstone was a very different man, and there is no record of his thoughts on greasy poles or similar matters. We do, though, have access to his thoughts as expressed in his diary. On his fifty-ninth birthday, less than a month after taking office as prime minister, he wrote:

> This birthday opens my 60th year. I descend the hill of life. It would be a truer figure to say I ascend a steepening path with a burden ever gathering weight. The Almighty seems to sustain and spare me for some purpose of His own deeply unworthy as I know myself to be. Glory be to his name.[1]

As so often, there was reference to God and a self-deprecating admission of his own inadequacy. Two days later, his year-end entry included:

> Swimming for his life, a man does not see much of the country through which the river winds, and I probably know little of these years through which I busily

work and live, beyond this, how sin and frailty deface them, and how mercy crowns them. Farewell great year of opening, not of alarming, change: and welcome new year laden with promise and with care.[2]

This time, there was no mention of the Almighty, but sin did feature. The last sentence shows that he approached the new year with optimism.

Gladstone took office with the expectation that he would only have one period as prime minister. He expected to then retire and devote the rest of his life to religion, Homer, writing, and his other interests. H. C. G. Matthew put it as follows:

> That Gladstone regarded the premiership which began in December 1868 as his last as well as his first, can hardly be doubted by any reader of his journal. Anticipation of retirement is perhaps the most frequently reiterated theme in moments of recorded private reflection and in hints in private correspondence.[3]

The rest of his life did not pan out in this way. He was prime minister three more times and is the only person to have served four non-consecutive terms. When he did finally retire, Gladstone was eighty-four, the oldest person to have held the office.

While Prince Albert was alive and able to advise the queen, Gladstone had enjoyed a good relationship with her, but it had deteriorated afterwards and it deteriorated further during his first term as prime minister. It was a problem throughout the rest of his career. He was the least favourite of the nine who served her, whereas Disraeli was the favourite. With due hesitation, I venture to suggest that Melbourne was her second favourite, and that Palmerston and Russell (in that order) were her second and third least favourites. In 1868, Victoria was still in deep mourning for Albert. She was very reluctant to appear in public and frequently complained about her health and the burdens placed upon her. This created difficulties and, in some quarters, it fuelled feelings of republicanism.

It is interesting to reflect on the relationship between different monarchs and their prime ministers, and to try and rank them in order from most liked to most disliked. At the time of writing, Elizabeth II has been served by fourteen prime ministers, and she has been meticulous about keeping her views private. We can speculate, but we do not know. When MacDonald resigned at the end of his second term, George V told him that he had been the prime minister that he liked the best.[4] Perhaps he was just being kind, but if he meant it, he was putting him ahead of Asquith, Lloyd George, Bonar Law, and Baldwin.

The relationship between George II and the duke of Newcastle (prime minister 1754–56 and 1757–62) was often very strained. On one occasion, Newcastle thought that the king was challenging him to a duel.[5] The misunderstanding was caused by the angry Hanoverian king's poor command of the English language.

Shortly before Gladstone took office in 1868, the dean of Windsor, who had been a contemporary at Eton, wrote to him and offered some friendly advice. He said that the queen was a woman (which would not have come as a surprise) and that she would need to be treated as such. He continued:

> Everything depends on your manner of approaching the Queen. Her nervous susceptibility has much increased since you had to do with her before, and you cannot show too much regard, gentleness, I might even say tenderness towards her. Where you differ, it will be best not at first to try and reason her over to your side, but to pass the matter lightly over, with expression of respectful regret, and reserve it, for there is no-one with whom more is to be gained by getting her into the habit of intercourse with you. Put off, until she is accustomed to see you, all discussions which are not absolutely necessary for the day.[6]

Disraeli got it right. He managed her brilliantly, if somewhat unscrupulously. He flattered her and lightly moved over points of disagreement. Gladstone got it wrong. His approach was to very respectfully, but relentlessly and at length keep putting his point of view in detail. It frequently annoyed her.

There is a story that illustrates the different ways that the two men communicated with women, not just the queen. It may or may not be strictly true, but it is widely believed and this alone makes it significant. It concerns Jennie Churchill, the wife of Lord Randolph Churchill and the mother of Sir Winston Churchill. As a young woman, she dined with both Gladstone and Disraeli. She later said: 'When I left the dining room after sitting next to Gladstone, I thought that he was the cleverest man in England. But when I sat next to Disraeli, I left feeling that I was the cleverest woman'.

Gladstone's relationship with the queen was subjected to a number of early tests. The first concerned Lord Clarendon, who Gladstone had promised the position of foreign secretary. He was an experienced diplomat and an experienced minister, who had held this position during the Crimean War. The problem was that he had a flippant manner and had taken to referring to the queen as 'the Missus'. She was aware of this and had taken offence, and as a result, she did not want him in the cabinet. It was potentially a major difficulty, but Gladstone got his way. He undertook to tell Clarendon that the problem was his fault and that he should be more cautious with his tongue. Victoria rather reluctantly dropped her objection and he took the appointment.

A second problem blew up in Gladstone's very first week in office. G. O. Trevelyan was a young junior minister at the Admiralty, and during an election address, he had said that the court and the duke of Cambridge (the queen's first cousin) as commander-in-chief were obstacles to Army reform.

The duke held this position for thirty-nine years from 1856–1895 and there was a lot of truth in the observation.

Gladstone was horrified and delivered a stinging rebuke to Trevelyan, who he wanted to keep. The junior minister apologised and this was conveyed to the queen. Gladstone told her that he was a man of character and ability, and that he had learnt his lesson. He left the matter of whether or not he should be sacked in her hands. The queen accepted the apology, but demanded that a similar one be given to the duke of Cambridge. This was done, and he kept his job. Gladstone again got the result that he wanted.

The third difference with the queen was not a success for Gladstone. Much to his dismay, she would not agree to open parliament in person. She had two reasons, the first one being her health and the fatigues and headaches to which she was prone. Her doctor, Sir William Jenner, probably wrongly accepted this, but her secretary, General Grey, did not, and neither did her daughter, Princess Louise. Grey told Gladstone: 'Princess Louise is very decided as to the ability of the Queen to meet any fatigue and is most indignant with Jenner for encouraging the Queen's fancies about her health'.[7] Jenner told Gladstone that her health was not the only reason that she refused. It was also because of 'an anxiety to avoid any personal interference in the great question pending with respect to the Irish Church'.[6] This was a way of saying that she was worried about one of his policies. The queen did not open parliament.

Rather surprisingly, and despite having several months' expectation of the general election, Gladstone did not take office with a list of legislative measures to enact. It was an example followed by Disraeli in 1874. Despite this, much was done in Gladstone's 1868–74 government. What he did have very firmly in mind as an early priority was the disestablishment of the church in Ireland, and he intended to follow it with an Irish Land Bill.

It was the disestablishment of the Irish Church that had dismayed the queen and was one of her reasons for not agreeing to open parliament. Gladstone had sent her two long and very detailed letters outlining his intentions. She had had great difficulty understanding them and had had a precis prepared. She still had problems grasping his meanings, but she knew enough to know that she did not like them. She told Gladstone that 'she greatly regretted that he had committed himself to so sweeping a measure'.[8] She did not, however, go as far as trying to block him, and she was helpful when the bill ran into difficulty in the Lords.

Parallel to his disestablishment bill, Gladstone wanted the royal family to have a closer connection with Ireland. To this end, he asked the queen to acquire a royal residence in the country and visit it from time to time—this being in addition to, or instead of going to, Balmoral in Scotland. She flatly refused. As far as we know, she did not make the point that her prime minister had never even visited Ireland, let alone acquire a house there and spend time in it. Disraeli had previously made a similar suggestion but had dropped it when he found it was unwelcome.

Gladstone also wanted the post of lord lieutenant to be abolished and the prince of Wales to be appointed as viceroy, assisted by a secretary of state. The queen had no hesitation in saying no to this. The prince of Wales (Bertie) was then twenty-seven, and in 1901, he became King Edward VII.

Had Gladstone's proposal been acted on, history might have been different. Victoria distrusted her son and would not let him assist her. He wanted a proper role but was not allowed to have one. Perhaps as a result of this, he became something of a playboy, and his interests included women, food, and pleasure in general. When his time came, he rather surprisingly turned out to be a good king. Had he been allowed to be viceroy, he might have done a good job and it might have paved the way for other achievements. On the other hand, it might have been a disaster. We will never know. Having the prince of Wales as viceroy would have risked bringing the future monarch into politics. This might not have mattered too much in England, but it might have mattered a lot in Ireland. That country was heading towards very turbulent times.

Gladstone took a very large part in securing the Irish Church Bill, which, when enacted, disestablished the Anglican Church in Ireland. He lobbied influential people, influenced the content of the bill, and guided it through the House of Commons. His powerful speech, introducing the bill, lasted three hours and fifteen minutes and exhibited a great command of detail. During his career, he was sometimes accused, not least by Disraeli, of verbosity, but Disraeli said that there was not a word wasted. The future Archbishop Temple wrote: 'The Irish Church Bill is the greatest monument to genius that I have yet known from Gladstone, even his marvellous budgets are not so marvellous'.[9]

The government won by 118 votes on the second reading, and then there was an arduous committee stage, again dominated by Gladstone. The third reading was secured by a majority of 114 votes and was marked by another Gladstone triumph, this time with a speech lasting an hour and fifteen minutes.

The House of Lords accepted the bill, but then mauled it in committee. The principle was agreed but not the details of the financial consequences. They twice rejected and returned to the Commons parts of the bill, and their amendments were not all acceptable to the Lower House. The situation had the makings of a possible Lords *v*. Commons constitutional crisis.

At Gladstone's request, the queen helped resolve the impasse. Without declaring for or against the disputed amendments, she conveyed, via Archbishop Tait, her concern at what was happening. Following this, the Lords withdrew most of their objections and the Commons agreed a few compromises. Gladstone and the Commons won.

The extended exertions had been physically and mentally draining for Gladstone and this may help explain his intense relationship with Laura

Thistlethwayte in the autumn of 1869. Another factor may have been the death of his friend, the dowager duchess of Sutherland. There was no impropriety in this friendship, but the duchess, who was four years older than him, had a very powerful intellect and he had greatly enjoyed her conversation and company. Mrs Thistlethwayte was a reformed courtesan and he was physically attracted to her, something that is confirmed by his diary. For a while, she took a lot of his time. An account of their relationship is given in Chapter 9.

Following his 1869 triumph with the Irish Church Bill in the spring of 1870, Gladstone introduced the Irish Land Bill into parliament. This was troublesome in a number of ways and it did not achieve all of its hoped for results. There were no cabinet resignations, but many of its members were distinctly unenthusiastic about it. Some Liberal MPs were also unhappy. Central to the problems requiring solution was that much of the land in Ireland was owned by absentee Protestant landlords. The tenancies were very fragmented and there were too many tenants for the land. Unfair evictions (as the tenants saw them) were greatly resented.

The bill provided that an evicted tenant should be compensated for improvements that he had made, rather than the benefits accruing to the landlord. This seemed obviously fair and was generally accepted in parliament. Gladstone had wanted to go further, but he came to recognise that this was not politically possible. There were fears that legal changes in Ireland would in time be extended to England and Scotland where the situation was different and they were not needed.

Issues left over for future legislation included fixity of tenure, fair rents, and freedom of sale (of the accrued rights of the tenant). The Irish Land Act addressed some problems but did not deal with others, some of which were not anticipated at the time. These were left until further legislation in Gladstone's 1880–85 government.

Following his 1868 election defeat, Disraeli was listless and out of sorts. Over the 1868–69 winter, his health was poor and he was concerned at Mary-Anne's increasing frailty. At the time of his election defeat, she had just turned seventy-six. To make matters worse, his brother, James, died at Christmas 1868, and he left an estate in chaos.

Disraeli's political inclination was to do little. Gladstone and the Liberals had recently won a resounding election victory and he thought that it was best to sit back, periodically make points when opportunities presented themselves, but generally let them get on with it. He thought that in time, and perhaps not too much time, the public would tire of the tide of legislation and what they might see as meddling. The Liberals would disagree among themselves and his time would come. This was prescient and it is what happened. However, in the meantime, some of his supporters became unhappy about his inactivity and some even wondered if they needed a new leader.

Disraeli's apparent lethargy was in one way deceptive. He had once said that if he wanted to read a novel, he would write one, and he did just that. In May 1870, *Lothair*, written in three volumes, was published. It was less than six months since he had been prime minister, and it seems reasonable to suppose that none of it was written while he was in government, so he must have worked very quickly and intensively.

He did the writing in secret and publication took the country by surprise. Obviously, his publisher knew and presumably his wife also knew, but virtually no one else did. Even his private secretary, Montagu Corry, did not know. Disraeli subsequently wrote: 'Montagu Corry who possesses my entire confidence in political matters, who opens all my letters, and enters my cabinet and deals, as he likes, with all my papers in my absence, never knew anything about *Lothair* until he read the advertisement in the journals'.[10]

The book was an immediate and enormous success. The first edition of 2,000 copies sold out in two days, and seven further editions were published in Britain by the end of the year. It was also a great success in America. Charles Dickens was among those who praised it. A street in Wandsworth was named 'Lothair Street', and Baron Rothschild named one of his horses after the book's heroine and it subsequently won the Cesarewitch. High sales continued and it made the author a lot of money.

The plot of *Lothair* seemed to me unlikely to secure it a place on the bestseller list, but readers in the 1870s took a different view. It was set in the very recent past when Disraeli was in office, but he does not feature in it. Lothair is a young English aristocrat, who is heir to a large fortune. During the course of the book, he is seeking a truth that is both religious and spiritual. In doing so, he is successively attracted to three beautiful and charismatic young women. One represents the Catholic church, one the Anglican church, and the third the Italian nationalists. Each has admirable qualities, which will appeal to the reader, and, we may speculate, also to the inner Disraeli.

Lothair fights for the possession of Rome at the side of the Italian nationalist, with Garibaldi and against the Pope. He is wounded and becomes unconscious, then he awakes in a hospital run by Catholic nuns. They almost persuade him that he has been fighting on their side against the nationalists, but he gets away. He falls under the spell of the Catholic young lady, but eventually he meets and marries the Anglican. Richard Aldous comments: '... the continental marvels were rejected in favour of English aristocratic virtues of winsome beauty, common sense, Protestantism and gardening'.[11]

This is a brief and inadequate summary of the novel, which is full of symbolism and witty epigrams. Oscar Wilde later said that the novel influenced his own epigrammatic style.[12] Despite the general acclaim, some critics were not impressed, and Disraeli received a number of complaining letters from Irish Catholics.

He included a number of thinly disguised real people. Lothair was the 3rd marquess of Bute, who after a soul-searching struggle had converted to Roman Catholicism in 1868. Henry Manning, the Catholic archbishop of Westminster, who had been close to Gladstone, was portrayed as the ruthless Cardinal Grandison. He was reported as being rather pleased. This was not the reaction of Samuel Wilberforce, the bishop of Winchester, who took offence at his portrayal. He told a friend: '... my wrath against D. has burnt ... so fiercely that it seems to have burnt up all the materials for burning and to be like an exhausted prairie fire—full of black stumps, burnt grass, and all abominations'.[13] Goldwin Smith, a professor of history, was outraged by his portrayal and in particular by the phrase 'like sedentary men of extreme opinions ... a social parasite'.[14]

Gladstone's diary records that he read the book, but it makes no further comment. There was no portrayal of him. That would have to wait until Disraeli's last novel. This was unfinished at his death in 1881 and poignantly ended in mid-sentence. Given all of the above, it is interesting to note that the 1872 wedding of the 3rd marquess of Bute was performed by Henry Manning, archbishop of Westminster (cardinal from 1875). Disraeli was one of the witnesses.

As mentioned earlier in this chapter, Gladstone took office without, apart from Ireland, detailed legislative plans. This state of affairs did not last long, and, in particular, education quickly engaged the attention of the government and himself. The two Irish Bills were exhausting for him and there were other measures in the pipeline. It may seem curious to us now but ecclesiastical appointments concerned him greatly and took up a lot of his time. In February 1970, he told Home Secretary H. A. Bruce: 'If you read in the papers some morning that I have been committed to Bedlam, and that a straight waistcoat is considered necessary, please to remember it will be entirely owing to the vacancy in the see of St Asaph'.[15]

Gladstone's very deep religious beliefs probably caused him to give the appointments more time and attention than has been the case with nearly all of the other prime ministers. It is still the practice of the prime minister to advise the sovereign, who is head of the Church of England, on the appointments.

An entertaining but fictional example is provided by an episode of the television series *Yes Prime Minister*. The prime minister (played by Paul Eddington) discusses with the Cabinet secretary (played by Nigel Hawthorne) the recommendation that he will shortly make for the position of bishop of Bury St Edmunds. The Cabinet secretary tells him that the church is trying to be more relevant and that it is a social organisation not a religious one. The prime minister asks 'what about God?' and receives the reply 'I think that He's what's called an optional extra'. Mr Gladstone would not have been amused.

Educational reform was not a subject in which Gladstone was instinctively very interested and it presented him with a number of problems. Despite this, W. E. Forster's Elementary Educational Bill was introduced into the House of Commons in February 1870 and reached the Statute Book later that year. The reform of higher education was left until the later part of Gladstone's first administration and this is covered in the next chapter. The period in between the reforms was not dealt with in 1868–74.

Gladstone's first problem was that the country was divided on what should be done. Another problem was Gladstone's background and educational experience. He had attended Eton College and Christ Church College, Oxford. In his view and the view of many others, this was England's premier university college. He had received a first-class classical education. Many members of the House of Commons and the House of Lords had also attended public schools and received a classical education, though by no means all to the standard enjoyed by Gladstone. Disraeli had received a classical education, but not at a public school and not at a university.

This education was marvellous for Gladstone, but it was very far removed from the experiences of the children that he and his party were trying to help. Despite his liberal leanings, he did not instinctively empathise with them. His third problem was religion. Education was closely linked with the different churches and the different views of Anglicans, Roman Catholics, Nonconformists, and others. Gladstone was a passionate, high church Anglican, which coloured his views and put him at odds with those who saw God in a different way.

It is instructive to consider the position in England and Wales before 1870. According to Roy Jenkins, there were a total of 4.3 million children of school age and 2 million of them were receiving no education at all.[16] A total 1.3 million were in state-aided schools and 1 million were in purely voluntary (and frequently unsatisfactory) establishments. It was widely felt that Britain's schooling lagged behind the schooling in several other European countries, especially Prussia.

The childhood of David Lloyd George, who was prime minister from 1916 to 1922, illustrates some of the things that needed fixing. He was born in 1863 and lived in the village of Llanystumdy near Criccieth in North Wales. He attended the Anglican Llanystumdwy National School. Most of the children at the school were nonconformists and this included himself. He was brought up to be a Baptist and, like nearly everyone in the village, Welsh was his first language. Despite this, the lessons were exclusively in English and the pupils could be punished if they were caught speaking Welsh.

Lloyd George did not get to be prime minister without being a rebel, and in 1875, there was an early indication of this tendency. School inspectors from the church visited the school annually, and during the inspection, the pupils were required to recite the catechism in unison. Lloyd George resented this because the words did not accurately reflect his beliefs or the beliefs of his fellow pupils. So he persuaded his classmates to stay mute when instructed to do this. They were ordered to do it several times by the headmaster but did not. Eventually, David's younger brother felt sorry for the headmaster and the boys and girls followed his lead in saying the words.[17] It is only fair to mention that the headmaster was well-liked and accounts say that, in many ways, it was a good school.

Gladstone wanted to increase the grants to existing Anglican and Roman Catholic schools, and to set up new state schools. These became known as Board Schools because they were controlled by Local Education Boards. These would provide just secular education, but would allow (presumably only with permission) priests and nonconformist ministers to visit the schools and give religious instruction to children who favoured their denominations. It is a fanciful thought, and one as far as I know that was never put to the test, but one wonders how an Islamic Imam would have been received. The Board Schools would be funded by the local ratepayers. Gladstone's views had progressed a long way from his former beliefs, which most people would now, and to a lesser extent at the time, consider to be narrow minded. However, he did not want to see church schools absorbed into a national secular system.

He did not get what he wanted. Roy Jenkins put it as follows:

> Hardly anyone except himself was in favour of the position. It did not satisfy the Anglican lobby, which was less tolerant of 'lesser breeds without the law' than Gladstone had become; it did not satisfy the Dissenters, who wanted simple Bible teaching on the rates; and it did not satisfy the mostly Erastian members of the Cabinet who wanted a more politically attractive solution.[18]

On 14 June 1870, Gladstone was defeated by a cabinet decision to accept the Cowper-Temple amendment. Cowper-Temple was a member of his party who had been a junior minister as far back as 1841. The amendment provided basic non-denominational, religious information, and instruction in the Board Schools. The word 'basic' should particularly be noted. Gladstone strongly disagreed, but he had to accept the decision of his cabinet.

Not for the first or last time, Gladstone vehemently advocated to parliament something with which he disagreed. Also not for the first or last time, he showed magnanimity to a person whose views had prevailed against his wishes. In 1880, he successfully recommended to the queen that Cowper-Temple be created Baron Mount Temple in the County of Sligo. Cowper-Temple was exceptionally well connected. His uncle was a prime minister, Lord Melbourne, and his stepfather was a prime minister, Lord Palmerston.

A further amendment allowed schoolboards to pay denominational schools the fees of poor children. In practice, very few of the boards did this, but it seriously annoyed many nonconformists. Joseph Chamberlain, who was about to be mayor of Birmingham and was not yet in parliament, was one of the many who were outraged. He was a future Liberal minister, a future Liberal Unionist minister, and a future Unionist minister. As told later in this book, he would become a serious thorn in the flesh for Gladstone. Joseph Chamberlain was Unitarian, as was his son, Austen Chamberlain, who became leader of the Conservative MPs in the Commons and his other son, Neville, who became prime minister.

The bill was not good for the reputation of Gladstone, and it was not good for the reputation of the Liberal Party. One amendment by a Liberal MP would have put beyond doubt that religious teaching in any Board School should not be in favour of or opposed to the tenets of any particular denomination. This was defeated by 251 votes to 130 votes. The 130 votes against were all cast by Liberals. The bill only got through with the assistance of the votes of over 100 Conservatives.

The Elementary Education Act 1870 was amended by Disraeli's Conservatives soon after Disraeli became prime minister in 1874. Gladstone regarded this as constitutionally improper because he thought that an incoming government was bound to accept the legislation of its predecessor. Many people thought differently at the time and almost everyone thinks differently now.

Ireland, education, and church appointments were not the only problems occupying Gladstone's time in the period to 1870. Another was throwing open to competitive examination all ranks in the Civil Service. The two exceptions to this were the Education and Foreign Offices.

This chapter has not so far touched on Gladstone's attitude to foreign affairs, but they became very important to him in the summer of 1870. The catalyst for this was the Franco-Prussian War, which started in the summer of that year. The pressure on him was intensified because the foreign secretary, Lord Clarendon, had died just two weeks earlier. His successor, Lord Granville, was not yet as effective.

The war was between the Second French Empire (and then the Third French Republic) on one side, and the German States of the North German Federation (led by the Kingdom of Prussia) on the other. The cause was the wish of the Prussians (led by Chancellor Otto von Bismarck) to extend German unification, and French fear of the consequences if this aim succeeded.

Very few people saw the war coming, and this included Gladstone, Clarendon, Granville, and the Foreign Office. Bismarck, though, did. History has generally blamed him for engineering the conflict. France, led by Emperor Napoleon III, declared war on 19 July 1870. Opinion in Britain was divided, and this was also true of the royal family, but there was most support for Prussia.

Queen Victoria strongly supported Prussia and, of course, she had strong family links to Germany. Through her father's side of the family, she was a Hanoverian, and her mother was Princess Victoria of Saxe-Coburg-Saalfield. Her late and much loved husband was German and her eldest daughter was married to the heir to the Prussian throne. This daughter was the mother of the future Kaiser Wilhelm II, who bore a lot of responsibility for the start of the First World War.

The prince of Wales, on the other hand, loved France, and Paris in particular. To his mother's annoyance, he favoured France. The princess of Wales, who was aged twenty-five at the time, hated Prussia and her feelings lasted until after World War 1. She was the daughter of King Christian VIII of Denmark and was bitter at what she saw as Prussia's actions in provoking then winning the war with Denmark six years earlier. This had resulted in the duchies of Schleswig and Holstein passing from Denmark to Prussia.

The queen was very partisan in her support for Prussia. On 19 July, the day that France declared war, she wrote to Gladstone: 'It is not a question of Prussia against France but of United Germany most unjustifiably attacked, fighting for hearth and Home—so no one can help feeling warmly for them'.[19] There were other letters in a similar vein.

Gladstone was not so sure. His sympathies for the time being veered towards Prussia, but he had reservations. He was firmly resolved to keep Britain out of the war, which was not hard and he easily accomplished it. He also successfully repulsed calls for a big increase in the country's military capacity. A further and much harder to achieve objective was to deter the Prussians and the French from violating Belgian territory, something that the Germans did in both 1914 and 1940. He was successful in this as well. He demanded that the War Office urgently study means of sending 20,000 troops to Belgium. This plus diplomatic pressure did the trick.

The war was very short and ended in a crushing victory for the Prussians. The Prussian (or German) Army marched on Paris in 1814, 1815, 1870, 1914, and 1940. Four times they got there, and in 1914, they were so close that the gunfire could be heard from Notre Dame Cathedral. In 1870, the war effectively ended on 1 September, though republicans seized Paris and kept it going a little longer. On 1 September, the French suffered a crushing defeat at the Battle of Sedan. The French emperor was with his troops and was among the large number who surrendered. Louis Napoleon was taken to see the Prussian King Wilhelm and the French emperor opened the conversation by congratulating him on the performance of his artillery. Wilhelm responded by saying that Louis Napoleon was a prisoner and that arrangements would have to be made. He proposed making his Summer Palace available and asked if this would be convenient. The conversation was very civilised, but there was no disguising the fact that Louis Napoleon and France had been humiliated.

Gladstone had done well, but he had committed a financial indiscretion, and he still had to face the problem of Alsace Lorraine. This proved to be unsurmountable.

Just a few days before war was declared, the conflict was seen to be almost inevitable. This was bad for the price of British government stocks, which fell accordingly. At this point, Gladstone bought Consols at the reduced price, and he did so with knowledge that Belgian neutrality was unlikely to be violated. This was good for the price, which recovered when it became generally known. Gladstone had made a significant profit because of this. He did not try to conceal what he had done and Roy Jenkins thought that it never occurred to him that he was doing anything improper.[20]

When the war was over, Bismarck moved to annex the prosperous French province of Alsace and part of the prosperous French province of Lorraine. This upset much of the British people who sympathised with France on this matter. Gladstone wanted to rally the European powers to put pressure on Prussia and stop it happening. However, the cabinet thought that this was a lost cause and that failure would damage British prestige. Accordingly, he was prevented from launching his initiative and it was a setback for the prime minister.

Bismarck did succeed in getting the provinces for his country, and it endangered bitterness that lasted nearly half a century. They were returned to France in 1919 under the terms of the Treaty of Versailles that followed the First World War.

16
1871–1874

Gladstone had become prime minister in December 1868, and he had done so after a resounding general election victory. His party and the country were behind him and he took office with the wind in his sails. Disraeli had thought that, in time, his opponent would antagonise at least part of the country and that people would tire of what they would come to see as too much government. He thought that, until that happened, it was best for the Conservatives to be relatively restrained. This did not please many of his supporters, and there were tentative thoughts about changing the leader, perhaps to the 15th earl of Derby.

The passage of time showed that Disraeli had been prescient. What he had foreseen came to pass. Gladstone, to some extent, lost his touch. He tried to do too much, exhausted himself, made a number of bad decisions, acted imperiously, and upset some of his supporters and part of the country. His 1868–74 ministry ended ignominiously. The years covered in this chapter were, from his point of view, much less happy than the years covered in the last one.

An early difficulty for him was the Universities Tests Act, which became law in 1871. This abolished religious 'Tests' and allowed Roman Catholics, Nonconformists, and non-Christians to study at Oxford, Cambridge, and Durham Universities, and to hold almost all the positions within them. There were a very few exceptions where the posts had specifically religious functions, such as theological professorships. This was the final departure from the position when Gladstone had been at Christ Church College, Oxford. There had been changes since then, but at the time, only Anglicans could attend the universities and hold positions in them.

Gladstone had come a long way from his earlier beliefs, expressed in a book, that only Anglicans should attend the universities, and indeed that only Anglicans should hold certain positions in public life. Nevertheless, this went against the grain for him. He told the solicitor general who instigated the bill that the measure was 'beyond anything odious' to him.[1] As was his wont, when he adopted a measure, he pursued it ferociously and he succeeded in securing the bill's passage. In practice, it had less effect than might have been expected. Roman Catholics to a large extent did not take up the opportunities.

A further 1871 Act was a step to legitimise the status of trades unions, and furthermore, it legalised strikes. However, it did not legalise peaceful picketing. It apparently did not occur to Gladstone that the effect of strikes would be greatly reduced or even nullified unless this was done. It did occur to Disraeli or perhaps to one or more of his ministers. Peaceful picketing was made legal in 1875 during his second term as prime minister.

In mid-1871, Gladstone suffered yet another problem in his relations with the queen. It concerned the Army Regulation Act 1871. This abolished the purchase of commissions and promotions, and made provision for officers who lost presumed property rights. Gladstone wanted more far-reaching reforms, but to his great annoyance, even the ones in the bill ran into difficulties in the House of Commons. Vested interests opposed these obviously sensible and overdue reforms, and the duke of Cambridge was among their number. As recounted in the last chapter, he was the queen's first cousin, and he was commander-in-chief of the Army from 1856 to 1895. He was not a moderniser.

The queen initially favoured the bill, and she never got as far as opposing it, but she became equivocal and listened to the forces ranged against it. Referring to the duke of Cambridge, she wrote to Gladstone and said that she was sure 'that Mr Gladstone and the Govt. must feel very grateful to [him] for the support that he has given to the Army Bill'.[2] This was not the opinion of the recipient. Gladstone thought that the duke was part of the problem not part of the solution. Later, when it came to a vote in the House of Lords, the duke abstained.

What the queen did strongly oppose was the prospect of parliament sitting into late August and delaying her departure for her late summer–autumn visit to Balmoral. This was Gladstone's intention when the bill floundered in the Lords. She therefore acceded to his next move, which was just about legal but verged on the edge of constitutional impropriety. The government proceeded by prerogative. The purchase of commissions had been made illegal in 1809, except where it was regulated and the price kept under control by royal warrant. By prerogative, the warrant was cancelled. Abolition could be accomplished without the bill but compensation could not. This was most definitely not the result that the vested interests wanted, so the Lords gave in and passed the bill.

What happened illustrated Gladstone's capacity for effective ruthlessness, and it outraged many members of the House of Lords. It left some of them looking for opportunities for taking revenge. Although the queen kept her counsel, she too was probably affronted. She perhaps showed this by departing for Balmoral before a Privy Council Meeting to approve her speech ending the parliamentary proceedings. The meeting was held in Scotland and a quorum including at least one cabinet minister was required. Following this, the speech was read on her behalf.

Shortly afterwards, relations between the queen and her prime minister plunged to a very low level. For two weeks, the queen really was ill and she was at a low ebb for several weeks after that. It was very understandable that Gladstone did not realise it. We all know the story about the boy who cried wolf and was not believed when the wolf came. The queen had so often metaphorically cried wolf about her health and the strain that she was under that he did not take much notice of her protestations. The year was 1871, and it was at the peak time of republican feelings in the country.

This problem with the queen was just one of many. She had been unhappy about the release of Fenian prisoners and she badgered the prime minister following a mock assassination attempt in February 1872. John Brown, her highland servant and very close friend, intervened, and as a consequence was awarded a life annuity of £25. The offender, a somewhat deranged seventeen-year-old youth called Arthur O'Connor, had approached her with an unloaded imitation pistol.

The sentencing judge thought that O'Connor was an inadequate and gave him only a year's imprisonment. The queen, understandably we may well think, became very alarmed about her vulnerability. She deluged Gladstone with letters complaining about the law and the leniency of the sentence. She wanted O'Connor to be deported. He voluntarily agreed to go abroad provided that it was to a place with a healthy climate. His shrewdness in making this stipulation raises obvious questions about the degree of his inadequacy, which had been a factor in obtaining the lenient sentence.

There are reckoned to have been seven so-called assassination attempts on Queen Victoria, though most of them, like this one, were really gestures rather than serious threats to her life. She was not to know this at the time, and she acted bravely and with dignity. There have been a number of examples of public figures acting with dignity and generosity following an attempt on their life. A really outstanding one is Lord Palmerston who survived a shot at him in 1818 when he was secretary at war. The offender was of unsound mind and had a grievance about his army pension. Palmerston personally paid for his legal defence, and after he had been sent to a mental institution he ensured that he was looked after.[3]

Gladstone had a lot to put up with and was often justified in feeling resentful, but it should not be overlooked that the queen's interventions were sometimes (but only sometimes) helpful. A good example was her letter to him shortly before the 1871 budget due to be presented by his chancellor of the Exchequer, Robert Lowe. It related to the tax on matches:

> Above all it seems *certain* that this tax will seriously affect the manufacture and sale of matches wh is said to be the *sole* means of support of a vast number of the very poorest people & *little* children, especially in London, so that this tax wh it is intended shld press on all equally, will in fact be only severely felt by the poor, wh wld be *vy wrong*—& most impolitic at the present moment.—The Queen trusts that the Govt will reconsider this proposal, & try & substitute some other wh will not press upon the poor.[4]

This plus other representations caused the cabinet to make the change. The new tax was not introduced and the required revenue was secured by putting 2 pence on income tax.

Around the time of Gladstone using prerogative to force through army reforms, he had twice more acted at the very edge of the rules to achieve his aims.

The first instance was the appointment of Sir Robert Collier, the attorney general, to the Judicial Committee of the Privy Council. Such appointments were restricted to those who had sat on the judicial bench in England or India. Sir Robert was an admirable man but he had done neither. Gladstone circumvented the problem by arranging for him to be appointed a High Court judge and to serve in this role for just two days. This caused outrage and eventually to votes in parliament. Gladstone secured a majority of twenty-seven in the Commons and just two in the Lords.

There were some similarities to the second case. Gladstone wanted to make a clerical appointment for which it was a requirement that the holder be a member of Convocation at Oxford. His chosen candidate did not fulfil this stipulation. Gladstone arranged for him to be technically incorporated as a member of Oriel College for the statutory forty-two days of residence. Once again, he succeeded, but again there was outrage and he had to defend his actions in parliament.

Gladstone's career so far had mainly been concerned with finance and home affairs. His exposure to foreign affairs had been limited. This would change and future chapters give accounts of, among other things, his furious disagreements with Disraeli over the so-called 'Eastern Question', the facing down of Russia, and the Bulgarian Horrors. They also give accounts of the two men's disagreements over colonial expansion. In the late 1870s, Gladstone became very disparaging about what he called 'Beaconsfieldism'. This was a reference to Disraeli's title after he moved to the House of Lords.

In the early part of his 1868–74 administration, Gladstone had done rather well in his handling of the Franco-Prussian War, though his cabinet had restrained his plans to try and stop the victorious Prussians annexing the French provinces of Alsace and Lorraine. It probably could not have been done anyway. There was now another Gladstone triumph, though not everyone saw it that way. Interestingly, the unusual co-operation of Disraeli and the Conservatives helped make it possible. The matter was the settlement of the long-standing dispute with the United States over the exploits of the warship *Alabama* during the American Civil War.

The steam-powered *Alabama* was built on the River Mersey for the Confederate States by John Laird and company. A civilian crew sailed her to the Azores, and there she was fitted with armaments and supplies, and fuelled with 350 tons of coal, all of this having been shipped from Britain. A replacement crew, many of them British, took over, and for nearly two years, she wreaked havoc on Union shipping and the shipping of other countries supplying the Union. There were military victories, but nearly all the targets were merchant ships. Efforts were made to avoid civilian casualties and captured foreign nationals were disembarked at neutral ports. She was sunk in June 1864 shortly before the end of the war. In the almost two years that she was operating, she caused great damage and greatly hindered the Union cause.

The fact that the ship was built, sailed, and supplied was partly down to the negligence of the British government, and it should be remembered that in the early part of the war, some members of it, Palmerston in particular, did not support the Union cause. Gladstone's speech in Newcastle (quoted in Chapter 13) was interpreted by many as a call to recognise the Confederacy. Customs officials in Liverpool were slow in sending reports to the Foreign Office. The foreign secretary, Russell at the time, was slow in responding and was waiting for legal advice when the ship sailed.

With much justification, the United States government demanded compensation from Britain after the war had been won, but the amount that they wanted was ridiculous. To use a modern phrase, everything but the kitchen sink was added to the claim. Consequential loss was included as well as the direct damage—almost to the point of wanting Britain to pay the cost of the war being lengthened. No British government could possibly agree and the American attitude provoked anger in Britain. Tennyson wrote to Gladstone in February 1872: 'If you let those Yankee sharpers get anything like their way in the Alabama claims, I won't pay my ship-money, any more than old Hampden'.[5] The writer was Poet Laureate from 1850 to 1892. In 1868, he had turned down the offer of a peerage by Disraeli, but he accepted in 1892 when the offer was made by Gladstone.

Gladstone wanted the matter settled, and he should take considerable credit for getting the Americans to agree to independent arbitration. It was not easy. Disraeli's short-lived 1868 government had tried but had not been successful. Disraeli supplied Stafford Northcote as one of the five commissioners who went to Washington to try and get agreement. Later, one of Gladstone's letters to the queen included: '... the signal prudence of Mr Disraeli during the anxious period of the Controversy with the United States and the value of the example he had set'.[6]

The five appointed arbitrators were representatives of Great Britain, the US, Italy, Switzerland, and Brazil. The American arbitrator jettisoned the absurd elements of his country's claims and a settlement of £3.25 million was agreed. A very sour period in the relationship with the US came to an end, which was an enormous benefit to both countries. Gladstone deserved his share of the credit.

Another 1872 Gladstone success, this time a domestic one, was the Ballot Act. He came to the measure late and reluctantly. It was yet another instance of him reneging on a former reactionary stance, then, having been persuaded, driving it through with great zeal. The country had a dispiriting history of corruption in conducting parliamentary and local elections. Numerous examples include the following.

In the Irish borough of Cashel, Henry Munster paid the very large sum of £30 to each of twenty-five of the town's twenty-six butchers to secure their votes.[7]

At Totnes, there was great disappointment when a candidate withdrew. The wives of the electors had come to the Conservative hotel to collect the money that was to be distributed and sadly departed without it.[8]

Also at Totnes, tenants of the duke of Somerset were paid between £60 and £150 to vote against his wishes—enormous sums at the time for bribes. They faced the consequence of certain eviction, but calculated that it was worth it.[9]

Part of the problem was that voting was in public. Landlords, employers, and others could see which way people voted. It was even legal for newspapers to print the names of voters and the way that their votes were cast. The following words are from the splendidly named MP for Wareham, John Samuel Wanley Sawbridge-Erle-Drax:

> Electors of Wareham! I understand that some evil-disposed person has been circulating a report that I wish my tenants, and other persons dependent on me, to vote according to their conscience. This is a dastardly lie; calculated to injure me. I have no wish of the sort. I wish, and I intend, that these persons shall vote for me.[10]

Secret voting ended this. A person paying a bribe could not know the way that the recipient had voted. Conversely, a voter could take more than one bribe without fear of discovery. One exceedingly flimsy argument against the secret ballot was that some people thought it right that manly voters should march to the poll with their heads held high and that the world should be able to admire the courage of their convictions. For many years, Gladstone had strongly thought this, and right up to 1872, he had nostalgic feelings for his former conviction. It should not be forgotten that corruption, much of which he was unaware, had helped secure his election for Newark in 1832.

After two private members' bills had failed, the third attempt became a government measure, but after its passage through the Commons, it was rejected by the Lords. The voting on an insultingly low turnout was 97 votes to 48. The ridiculous grounds for the reverse was that the bill had not been adequately scrutinised in the Commons. It had in fact had eighteen days' consideration in the lower chamber.

A justifiably outraged Gladstone resolved that this was something up with which he would not put. He said that the bill would return to the Lords with 'an authoritative knock', and if necessary, there would be an autumn session. Their lordships and honourable members did not like this idea at all, and Disraeli feared that continuing to block the bill in the upper house would not be good for his party's prospects. There were words in ears and the lords gave way. It was Gladstone's last legislative success in his 1868–74 government.

The secret ballot was first employed at a by-election held in Pontefract in August 1872. The actual ballot box is today preserved in a local museum, and it is still marked with the seal used to ensure that there was no tampering with the votes. Rather charmingly, the seal was made with a liquorice stamp used to make Pontefract cakes at a local liquorice factory.

During Gladstone's 1868–74 administration, the balance of power and influence between Disraeli and himself shifted very markedly. Fixing the date when this occurred is not possible because it happened over a period. The shift was perhaps just in time for Disraeli because, on 1 February 1872, a number of leading conservatives gathered at the home of Lord Exeter. Disraeli and the 15th earl of Derby, his likely successor, were not among their number. Many of them were dissatisfied with Disraeli's leadership, which they thought should be much more active, and the Chief Whip reported that this view was widely held on the back benches. Only Stafford Northcote and Lord John Manners spoke strongly in his defence. Fortunately for Disraeli, no one could be persuaded to be the person to give him the bad news.

Despite this, the tide was already turning and there was a strong indication of this just twenty-six days later. The prince of Wales had very nearly died of typhoid, the illness that had killed his father ten years previously. On 27 February, there was a national service of thanksgiving at St Paul's Cathedral to celebrate his recovery. Cheering crowds saluted the queen and the prince, and Disraeli (travelling separately) was also greeted in this manner. This was not the case for Gladstone. He passed the crowds in silence and there were even one or two jeers. Disraeli was back.

A string of Conservative by-election victories commenced and the Conservatives built up a very effective party organisation. They were much more successful in this than the Liberals, and it made a big difference when the general election came. At the same time, it became clear that Gladstone was losing his grip and that he and his colleagues had become weary of office. It was now downhill for them.

Gladstone had become known for his massive, barnstorming orations to very large public audiences around the country, but he had not recently done them. Disraeli did not operate in this way, but he now undertook two of them. Both were very successful indeed. His speaking style was, of course, very different from Gladstone's. He employed wit, sarcasm, epigrams, and the like. Gladstone was noted for blazing sincerity.

The first of Disraeli's two speeches was in the Free Trade Hall in Manchester, and it took place on 3 April 1872. It was ironic that the venue had been named after Peel's policy, which all those years ago Disraeli had challenged. The consequence had been that the Conservative Party had split.

The crowds were enormous, so much so that Disraeli and his wife, Mary Anne, had difficulty disembarking from the train. The carriage horses were taken away and a group of strong men pulled the couple through the cheering crowds. Around 6,000 people were in the hall to hear the speech. It was hot and the atmosphere was oppressive, which made it all the more remarkable that Disraeli spoke for more than three and a quarter hours. His speech was in the most part detailed and worthy, perhaps even a little dull, but perhaps that made it valuable. There should be a place for worthy speeches. However, it is mainly remembered for a number of denunciations of Gladstone. One in particular electrified the audience and included:

> Their paroxysms ended in prostration. Some took refuge in melancholy, and their eminent chief alternated between a menace and a sigh. As I sat opposite the Treasury bench the ministers reminded me of one of those marine landscapes not very uncommon on the coasts of South America. You behold a row of exhausted volcanoes. Not a flame flickers from a single pallid crest. But the situation is still dangerous. There are occasional earthquakes, and ever and anon the dark rumbling of the sea.[11]

This speech and his equally successful one for the National Union of Conservative Associations at the Crystal Palace in London were noted for his commitments to such matters as public health. He heralded Caring Conservatism. There was a joke in Latin to back this up. He spoke of '*Samitas, Samitatum, Omnia Samitas*'.[12] His normal audience in Westminster would have understood this, but one wonders what the mighty 6,000 made of it. His speeches also laid the way for reconstructing the colonies to secure closer ties, which he said would be good for them and good for the mother country.

The two speeches were so successful that an obvious question is why he did not do a series of them. Part of the answer is that they exhausted him and that his health had recently been bad. He needed to conserve his energy. However, the main reason was that his wife's health was very bad. In fact, she was dying.

Mary Anne almost certainly had cancer. She knew but did not tell her husband. This was because she thought that he did not know and she did not want to upset him. He knew, but he did not tell his wife. This was because he thought that she did not know and he did not want to upset her. Mary Anne, who was twelve years older than her husband, was seventy-nine in the summer of 1872.

Her illness was a terrible ordeal for Disraeli, and for her too of course. Their marriage was a very curious one, but it was a genuine love affair. He devoted a great deal of time to her care and they often took carriage rides together into London's suburbs and the surrounding countryside. Sometimes Disraeli would afterwards write to the queen to give her an account of the ride. On one occasion, he wrote: 'What miles of villas! And of all sorts of architecture! What beautiful churches.... One day we came upon a real feudal castle, with a donjon keep high in the air. It turned out to be the new City prison in Camden Road, but it deserves a visit, I mean externally'.[13]

In late November, Mary Anne made a great effort and the couple entertained their friends in a final house party at Hughenden. As she stood at the door and waved them goodbye, everyone knew that it would be the last time. She died on 15 December, and five days later, she was buried outside Hughenden Parish Church. Her grave was next to the grave of Disraeli's benefactor, Sara Brydges-Williams, who had died nine years previously. The grave of Mary Anne's husband would join the two of them eight years later. After the funeral, Disraeli stood alone for several minutes staring at the grave. He was bareheaded and it was pouring with rain.

Gladstone was sad at Mary Anne's passing and he behaved with sympathy and propriety. During her final weeks, he several times called at their London home to enquire after her health. After her death, he sent Disraeli the following letter:

> You and I were, as I believe, married in the same year. It has been permitted to both of us to enjoy a priceless boon through a third of a century. Spared myself the blow which has fallen on you, I can form some conception of what it must have been and must be. I do not presume to offer you the consolation, which you will seek from another and higher quarter. I offer only the assurance which all who knew you, & and all who knew Lady Beaconsfield & especially those among them who like myself enjoyed for a length of time her marked though unmerited regard, may perhaps tender without impropriety; the assurance that in this trying hour they feel deeply for you and with you.[14]

Disraeli's reply read as follows:

> I am much touched by your kind words in my great sorrow. I trust, I earnestly trust, that you may be spared a similar affliction. Marriage is the greatest earthly

happiness, when founded on complete sympathy. That hallowed lot was mine, and for a moiety of my existence; and I know it is yours.[15]

My dictionary defines 'moiety' as 'a part or share of something, especially when it is divided into two parts'. Gladstone kept a copy of the letter that he sent, which is why it can be reproduced here. Disraeli kept most of the letters of condolence that he received, but the one from Gladstone is not among them. One wonders if it was mislaid or if he deliberately disposed of it.

Disraeli missed his wife badly and he had to face financial and practical difficulties as well. Their London home at Grosvenor Gate reverted to her family and her income of £5,000 a year stopped. He retained Hughenden, but in order to be ready for the imminent parliamentary session, he was compelled to move into a London hotel. It was comfortable, but he was lonely and unhappy.

Some years before dying and conscious of the age difference between them, Mary Anne had told him that, in the event of her death, he should seek a new female companion. Disraeli acted on this advice and there was no shortage of candidates for the honour of filling the role. One of them was the notorious Adeline, countess of Cardigan and Lancaster, who was the widow of the man who had led the Charge of the Light Brigade at Balaclava in 1854. She proposed marriage to Disraeli, but he turned her down. She took the rejection badly and spread rumours about him, including that he had bad breath.[16]

The countess was forty-eight at the time and she should perhaps have remembered that Disraeli had a long history of preferring older women. He rapidly formed very close relationships with two sisters, both of them grandmothers. One was older than him, and the other was married and in her sixties. There are 1,100 surviving letters to one sister and 500 to the other.[17] He got a lot of comfort from the friendships and writing the letters. They were gossipy and political. He also got satisfaction from his continuing political activities, and he rapidly scotched rumours that he was about to retire.

From early in the 1873 parliamentary session, Gladstone and his government were in deep trouble. The cause was the Irish University Bill. Its laudable aim was to establish an Irish university and certain other colleges. This was mainly intended to help Roman Catholics who had been prevented by their own bishops from attending the fiercely Protestant Trinity College. Irish Catholics were under-represented in higher education in Ireland. The bill provided that there was to be no teaching of theology, moral philosophy, or modern history. This was because Ireland's history and the likely entrenched views of the prospective students made these subjects unacceptably divisive. Furthermore, teachers could be suspended or sacked if they upset students because of their religious beliefs.

The bill upset all sides, including much of Gladstone's cabinet. Some of them grumbled and the chief secretary of Ireland, Lord Hartington, threatened to resign. The duke of Argyll stayed away from cabinet meetings when the bill was under discussion. Outside the cabinet, former Prime Minister Earl Russell did not like it. Besides all this discontent, there was very little support from the Catholics that the bill was designed to help. The archbishop of Dublin, Cardinal Cullen, said that the Anglican Trinity College would use its wealth 'as a bait to poor Catholics to desert their denominational tutors'.[18] Then he asked Irish MPs to vote against the bill.

Gladstone's speech introducing the bill was superb and it lasted more than three hours, but he was pushing at a closed door. Disraeli's criticism of the bill was also very effective and he was pushing at an open door. His denunciation included: 'You have despoiled churches. You have threatened every corporation and endowment in the country. You have examined into everybody's affairs. You have criticised every profession and vexed every trade. No one is certain of his property and nobody knows what duties he may have to perform tomorrow'.[19] Despite admiration for Gladstone's performance, on 12 March at 2 a.m., the vote went against him by 287 votes to 284.

Gladstone had a number of options, all of them unattractive. He could abandon the bill and carry on; he could resign and let Disraeli form an administration in his place; or he could ask for a dissolution. Twelve hours after the lost vote, he told the cabinet that he had decided to resign, and he followed this by thanking them for all that they had achieved together. Shortly afterwards, he told the queen of his decision and advised her to send for Disraeli. The delighted Victoria had no hesitation in swiftly accepting the advice and acting on it.

What the queen had not expected was that Disraeli would decline the invitation. He did not want to lead another minority government, and not a big minority at that. Despite the Conservatives by-election successes, the Liberals still had a majority of eighty. He had never served in a majority government. His experience was of three short terms as chancellor of the Exchequer and nine months as prime minister, all of the four periods in minority governments. It had been frustrating and he did not want to do it again. He wanted power as well as the position.

In addition, there was the matter of cool political calculation. The government was in a bad way, and he thought that its plight would get worse and worse. Conversely, his prospects and the prospects of the Conservative Party would get better and better. He could have taken office then immediately ask for a dissolution, but he rejected this course. It was done by Henry Campbell-Bannerman when Arthur Balfour resigned in December 1905. He was rewarded by the January 2006 Liberal landslide

Gladstone was outraged by Disraeli's refusal to take office. He thought that having defeated the government, he had a moral obligation to form its replacement. Disraeli thought that this was nonsense. He told the queen's private secretary: 'We did not defeat the government. We threw out a stupid, blundering Bill which Gladstone, in his *tête montée* way, tried to make a vote of confidence. It was a foolish mistake of his'.[20] There followed an acrimonious exchange of letters addressed via the queen, but Disraeli held firm. The queen had to have a government, so eventually Victoria reluctantly acted on Disraeli's advice and asked Gladstone to carry on. He reluctantly agreed to do so. The episode further fuelled the feud between the two men. It is probably fair to say that the following ten months vindicated Disraeli's intransigence.

Not long after his aborted resignation, Gladstone faced a minor scandal that caused him to reshuffle some of his ministers. It pained him and he did not do it very well. Furthermore, it led to an unwise decision concerning his own responsibilities. There was no dishonesty, but public money had wrongly been allocated to the telegraph service. The two ministers at fault were Monsell, the postmaster general, and Ayrton, the first commissioner of works. The chancellor of the Exchequer, Lowe, had some responsibility, but less because of his remoteness from what had happened.

Monsell left the government but was awarded a peerage in the next honours list. Ayrton was moved to the position of judge advocate-general. He caused anger by speaking in the Commons in defence of his actions and defining ministerial responsibility in unrealistically limited terms. This was so unacceptable that Gladstone spoke immediately afterwards and contradicted what his minister had just said. Despite this, Gladstone did get the new position for him. It was not easy because the position involved speaking directly to the queen. Victoria was so upset by what he had done that this was not acceptable to her. A compromise was reached. He was made judge advocate-general, but with the condition that he would only communicate with the queen in writing.

Bruce, the home secretary, went to the House of Lords as lord president and Lowe was given his former position as home secretary. This left a vacancy at the Exchequer, and on 11 August 1873, Gladstone took it himself. This was not a good idea. Chancellor of the Exchequer is a demanding job, and he already had a demanding job. He was already feeling the strain, so why did he do it? There is a view that he was persuaded by his colleagues, though it is not easy to see why they might have done so. If it was the case, they did not have to persuade very hard. He wanted his old job and he had plans. They included the abolition of income tax and sugar duties, and partially replacing the lost revenue with death duties and duties on spirits.

There have been a number of instances of prime ministers simultaneously holding other cabinet positions and the results have been mixed. William Pitt the Younger was a good chancellor of the Exchequer for all the nineteen years that he was prime minister. Ramsay MacDonald was his own foreign secretary throughout his brief first ministry, and Lord Salisbury also held this position for more than four years during his final term as prime minister. During the Second World War, Churchill was both prime minister and minister of defence, and he repeated this double for a few months in the 1950s. In 1834, the duke of Wellington was prime minister for just twenty-six days while Sir Robert Peel was summoned home from Italy to take the position. During this time, he was first lord of the Treasury and secretary of state for the Home Office, Foreign Affairs, and War.

When Gladstone had become chancellor of the Exchequer he had not taken full account of an embarrassing problem. This related to the possible requirement for him to fight a by-election because he was taking an office of profit under the crown. It was not an academic point because the Conservatives were riding high and might well defeat him in his Greenwich constituency. The rule lasted until 1919, and there were some notable casualties, Winston Churchill in 1908 being one.

There was a clear requirement if the office of profit was the only one held, but Gladstone was prime minister so it was the second one. Old precedents indicated that a by-election was not necessary, but their relevance had perhaps been invalidated by the Representation of the People Act 1867. Its wording on this point was ambiguous.

Gladstone took legal advice from a number of authorities, but the opinions expressed differed. The new law officers expressed the view that there were very strong arguments both for and against. This hardly helped. Jessel, the previous solicitor general, had advised that a by-election was not necessary. He is supposed to have said of himself: 'I may be wrong, and sometimes I am, but I never have any doubts'.[21] The problem would not come to a head while parliament was not sitting, and on 20 January 1874, the great Sir Erskine May, clerk of the House of Commons, told Gladstone that, in his opinion, a by-election was not required.

A few days later, all concerned were able to turn their minds to other matters, because Gladstone called a general election. This had been expected during 1874, but not so early in the year. Nearly everyone was caught by surprise, and this included Disraeli. The tired prime minister, who was also chancellor of the Exchequer, wanted to break free and get a new mandate. Especially, he wanted the freedom to implement his budgetary plans. It was a bad mistake.

Gladstone was obsessed with his long-standing wish to abolish income tax, which at that time stood at 3 pence in the pound, and he thought that this would be very popular with the voters. As already mentioned, he also wanted to abolish sugar duties and raise some of the revenue that he needed by raising death duties and the duties on spirits. This would leave a shortfall, and he was in the fortunate position of having £5.25 million in the government's coffers. Perhaps the word 'fortunate' is misplaced, because it was his government that had put it there.

Even allowing for this, he needed more money, and he strongly believed that a government should not run a deficit in peacetime. He intended to try and end a war with the Ashantis in the Gold Coast (now Ghana) and to strictly control government expenditure in all departments. In particular, he intended to ruthlessly limit expenditure on the armed forces, especially the Royal Navy. This intention had been giving him severe problems with Goschen, the first lord of the Admiralty, and Cardwell, the war secretary. Their money had already been limited and they had accepted this so far. They were on the brink of resigning. Roy Jenkins said: 'The dissolution was as much against the Admiralty and the War Office as it was against the Tories'.[22]

Gladstone had the initial advantage of surprise. His address to the electors of Greenwich was printed in *The Times* on the morning of Friday 24 January. The first that Disraeli knew of it and the forthcoming general election was when he was woken early on that morning and given a copy of the newspaper. He immediately set about getting his own election address in the same paper on the morning of Monday 27 January. He worked furiously for three days, assisted by an *ad hoc* group of advisers coming in and out, and he achieved the deadline.

Disraeli's address was only a quarter the length of Gladstone's, but it was on the whole more favourably received. *The Times* commented: 'Where one is conscientiously argumentative, the other is brisk, curt and rapid'.[23] Gladstone's address relied heavily on the plan to abolish income tax, whereas Disraeli's promised attention to the condition of the people. What is more, this was to be done without 'incessant and harassing legislation'. This was shrewd. The voters were fed up with it. Disraeli promised more attention to Britain's interests overseas and less meddling at home.

The election was fought more on a national basis than its predecessors. There was less attention to individual candidates in local constituencies, and there was more attention on the party leaders. It was, in the words of part of the title of this book, Disraeli *v.* Gladstone. The size of the electorate had almost doubled since the Representation of the People Act 1867, and this resulted in the need for more effective national organisations. Both parties had paid attention to this, but the Conservatives had done it better and on a bigger scale. They had more organisation, more money, and more candidates. It made a difference.

Gladstone soon realised that his plan to abolish income tax and bear down heavily on government expenditure was not going to have the widespread approval that he anticipated. It was against the spirit of the times. After the election had been lost, Joseph Chamberlain, then the Liberal mayor of Birmingham, said that Gladstone's election address was 'the meanest public document that had ever, in like circumstances, proceeded from a statesman of the first rank. His manifesto was simply an appeal to the selfishness of the middle classes'.[24] This is the man who would soon become an MP and then lead the radical wing of the Liberal Party in Gladstone's 1880 government. He would go on to split the Liberals over Irish Home Rule and then split the Conservatives over tariff reform.

Among other things, the election campaign is remembered for an especially vituperative attack by Disraeli. Speaking at Aylesbury, he said:

> I read something the other day. A person entered a jeweller's shop and asked to look at a costly trinket that was before him, and when the respectable tradesman ... handed him the trinket, the customer threw a quarter of an ounce of snuff into his eyes, and when the unfortunate tradesman recovered his sight and senses he found that his customer had disappeared and his trinket too. And so it is that Mr Gladstone throws gold dust into the eyes of the people of England, and, before they clearly ascertain what it is like or worth, they find that he has disappeared with a costly jewel as the price of his dextrous management.[25]

Gladstone's response came two days later at New Cross:

> I have been sharply opposed to Mr Disraeli in political life for more than twenty years, but certain bounds and limits have been imposed on the character of the language which has been used between us. I do not wish to pass those limits; and if an example has been unfortunately set which I am sure he himself will regret, I for the moment undoubtedly will not follow him.[26]

Disraeli was delighted with what he had said, and he was delighted with the furore that it had provoked. He thought that it would gain him votes, and he was probably right. Nevertheless, it was shocking and unfair, and various commentators said so. It ranks with Aneurin Bevan's remark in 1948 that the Tory party was 'lower than vermin'.

Disraeli secured a crushing victory, which was the first Conservative majority since Peel's in 1841. The distribution of seats was as follows:

Conservative:	350
Liberal:	245
Home Rule:	57
Total:	652

William Gladstone is kicked out of power.

The Home Rulers were Irish and had taken seats for the first time. Their success had been facilitated by the 1872 Ballot Act. Vulnerable Irish voters were now able to cast their votes out of the scrutiny of potentially vengeful landlords and employers. Home Rulers and their successors have caused problems ever since. In the 1918 general election, Sinn Féin won in seventy-three constituencies, but their victorious candidates did not take their seats at Westminster. One of them was Countess Markievicz, who had been sentenced to death for her part in the 1916 Easter Rising.

Gladstone was re-elected at Greenwich, which was a two-member constituency, but only in second place behind a Conservative.

Both Gladstone and his wife were bitter at the result and bitter about Disraeli. They resented the obligation to hand over the government's £5.25 million surplus to him, and Gladstone unsuccessfully tried to think of ways to avoid doing so. In a letter to their son, Herbert, Catherine wrote: 'Is it not disgusting after all Papa's labour and patriotism and years of work to think of handing over his nest egg to that Jew'.[27] There is no question mark because it is a rhetorical question. It was not the first time that she could be criticised for anti-Semitism.

The upset Gladstone mistakenly believed that Disraeli would not run a stable government. In a letter to the Lord Advocate, he wrote: 'I am confident that the Conservative Party will never arrive at a stable superiority while Disraeli is at their head'.[28] Seeking reasons for the defeat, he wrote to his Irish Envoy, Earl Spencer: 'We have been swept away, literally, by a torrent of beer and gin. Next to this comes Education: that has denuded us on both sides for reasons dramatically opposite: with the Nonconformists, and with the Irish voters'.[29] Perhaps his views about beer and gin were influenced by the fact that the man who had topped the poll at Greenwich was a gin distiller.

Not surprisingly, the queen shed no tears at Gladstone's defeat. Writing to her daughter, she said that Palmerston had told her that he was a dangerous man. She added: 'So very arrogant, tyrannical and obstinate, with no knowledge of the world or human nature'. She added: '... all this and much want of regard towards my feelings ... led to make him a very dangerous and unsatisfactory premier'.[30] She wanted him to resign immediately as Disraeli had done in 1868, and not wait to be dismissed by the new parliament.

Gladstone thought that it was constitutionally preferable to wait for parliament, and he was loth to follow a precedent set by Disraeli. However, the queen was insistent and complained that the likely date of his dismissal by parliament clashed with the date of the return from St Petersburg of her second son after his marriage to the daughter of the tsar. Writing to Gladstone in the third person, she said: 'People are apt to forget as she told Mr Gladstone the other day, that the Queen is a *woman* who has far more on her hands and far more to try mind and body than is good *for anyone* of her sex and age'.[31]

At this point, Gladstone conceded, and on 20 February, he went to Windsor and resigned. She acknowledged his loyalty and offered him a peerage, which he had no hesitation in declining. Then the delighted Victoria sent for Disraeli. He was once again at the top of the greasy pole, this time with power and the prospect of a lengthy tenure.

17
1874–1875

The dream of his life was ended
The hurricane winds might blow,
A shout from the lofty masthead,
Land, land to the leeward ho.

The words are from a song that I learnt as a child, and they have remained with me ever since. It is an indulgence to include them in this chapter, but they seem appropriate. The words celebrate the achievement of Christopher Columbus in discovering the New World in 1492, and his feelings when he sighted it. He had been proved right and achieved his ambition. Perhaps the words are relevant to Disraeli too—on 20 February 1874 when he became prime minister for the second time. He had believed in himself and he had been trying to achieve it for much of his life. Now he had the position, he had the status, and, unlike the previous time, he had the power.

Proud and delighted as he was, the achievement of the sixty-nine-year-old prime minister was to some extent overshadowed by his various ailments and awareness of his advancing years. He said: 'Power had come to me too late. There were days when on waking I felt I could move dynasties and governments, but that has passed away'.[1] He suffered from gout—which affected an eye—bronchitis, and asthma. He sometimes wore velvet slippers in the Commons, and he walked with a stick. He had never visited Ireland, but planned to do so in the winter of 1874–75, but problems with his health forced him to cancel it. He never did get to Ireland. His health was a handicap in 1874–75 and it remained so until his defeat in the 1880 general election.

In April 1874, Lord Derby wrote: 'I hear also much talk as to Disraeli and his state of health. Many of his friends think that he has lost his energy … and will not long bear the strain of parliamentary life'.[2]

Gladstone's spirits and plans at this time could hardly have been more different. Although intending to retain his seat in the Commons, he planned to retire from active politics and give up his position as leader of the Liberal

Party. On 7 March 1874, while taking his breakfast alone at Grillon's Club, he wrote down his reasons for the decision:

(1) To engage now, is to engage for the term of Opposition, & the succeeding term of a Liberal Government.... This is not consistent with my views for the close of my life.

(2) Failure of 1866–8. [That is, his realistic appraisal of his lack of success as either leader of the House of Commons in a government of which he was not Prime Minister or as leader of the opposition.]

(3) My views on the question of Education in particular are I fear irreconcilable with those of a considerable proportion of [the Liberal party].

(4) In no case has the head of a Govt. considerable in character & duration, on receiving what may be called an emphatic dismissal, become Leader of the Opposition.

(5) The condition of the Liberal party requires consideration.
a. It has no present public *cause* upon which it is agreed.
b. It has serious & conscientious divisions of opinion, which are also pressing, e.g. on Education.
c. The habit of making a career by & upon constant active opposition to the bulk of the party, & its leaders, has acquired the dangerous predominance among a portion of its members. This habit is not checked by the action of the great majority, who do not indulge or approve it: & it has become dangerous to the credit & efficiency of the party.[3]

Gladstone was dispirited, and he felt insulted by the result of the general election. There were other things outside government that he wanted to do. Nevertheless, his former cabinet colleagues did not want him to give up the leadership and nor did the party as a whole. His colleagues tried very hard to make him change his mind. A pressing practical problem was that there was no obvious successor. Several of the possible candidates did not want the job and none of them had clear support.

A further factor was that Gladstone's wife, Catherine, was very cautious about the implications of him giving up the leadership. This was on account of her wish that her husband's life should be fulfilled, and her suspicion that the role that he was currently playing was the one most likely to achieve that aim. However, one cannot help but wonder if she was worried that he would be too much under her feet. Numerous women have felt this when their very active husbands retired and found that they had time to manage how their wives ran the house. This was probably unlikely to have happened, not least because Gladstone did not plan to retire. He intended to do other things. The consequence was a rather unhappy compromise. He would retain the leadership through the 1874 parliamentary session, but more of the job would be delegated than had been his practice in the past. He would definitely give up the position by the start of the 1875 session and this would be announced following his colleagues' agreement being reached. This is what actually happened and until he handed over he operated in a lacklustre fashion—very different from being a bundle of energy that had been his usual manner. In February 1875, Hartington reluctantly took the leadership in the Commons and Granville became leader in the Lords.

After relinquishing the leadership, Gladstone continued to sit on the Liberal front bench. It seems a curious thing to have done and it carried the risk of making his colleagues uncomfortable, but he said that it was the wish of both Hartington and Granville. His periodic interventions, sometimes unexpected, often caused excitement. In March 1875, one of them prompted Disraeli to report the event to the queen in the following terms: 'Mr Gladstone not only appeared but rushed into the debate. The new Members trembled and fluttered like small birds when a hawk is in the air'.[4]

The new prime minister did not neglect the official entertaining that was expected, and he had to do it without Mary Anne. Furthermore, he attended receptions given by others. Sometimes he and Gladstone were at the same event, though they rarely spoke to each other. On one occasion, Disraeli decided to leave early and before the time that he had arranged for his carriage. Embarrassingly for the staff, the carriage was not there. Shortly afterwards, Gladstone came out too and seeing his difficulty offered him a lift. The ride would probably not have been enjoyable for either of them, but fortunately a cab unexpectedly became available and Disraeli was able to decline the offer.

As Disraeli set about forming his cabinet, he was bolstered by some good news. British forces had captured the capital of the Ashanti in the Gold Coast (now Ghana). Gladstone had planned to wind down this small colonial war, and among his reasons was a wish to save money to help fund his planned abolition of income tax. This benefit had fallen to Disraeli, and he also had the £5.25 million surplus unwillingly bequeathed by Gladstone.

Disraeli had a preference for small cabinets and the one that he now formed was the smallest since 1832. It contained twelve members, six sitting in the Commons and six in the Lords. Derby was once again foreign secretary, and his advice led to the appointment of Richard Cross as home secretary. Cross, who was hardly known to Disraeli and had never served in government, was an able, middle-class businessman very committed to social reform. He would play a significant part in the government's legislative programme. W. H. Smith was made financial secretary to the Treasury. This was the man who, with his father (also W. H. Smith), built up the great chain of bookshops that is still with us. He was made first lord of the Admiralty in 1877 and went on to have a further distinguished career in government. It is suspected that W. S. Gilbert based the character of Sir Joseph Porter KCB on him in the comic opera *HMS Pinafore*.

An important and surprising appointment was the 3rd marquess of Salisbury, who became secretary of state for India. As Viscount Cranborne, he had led the three ministers who had resigned from Lord Derby's government in 1867. Salisbury was a very able man, as proved by his subsequent career, and a man capable of causing a lot of problems for the government. Disraeli wanted him on board and used his very considerable talents of persuasion, cajolery, and flattery to secure this end. Salisbury, by then foreign secretary, later played a key part in Disraeli's triumph at the Congress of Berlin in 1878.

The cabinet ministers all had portfolios, but Stanley Weintraub suggested, probably not intending to be taken literally, that Victoria required a cabinet portfolio.[5] He meant that pleasing the queen, liaising with her, and managing her took up a great deal of Disraeli's time. It did indeed. On taking office, he had told her that whatever she wished would be done 'whatever the difficulties'.[6]

Victoria was very pleased that Gladstone had gone and delighted that Disraeli was back. The two regularly sent flowers to each other and he flattered her outrageously, which greatly pleased her. She soon allowed him to sit during his audiences, which was an almost unique privilege. She was very concerned about his health and frequently enquired about it. Letters and telegrams were sent to him almost daily and sometimes two or three times a day. They took a lot of his time. She demanded frequent audiences, not always in convenient places, and these demands extended to other ministers. She had ideas and projects, and demanded that Disraeli take action on them.

The power of the queen's demands is illustrated by a note made by Derby in February 1876 following a conversation with Montagu Corry, Disraeli's secretary: 'He thinks there is no flaw anywhere in her intellect, which is shrewd and acute: but she is selfish and despotic beyond measure: that if her power were equal to her will, some of our heads would not be on our shoulders'.[7]

Richard Cross, the new home secretary, shortly had an unwelcome surprise. In his memoirs, he wrote:

> When the Cabinet came to discuss the Queen's Speech I was, I confess, disappointed at the lack of originality shown by the Prime Minister. From all his speeches I had quite expected that his mind was full of legislative schemes; but this did not prove to be the case. On the contrary, he had to rely on the various suggestions of his colleagues, and as they themselves had only just come into office, there was some difficulty in forming the Queen's Speech.[8]

Disraeli's mind was attuned to lofty ideas and sweeping principles, not to the burdens of detailed legislation and administration.

Despite this inauspicious start, the government achieved a lot in its first two years, especially the second one. There were many valuable Acts of Parliament affecting public health, trades union, merchant shipping, rights for tenant farmers in England, and other matters. Many of the measures were to improve existing legislation rather than to strike out with new initiatives. It does not sound exciting, but it was valuable. Some years later, radical MP Alexander Macdonald told his constituents that 'The Conservative Party have done more for the working classes in five years than the Liberals have in fifty'.[9]

The only act managed by Disraeli personally was the Agricultural Holdings Act. All the others were managed by his cabinet colleagues, Cross in particular. Nearly all of the ideas came from them too. This poses a question of how much of the credit should go to Disraeli and was he just lucky with his colleagues. The answer to the latter part of the question is surely no. For a start, he chose them and encouraged them to perform. To use the rather ugly modern word, he facilitated it. He listened to their ideas, allowed challenges, and then gave the go ahead. A sporting analogy seems appropriate. In a football match, the goalkeeper might make good saves and the striker might score a vital goal, but it is a mistake to underestimate the importance of the captain, who has a vital role in influencing the team's performance.

Although Disraeli's government had a string of successful legislative measures, an early one presented him with problems. However, it turned out very well for him and very badly for Gladstone. The queen wanted a bill to limit ritualistic practices among Anglo-Catholics in the Church of England. The possibility of such a measure had been live for some time, and it risked being highly divisive. When in government, Gladstone had seen the likely dangers and very sensibly left it alone.

In 1874, the Anglican bishops in the House of Lords introduced such a bill. The queen was very pleased and pressed Disraeli to give it his support. The prime minister, like Gladstone before him, could see the dangers and was hesitant about doing so. The cabinet, particularly Lord Salisbury, wanted him to have nothing to do with it. Then the high church Gladstone inadvisably barged in. He had always opposed attempts by parliament to control religious practice and he did so now. When the bill came to the Commons, he tabled six resolutions to stop the bill to put down ritualism. This stirred up feelings in several quarters and it infuriated many of his MPs. Nonconformists were well represented on the Liberal benches and they did not like, as they saw it, Gladstone protecting near 'Popery' in the established church.

The queen asked Disraeli: 'What has become of the Protestant feeling of Englishmen?' And told him that Gladstone's behaviour was 'much to be regretted, though it was not surprising'.[10] Disraeli saw that Gladstone was in great trouble and was delighted to accommodate the queen's wish. He threw the government's support behind the bill and the humiliated Gladstone withdrew his resolutions. The bill duly became law and it was a Disraeli triumph. Not long afterwards, Gladstone to some extent mended his fences with his disaffected supporters, though at the price of upsetting the Catholics. Writing about converts to Catholicism, he expressed the view that 'no one can become her convert without renouncing his moral and mental freedom and placing his civil loyalty and duty at the mercy of another'.[11] This was swiftly repudiated by, among others, Archbishop Newman (later Cardinal Newman) and the marquess of Ripon. The latter had served in Gladstone's cabinet and, much to Gladstone's annoyance, had recently converted to Catholicism. Gladstone then followed up his provocative remark by publishing a pamphlet that developed his reasoning on the point. It was very successful and sold 70,000 copies in its first month. He continued with yet more invective, though the public was getting rather bored. Cardinal Cullen, the primate of Ireland, ordered prayers to be said for him in all churches to the end that he might be made sensible of his errors and of the wrong which he was seeking to do to the Pope and the Catholic Church.[12] Around this time, Gladstone became mildly interested in spiritualism and attended some séances.

Worries about the Pope's authority over Roman Catholics was a factor in the American Presidential Campaign of 1960. The USA had never had a Roman Catholic President and fears were expressed that the Pope would have undue influence over the successful candidate, Jack Kennedy. Former President Harry Truman said that he was more worried by the 'Pop' than the Pope. The 'Pop' was Jack Kennedy's father, Joe Kennedy, who influenced his son's campaign and gave it a great deal of money.

As might be expected, Gladstone kept busy during the time that he was less involved in politics. Among other things, he returned to his fascination with Homer and wrote a number of articles. In one of them, he contended that the Trojan War had not been a war of aggression. It had served 'the worthy, nay the paramount end of establishing on a firm and lasting basis the national life, cohesion and independence' of the Greeks.[13] In a later article, he proved, to his own satisfaction at least, that the Greeks were among the descendants named in Chapter 10 of the Book of Genesis as survivors of the flood.

In November 1875, a Disraeli initiative secured a personal triumph. It pleased the queen, and it pleased the British people, but it did not please Gladstone. The Suez Canal had opened in 1869 and Britain had turned down a chance to buy some of the company's shares. This was a mistake because the canal was a success, Britain was the biggest user of it, and it was very important in considerably shortening the route from Britain to India.

The majority of the Suez Canal Company was French owned, but the Khedive of Egypt owned 44 per cent. The Khedive was desperately short of money and needed to sell his shares. He was negotiating with two French banks when Disraeli was made aware of what was happening. He wanted the shares for Britain and he moved swiftly and decisively to get them. Parliament was not sitting, and it would be difficult to get the money quickly from the slow moving Bank of England. Disraeli persuaded his worried and indecisive cabinet, then got Rothschild's bank to advance the required £4 million. The bank was well rewarded with commission and interest, but it was taking a risk because parliament had not given its approval. However, everything went to plan and Britain owned 44 per cent of the Suez Canal Company. French interests owned most of the remainder.

It was brilliant for British prestige and public opinion was very favourable. The queen was even more pleased with her prime minister. Somehow, it was overlooked that it was a minority interest and the shares were mortgaged, and for this reason did not have votes until 1895. Never mind all of that—it was a Disraeli triumph. Gladstone did not think so. Roy Jenkins wrote: 'He reacted strongly against what he regarded as this showy, vulgar and internationally disruptive *coup de théâtre*'.[14] Gladstone had problems in Egypt during his 1880–85 government.

18
1876–1878

Disraeli had a policy of trying to please the queen, and he often succeeded. It caused him a problem early in the 1876 parliament. Victoria was very conscious of her status and for some time had been irked by the fact that she was a mere 'Queen', whereas a number of other monarchs were emperors. The *'Dreikaiserbund'*, an informal alliance of Russia, Austria, and Germany, were all headed by emperors. Worse, Victoria's eldest daughter was married to the heir to the German emperor and would, in time, become empress of Germany. She would then outrank her mother. Victoria found this upsetting and she asked Disraeli to arrange for her to be made 'Empress of India' in addition to her existing title.

Disraeli was dismayed by the request and realised that there would be dissent. He was right, there was. However, despite his forebodings and after an initial refusal he agreed to try and accommodate the queen's wish. In return, she agreed to open the 1876 parliament in person, something that she had rarely done since the death of her husband. The Liberals took exception to a breach of protocol. It was normal for the opposition leaders to have prior notice of any proposed legislation affecting the monarch. This was not done, and the first they heard of it was the queen's words when delivering the speech.

There was much opposition to the bill. Opponents pointed out that being an emperor was not a guarantee of respect. Napoleon III of France had been deposed, and Maximillian of Mexico had been both deposed and executed. Strong objectors to the bill included Gladstone, who called it 'tomfoolery'. Lowe, his former chancellor of the Exchequer, went even further.

Disraeli and the queen were saved by the vehemence of Gladstone and Lowe. They went too far for the Liberal leader, Hartington, and others, and on 5 May 1876, the Royal Titles Bill was passed. The delighted Victoria added 'Empress of India' to her title. However, the controversy did Disraeli no good at all and it weakened his authority.

After the passage of the Royal Titles Bill, foreign and colonial affairs dominated Disraeli and his government until he lost the 1880 election. He and

Gladstone had violently different views and they were metaphorically at war over foreign and colonial matters for the next four years. It was very personal and it is probably true to say that their enmity peaked at this time.

Until the Congress of Berlin in the summer of 1878, the issue was the so-called 'Eastern Question'. The heart of this was the implications of the decay of the Ottoman Empire. The Ottomans, based in Constantinople, had for centuries been a major power and their empire included many large territories outside of Turkey. Their control peaked in 1683 when they almost captured Vienna. The Ottomans were Muslim and many of the peoples and territories that they dominated were Christian.

During the nineteenth century, the military power of the Ottomans progressively diminished and they had serious financial problems. In fact, it could be seen that the empire would disintegrate. In the 1870s, various peoples within it wanted independence and a power vacuum was developing. Britain and some other European countries wanted to preserve and perhaps increase their influence in the area. In particular, Britain was anxious to prevent a build-up in the territory controlled by Russia.

There was no disguising the fact that Disraeli's health and weariness were increasing problems, and whether or not he could carry on had become an issue. He had no obvious successor as prime minister, and the queen was appalled at the thought she might lose him. The consequence was that he moved to the House of Lords, still as prime minister, and Sir Stafford Northcote became Leader of the Commons. Disraeli still had his work and duties as prime minister, but the time and stress devoted to his parliamentary duties were greatly reduced.

Disraeli had sat in the Commons for thirty-nine continuous years and leaving it was a wrench. He had dominated the chamber as few others had done. In an admiring tribute, an opponent, Harcourt, said: 'Henceforth the game will be like a chessboard when the Queen is gone – a petty struggle of pawns'.[1] Salisbury warned him that he was going to 'the dullest assembly in the world'.[2] Disraeli remarked: 'I am dead, dead but in the Elysian fields'.[3] The words are apt because in Greek mythology the Elysian fields is the final resting place of the souls of the heroic and virtuous.

Disraeli took the title 'Earl of Beaconsfield' as a tribute to his late wife, Mary Anne, who had become Viscountess Beaconsfield in 1868. Beaconsfield is a small town in his Buckinghamshire constituency, not far from his home in Hughenden. For the sake of continuity, the rest of this book continues to refer to him as Disraeli.

Shortly before Disraeli went to the Lords, he was confronted by reports of Turkish atrocities in Bulgaria. He did not handle them well and he did not handle them well after he had gone to the Lords either. Soon after his elevation to the Upper House, an incandescent Gladstone burst on to the scene. He lambasted the Turks, violently criticised Disraeli, and stirred the pot of discontent in the country.

The Turks had badly misruled the desperately poor Bulgarians, and there had been extensive financial corruption and violence directed at the unfortunate Bulgars. All of this had provoked a doomed uprising, which had been swiftly and savagely repressed.

On 23 June, the *Daily News*, a Liberal-leaning newspaper, reported that 25,000 men, women, and children had been massacred, then it continued to publish further reports about what had happened. British public opinion was outraged, and in parliament, the Liberal opposition pressed Disraeli to make a satisfactory response. This he failed to do.

Disraeli's first priority was to look after British interests in the area, and he believed that bolstering the Turks against the Russians was the way to do it. This was also the view of the queen. A further factor was his suspicion that reports of the Turkish atrocities had been exaggerated. His scepticism was well founded, but even so, there was enough truth in them to make the Turkish behaviour reprehensible. Accounts included rapes of Christian women and the burning of churches with Christian men, women, and children inside.

Disraeli's responses were disastrous. Among other things, he said that 'oriental people seldom I believe, resort to torture, but generally terminate their connection with culprits in a more expeditious manner'.[4] The word used was 'culprits' not 'victims', and it amounted to saying that Turks murdered people without bothering to torture them first. He called the reports 'coffee house babble'. He admitted that 12,000 Bulgarians had been massacred, but denied that it was 30,000 as claimed.

In late August, Gladstone wrote an explosive pamphlet, which he entitled *The Bulgarian Horrors and the Question of the East*. Then, on 3 September, he travelled overnight from Hawarden and arrived at Granville's house at 5 a.m. In a frantic couple of days, he accomplished the final revisions to the pamphlet, saw the editor of *The Times* and others, sent a copy to Disraeli, and launched it on the country. In a letter to the foreign secretary, Disraeli described the pamphlet as 'vindictive and ill written—that of course. Indeed in that respect of all the Bulgarian horrors perhaps the greatest'.[5] He was so pleased with the memorable phrase that he repeated it publicly afterwards.

The pamphlet had a great impact. The initial print run was 2,000, but the eventual total sold was 200,000. Shortly after the publication, Gladstone followed it up with a public meeting at Blackheath in his Greenwich constituency. For an extended period, he addressed 10,000 people in the pouring rain.

The following is a violent extract from the pamphlet that shows the strength of his feeling:

There is not a cannibal in the South Sea Islands, whose indignation would not arise and overboil at the recital of that which has been done, which has too late been examined, but which remains unavenged: which has left behind all the foul and all the fierce passion that produced it, and which may again spring up in another murderous harvest from the soil soaked and reeking with blood, and in the air tainted with every imaginable deed of crime and shame.... No Government ever has so sinned; none had proved itself so incorrigible or, which is the same, so impotent for reformation.[6]

The most famous phrase in the pamphlet is 'bag and baggage'. In context, it appears as follows:

Let the Turks now carry away their abuses in the only possible manner, namely by carrying off themselves. Their Zaptiehs and their Mudits, their Bimbashis and their Yuzbashis, their Kaimakams and their Pashas, one and all, bag and baggage, shall I hope clear out from the province they have desolated and profaned. This thorough riddance, this most blessed deliverance, is the only reparation we can make to the memory of those heaps on heaps of dead; to the violated purity alike of matron, maiden, and of child...[7]

Disraeli had a considerable talent for denouncing his opponent. In one of his retorts, he described Gladstone as 'a sophistical rhetorician inebriated with the exuberance of his own verbosity and gifted with an egotistical imagination that can at all times command an interminable and inconsistent series of arguments to malign an opponent and glorify himself'.[8]

The key supporters of both Disraeli and Gladstone were more moderate and refrained from joining in fully. For Disraeli, both Derby and Salisbury were restrained, though they did support the prime minister. One presumes that they shared the shock concerning the atrocities. Hartington in the Commons and Granville in the Lords were Gladstone's leaders, at least in theory, and they gave him their restrained support. One presumes that they saw some merit in the need to put Britain's interests first.

The region was in turmoil. Serbia and Montenegro were at war with Turkey and Russia was mobilising. Opposition to Russian expansion and its control of Constantinople was a key British aim. On 29 October, the war minister noted in his diary: 'The Queen was ... strongly Anti-Russ[ian] and still more Anti-Gladstone'.[9] It did not help that around this time Gladstone had formed a close and worrying friendship with Olga Novikov, the wife of a member of the Russian General Staff. There were fears that she was influencing him in the interests of her country.

In St Petersburg, there was a war party and a peace party and the war party got the upper hand. Russia wanted more influence, more territory, and it threatened the Dardanelles and Constantinople. The situation was fluid, confused, and tense for the next two years. Disraeli wanted to be very firm but had great difficulty carrying his cabinet. Meanwhile, British public opinion moved away from its revulsion at the Bulgarian atrocities, and in the main became strongly anti-Russian. A second Gladstone pamphlet was not a success. War fever is perhaps too strong a term, but a popular music hall song put the word 'jingoism' into the English language:

> *We don't want to fight but by jingo if we do*
> *We've still got the ships, we've got the men, we've got the money too*
> *We've fought the Bear before, and while we're Britons true*
> *The Russians shall not have Constantinople.*

Salisbury represented Britain at a conference to try and resolve the problems, but Turkey was intransigent and it was a failure. In April 1877, Disraeli wanted to mount a pre-emptive occupation of the Dardanelles, but the cabinet successfully stopped him. Disraeli received a note from the queen telling him that she would rather abdicate than kiss the feet of the tsar. Then, on 24 April, Russia declared war on Turkey.

Gladstone put down five belligerently anti-Turkish resolutions in the House of Commons, which caused difficulties for his leaders, Hartington and Granville. He was persuaded to withdraw three of them, then made a fine two-hour and thirty-minute speech. The Conservatives comfortably won the subsequent vote.

Although a lot of Britain had swung to support Disraeli's policy of opposing Russia, Gladstone was still capable of attracting very large crowds to hear him espouse his pro-Russia and pro-Christian views. This was particularly the case away from London and the south. One of the biggest meetings of all was on 31 May 1877 at Bingley Hall in Birmingham when he was the guest of Joseph Chamberlain. The hall was an enormous structure with hardly any seating. Gladstone had been told to expect more than 10,000, but this number was greatly exceeded. He thought that there were about 25,000 and Chamberlain put it at 30,000.

Estimating the size of a crowd is notoriously difficult, and we should be sceptical, but by any standard, making the speech was an enormous challenge. Needless to say, he rose to it and he spoke for an hour and fifteen minutes. There were, of course, no microphones and relays of shouters relayed the great man's words to those at the back. One wonders if the words were sometimes distorted. There is an old wartime joke about a military commander using a relay of whisperers to pass on the message 'send reinforcements we are going to advance'. At the end of the chain, it had changed to 'send three and fourpence we are going to a dance'.

In the early stages of the Russo-Turkish War, the Russians had the upper hand, and in July 1877, Disraeli came close to advocating intervention on the Turkish side. This would have pleased the queen, but his reluctant cabinet led by Derby would not support him. Then the Turkish forces rallied and held out for five months. However, in December, the Russians got close to Constantinople. A British fleet was sent to the Dardanelles and there was a Russo-Turkish armistice. In March 1878, the protagonists concluded the Treaty of San Stefano.

Among other things, the treaty almost completely removed the Turks from Europe. It gave Russia big gains in the Balkans and Central Asia, and it created a large and independent Bulgaria, which would be vulnerable to Russian influence. This was unacceptable to Disraeli. However, the whole matter was to be decided at a European Congress.

Indian troops were sent to Malta and British reserves were called up. Gladstone was part of a small minority who voted against calling up the reserves. Derby was unhappy and finally resigned as foreign secretary. He had been a friend and associate of Disraeli for a very long time. He later moved to the Liberals and held office in Gladstone's 1880–85 government. His replacement was Salisbury, which might have been seen as surprising because he shared most of Derby's views and had consistently opposed Disraeli in cabinet. His views or at least his behaviour changed on the appointment and he became a supporter of Disraeli. One wonders how big a part personal ambition was a factor in this. He played a prominent role in the forthcoming Congress of Berlin.

During the crisis of the Eastern Question and the build up to a possible war with Russia, some of Disraeli's opponents resorted to highly regrettable anti-Semitism. The basis of it was that he was siding with the Muslim Ottomans against Christian Russia. Jews, the crucifiers of Christ as they saw it, were opponents of Christianity, again as they saw it. Jews, including Disraeli, were suspect. Never mind that as a child he had been baptised into the Church of England. He had been born a Jew, he had a Jewish name, and he looked Jewish.

There are many examples that could be quoted. Edward Freeman, the Liberal historian, referring to Russia, wrote: 'There is a nation in the freshness of a new life, having to go on the noblest of crusades and one loathsome Jew wants to stop them'.[10] Freeman was no stranger to racial prejudice. On a separate matter, writing to a friend about America, he put: 'This would be a grand land if only every Irishman would kill a negro then be hanged for it'.

The writer, Henry James, wrote: 'London smells of gunpowder, and the tawdry old Jew who is at the head of this great old British Empire would like immensely to wind up his career with a fine long cannonade'.[11] Gladstone himself was capable of expressing anti-Semitic sentiments. He wrote:

> No small portion of excitement finds its way to me personally, in the shape of an idolising sentiment among the people such as I never before experienced.... I have watched very closely [Disraeli's] strange & at first sight inexplicable proceedings on this Eastern Question and I believe their fountainhead to be race antipathy, that aversion which the Jews, with a few honourable exceptions, are showing so vindictively towards the Eastern Christians. Though he has been baptized, his Jew feelings are the most radical & the most real, & so far respectable, portion of his profoundly falsified nature.[12]

The great European powers convened a congress to meet in Berlin in order to resolve the Eastern Question. It started on 13 June 1878 and concluded a month later. The six powers were Germany, Austria-Hungary, Russia, France, Italy, and Britain. Also represented were the Ottoman Empire and four Balkan states (Greece, Serbia, Romania, and Montenegro). The congress was chaired by Bismarck, the German chancellor.

Salisbury took office as secretary of state for foreign affairs only two months before the start of the congress. He was busy and he was successful. Despite their previously difficult relationship and his history of supporting the views of Derby, his predecessor in the office, Disraeli, gave him a great deal of freedom. His actions ahead of the congress were a big factor in the success of it, at least from the British point of view.

Due to Disraeli's poor health, the queen thought that he should not go to Berlin, but he disregarded her advice and decided to go. His journey took a leisurely four days, with nights spent in Calais, Brussels (where he dined with Leopold II), and Cologne. He arrived in Berlin at 8 p.m. very tired from the journey and was confronted with an invitation to dine with Bismarck that evening. He reluctantly decided that he had better go and arrived at 10.30 p.m. The meeting was a great success. Bismarck formed a very favourable impression of the British prime minister, and he retained it throughout the congress. '*Der alte Jude, das ist der Mann,*' was how Bismarck described him. This translates as 'The old Jew, he is the man'.

At the congress, Disraeli was the front man who led and dealt with broad principles. Salisbury was the details man and it was a powerful combination. An inspired piece of flattery by the British ambassador was of great service. French was the language of diplomacy but, unlike Gladstone, Disraeli was only fluent in English. Despite this, he could make himself understood in French and intended to do so. The ambassador told him that the delegates were very much hoping to hear the great English novelist speak in his mother tongue. Disraeli agreed to accommodate their reported wishes.

Towards the end of the congress, a piece of Disraeli brinkmanship was successful. The Russians gave in to his refusal to allow Bulgaria access to the Aegean Sea, but would not accept that Turkey could garrison what was left of Turkish Bulgaria. Disraeli said that he would leave and called for his special train too be made ready. Bismarck realised that he was not bluffing and pushed the Russians into accepting Disraeli's demand. The special train was not boarded.

As a result of the treaty, Ottoman territory in Europe was considerably reduced. Bulgaria was established as an independent principality within the Ottoman Empire. Eastern Rumelia was restored to the Turks under a special administration. Macedonia was returned to the Turks who promised reform. Romania became fully independent, and it both gained and lost territory. Austria-Hungary took Bosnia and Herzegovina and other land. Turkey ceded Cyprus to Britain. This had been agreed before the congress, but was announced at the end. The congress increased British power and prestige in the region, and it achieved Disraeli's aim of keeping the Russian Navy out of the Mediterranean.

It was seen at home as a British triumph and a Disraeli triumph. It should not be overlooked (though it sometimes is) that it was also a Salisbury triumph. The queen wrote to Disraeli and told him that 'high and low are delighted'. She added: '… excepting Mr Gladstone, who is frantic'.[13]

Disraeli and Salisbury got a great reception on their return home, first at Dover then at Charing Cross Station in London. There was bunting and a band at Dover, and flags, flowers, shields, and other things at Charing Cross. Cheering crowds were at both places. Then the two men travelled in triumph to Downing Street in an open carriage. Once there, Disraeli told his supporters: 'Lord Salisbury and I have brought you back peace—but a peace I hope with honour'. The phrase was used again in 1938, this time by Neville Chamberlain when he returned from Munich. He said: 'My good friends, for the second time in our history, a British Prime Minister has returned from Germany bringing peace with honour. I believe it is peace for our time'. Sadly he was wrong. The Second World War started the following year.

The queen offered to make Disraeli a duke, but he declined. He did, however, accept the garter on condition that it was also given to Salisbury.

At the time, the Congress of Berlin was hailed as a triumph of peace-making, but the verdict of history has been less favourable. Russia had been successful in the war that preceded it but felt humiliated. The Ottoman Empire lost land and resented it. Austria-Hungary gained a lot of territory but without the blessing of many of the people who lived in it. Tensions between Russia and Austria-Hungary intensified. There were two Balkan wars in 1912–13 and the region was the flashpoint for the start of the First World War.

19
1878–1880

Although Gladstone and part of the country dissented, following the Congress of Berlin, Disraeli was generally very popular, and this was evidenced in a number of ways. Memorabilia such as mugs and plates featuring his face were produced. This was unusual for a politician, though Churchill and one or two others are exceptions and I am the proud possessor of a Margaret Thatcher teapot. The cutlers of Sheffield presented Disraeli with a pair of carving knives with 'Peace with Honour' engraved on the handles.

This popularity did not last long and it is widely believed that Disraeli missed a window of opportunity to triumph in a general election. The possible calling of one was discussed and rejected at a cabinet meeting held on 10 August 1878. The law at the time provided for parliaments to last for a maximum of seven years and the current one still had two and a half years to run. In a perhaps rare moment of propriety, Disraeli felt that to call an election then would be opportunistic and verging on unconstitutional.

We will never know, but perhaps an election would not have delivered the expected Conservative triumph. Agriculture and the economy in general were not thriving and this is usually bad for the ruling party. There are many examples of general elections not giving the expected results. A possibly particularly relevant one was 1945 when the triumphant war leader, Winston Churchill, was defeated by a Labour landslide. Nevertheless, it was probably a missed opportunity for Disraeli. Afterwards, things went wrong and he was decisively beaten twenty months later in April 1880.

Gladstone was most certainly not ready to join the paean of praise for Disraeli, and he had taken personal offence at some remarks made by the prime minister. Only a few days after his return from Berlin, he wrote to him complaining about remarks that he had made. He claimed that Disraeli had said that he (Gladstone) had among other things described him as 'a dangerous, devilish character' and that he had 'indulged in criticisms complete with the most offensive epithets'.[1,2] Gladstone demanded evidence that he had actually said these things.

Two cartoons by Sir John Tenniel (1820–1914). *Punch*

Disraeli replied in the third person (Lord Beaconsfield), which was guaranteed to annoy Gladstone, and he gave details of remarks made by Gladstone that he thought could be construed in the way that he had done. In regard to the word 'devilish', he said:

> He is informed that it was not Mr Gladstone at Hawarden who compared Lord Beaconsfield to Mephistopheles but only one of Mr Gladstone's friends, timidly enquiring how they are to 'get rid of this Mephistopheles'; but as Mr Gladstone proceeded to explain the mode, ... Lord Beaconsfield may perhaps be excused for assuming that Mr Gladstone sanctioned the propriety of the scarcely complimentary appellation.[3]

Disraeli ignored Gladstone's charges about 'the most deadly mischief which *that alien* would drag [us] into'—that Disraeli was 'going to annex England to his native East and make it an appanage of an Asiatic empire'.[4] These offensively anti-Semitic comments had been written by Gladstone in the previous year. The bad feeling was a foretaste of things to come, especially during Gladstone's Midlothian campaign, which features later in this chapter.

Disraeli and Gladstone had differing views on imperial policy. Disraeli was inclined to preserve and increase the size of the British Empire, while Gladstone tended to favour self-determination of the people affected. Disraeli's activities in these areas involved military and other expenditure, which had to be financed, and which was a problem for his government. His imperial policies were a feature of what Gladstone came to disparagingly call 'Beaconsfieldism'. After the Congress of Berlin, things went wrong for Disraeli in two places—namely Afghanistan and Southern Africa. Neither were directly his fault, but the problems happened on his watch and some of the blame attached to him. They were contributory factors in his 1880 election defeat.

Undivided India, which at the time included what is now Pakistan, was the jewel in the crown of the British Empire. This was emphasised by the not generally welcomed recent decision to make the queen 'Empress of India'. British policy was to be very alert to any developing threats to it, especially from Russia, and the Russian route to India passed through Afghanistan. Britain was keen to have good relations with the Ameer of that country.

In the summer of 1878, Russia sent a military delegation to Kabul, the capital of Afghanistan, and it was received. The move was in response to the movement of Indian troops to the Mediterranean as detailed in the last chapter. Britain had been trying to get a military delegation into the country for a long time and its attempts had been rebuffed. Now Russia appeared to be threatening northern India. The situation was seriously upsetting for the viceroy and the officials.

The viceroy was Robert Lytton, the son of Disraeli's old literary friend Bulwer-Lytton. He had recently been appointed by Disraeli and he was known for his volatile temperament. He planned to send a British military delegation up the Khyber Pass to Kabul, but in London, the British government, although protesting to Russia, only moved slowly. Eventually, Lytton was told to delay the delegation and take a different route. Notwithstanding this, the delegation did set off and it did use the Khyber route. The consequence was humiliating. The delegation was stopped at the border and forced to turn back.

Despite deep government reservations, British prestige was at stake. In October, parliament was recalled and an ultimatum was sent to the Ameer. No reply was received, so Afghanistan was invaded. The Afghans were rapidly defeated and the Ameer fled. He was replaced by his son and a permanent mission was installed. The invasion had been a success and Russia had been rebuffed, but the episode had been both annoying and expensive.

Unfortunately for Britain, this was not the end of the story. Almost a year later, the entire British mission in Kabul was massacred and the resident envoy, Sir Louis Cavagnari, was among those murdered. The British response had to be and was decisive. Afghanistan was invaded and all resistance was crushed. Britain took control of the country's southern hills, but left the rest of it to the various warlords. This effectively sealed the route to India, but the events had seriously harmed the reputation of Disraeli and his government. Once again, it had been expensive.

Gladstone, now engaged in his Midlothian campaign, was not slow to make his views known. He asked his audience to 'remember that the sanctity of life in the hill villages of Afghanistan, among the winter snows, is as inviolable in the eyes of Almighty God as can be your own'.[5] As so often with Gladstone, God featured in his rhetoric.

Parliament reassembled on 13 February 1879. Two days earlier, news had reached London that more than 1,200 troops had been massacred at Isandlwana in the Transvaal. Disraeli was devastated and the country was horrified.

The massacre took place in the Zulu War, which had its origins in clashes in the Transvaal between the Zulus and the Boer settlers. The colonial secretary, Lord Carnarvon, had pursued a policy of confederation across South Africa, and the Boer settlers of the Transvaal had somewhat reluctantly joined it. This meant that the British took over the Boers' problems with some of the indigenous tribes. Some of them welcomed the change, but the warlike Zulus did not. Following their intransigence, the governor of Cape Colony, Sir Henry Bartle Frere, took a tough line with the Zulus under their leader King Cetshwayo. He demanded that they change their warlike culture and submit to British rule.

The government wished Frere to move cautiously, but communications with London took a long time. He either ignored the instructions or did not receive them in time. He pursued his aggressive policy and asked for reinforcements. They were sent but with instructions that they were to be used for defensive purposes only. Frere disregarded this and issued an ultimatum to Cetshwayo. No response was received, and to his dismay, Disraeli found that the country was involved in another colonial war.

On 22 January 1879, just eleven days after the British invasion of Zululand, a force of around 20,000 Zulus attacked a portion of the British main column at Isandlwana. The British troops were under the command of Lord Chelmsford who was not there at the time. Present were about 1,800 British, colonial, and native troops and about 400 civilians. More than 1,200 were slaughtered. The British had greatly superior weapons and nearly all the Zulus fought with spears and shields. The horrified Disraeli wrote to the queen: 'It will change everything, reduce our Continental influence, and embarrass our finances'.[6]

On the same day as Isandlwana, 144 British troops successfully repulsed an attacking force of 4,000 Zulus. The extraordinarily high number of eleven Victoria Crosses were awarded to the valiant defenders. The action is commemorated in the 1964 film *Zulu* starring Stanley Baker and Michael Caine. News management was not practised in the way that it is now, but it suited the government (and the Army) to play down the significance of Isandlwana and play up the significance and valour of Rorke's Drift.

The cabinet was angry with Frere, but thought that it would be unwise to dismiss him at this time. So they kept him in his job but issued a public reprimand. This was a gift to the scornful Liberals. Sir William Harcourt read out an imaginary note sent to Frere by the colonial secretary: 'My dear Sir Bartle Frere; I cannot think you are right. Indeed I think you are very wrong; but after all, I feel you know a great deal better than I do. I hope you won't do what you are going to do, but if you do, I hope it will turn out well'.[7]

Further reinforcements were sent to South Africa, and Sir Garner Wolseley was sent to be in overall charge. Just as he arrived, Lord Chelmsford, with his regrouped forces, inflicted an overwhelming defeat on the valiant Zulus at Ulundi. Cetshwayo was taken prisoner, but later restored to his position, though this time under the British. In 1882, he visited Britain and met both Gladstone, by then prime minister, and Queen Victoria.

Disraeli was the queen's favourite prime minister and they got on very well, not least because he often acceded to her wishes, but there was a sharp difference in connection with the Zulu War. Disraeli thought that Lord Chelmsford's performance was deplorable. In the early stages of the war, he had been indecisive and had to take a lot of the blame for the disaster at Isandlwana. The queen thought that he had redeemed himself later and deserved credit for the triumph at Ulundi, and she wanted the prime minister to receive him at Hughenden.

Disraeli refused and gave him a formal interview in Downing Street. Disraeli wrote to the queen:

Lord Beaconsfield charges Lord Chelmsford with having invaded Zululand '*avec un Coeur léger*' with no adequate knowledge of the country he was attacking, and no precaution or preparation. A dreadful disaster occurred in consequence, and then Lord Chelmsford became panic-struck; appealed to yr. Majesty's Govt frantically for reinforcements and found himself at the head of 20,000 of yr. Majesty's troops, in order to reduce a country not larger than Yorkshire.[8]

Gladstone severely criticised Disraeli over the Zulu disaster. His comments included: 'The Zulus had been slaughtered for no other offence than their attempt to defend against your artillery with their naked bodies, their hearths and home, their wives and families'.[9]

Disraeli had not expected that Gladstone's decision to retire from front line politics would be permanent, and his scepticism turned out to be well founded. Gladstone became so incensed with what he termed 'Beaconsfieldism' that he burst back on to the scene. He strongly disapproved of Disraeli's actions concerning the Eastern Question and the Congress of Berlin. He did not think that the country should have taken Cyprus and he was disgusted with events in Afghanistan and Zululand. He thought that Disraeli and the government lacked principles, and he disapproved of the way that they managed the country's finances.

Gladstone decided to find a different parliamentary constituency. He had not been happy at Greenwich and he had felt insulted to only come second (in the two seat constituency) in the 1874 election. He received overtures from the two very different parliamentary constituencies of Leeds and Midlothian. Leeds had nearly 50,000 electors, whereas Midlothian had the precise number of 3,620. It had the alternate name of Edinburghshire and voted under the very restricted pre-1886 Scottish county franchise.

Gladstone chose Midlothian and Leeds went to Herbert, his youngest son who was aged twenty-six at the time of the election. Herbert had a distinguished career and, among other things, went on to be home secretary and governor general of South Africa. However, Lloyd George once said that he was living proof that talent was not always hereditary.

William Gladstone's extraordinary Midlothian campaign is famous. Over fourteen days and at nearly the age of seventy, he exhibited almost unbelievable energy. Lord Rosebery, the youthful future prime minister, played a large part in sponsoring it. Gladstone travelled from Liverpool to Edinburgh on 24 November 1879 and he made speeches at the stations at which his train stopped. Lord Morley, a distinguished Gladstone biographer and a man who served in future Gladstone cabinets, says that he was heard by 500 at Carlisle, 4,000 at Hawick, and 8,000 at Galashiels.[10] His reception at Edinburgh was co-ordinated by Rosebery. Cheering crowds thronged the station, and he was driven through the streets to Rosebery's house in a torchlight procession. There were triumphal arches, fairy lanterns, and fireworks.

'Little Bo Peep', the Earl of Rosebery caricatured by Spy in *Vanity Fair* 14 March 1901. He co-ordinated Gladstone's Midlothian Campaign.

During the first week of the campaign, he made nine speeches, five of which were regarded as very major. They were very major because of their content, importance, length, and the size of the audiences. According to Roy Jenkins, 2,500 heard him at the Edinburgh Assembly Rooms, 3,500 at the Dalkeith Corn Exchange, 3,500 at the West Calder Assembly Rooms, 5,000 at the Edinburgh Corn Exchange, and 20,000 at the Waverley Market.[11] The audience at the last of these was standing and people who fainted were passed over the heads of others in the crush. It was rather like major football matches before the advent of all-seater stadiums.

In the country as a whole, just over 40 per cent of adult men had the vote and no women, but the proportion of voters in the Midlothian constituency was particularly small. Many people came a long way to hear him speak. It follows that the great majority of those who heard him did not have the vote. It is a great tribute to Gladstone and them that so many came. He did not patronise his listeners. He gave them his views passionately and he explained them in detail in conjunction with his principles. He spoke to them as an educated audience. They repaid the compliment by giving him their full attention.

For the second week of his campaign, he moved away from Edinburgh and its surrounding area, and he carried on at the same frenetic pace in other parts of Scotland. For one speech in Glasgow, nearly 50,000 applications were made for a venue where the accommodation was limited to 6,000. All the major speeches had different themes, which makes his achievement all the more remarkable. This was partly because they were all reported in great detail in the national newspapers. He wanted to influence the national audience, not just the Scottish one.

On the fifteenth day, Gladstone returned to Hawarden by train and, as on his journey north, he made whistle-stop speeches at stations on the way, this time at Carlisle, Preston, Wigan, Warrington, and Chester. On his first day back, he stayed in bed until mid-morning, then he felled a tree in the afternoon. In the evening, he started revising his Midlothian speeches for publication in a book. When published, it contained 255 pages.

The country most certainly noted the Midlothian campaign. It roused and invigorated a large number of Gladstone's supporters and converted some to his cause. It also antagonised many who were not like minded. Predictably, the queen was one of these. She said that it was 'a series of violent, passionate invective against and abuse of Lord Beaconsfield'.[12] Disraeli said, probably untruthfully: 'It is certainly a relief that this drenching rhetoric has at length ceased—but I have never read a word of it'.[13]

Following his Midlothian campaign, Gladstone was in a buoyant mood over Christmas and the new year, a period which included his seventieth birthday. He was looking forward to the election, and a new Liberal government in which he expected to be in the leading role. Sadly, the latter part of January 1880 was dominated by the illness then the death of his sister, Helen, in Germany, then her burial in Scotland. He took some slight comfort from the fact that there were some doubtful indications that she had abandoned Roman Catholicism and reverted to her Anglican faith.

Disraeli's spirits, on the other hand, were low. Several members of his cabinet were ill. He had persuaded the queen to open parliament, but he himself was ill and could not attend. He did manage to get to the Lords for the debate on the Queen's Speech, but he gave an unusually feeble performance. His prospects for the next general election did not look good.

There had to be a general election within a year, and Disraeli saw it as a choice between the spring and autumn of 1880. A gloomy cabinet meeting decided to leave it to the autumn and hope that their fortunes would improve. Then, almost immediately afterwards, came news that the Conservatives had triumphed in a by-election at Southwark. This was a welcome and enormous surprise because the seat had been Liberal for a long time. Shortly afterwards, a telegram and Valentine gift from the queen were received. The telegram read: 'I am greatly rejoiced at the victory at Southwark. It shows what the feeling of the country is'.[14] It hardly exhibited the impartiality that the country expects its monarch to exhibit.

Disraeli responded to Victoria's Valentine with a gloomy and elaborately flowery message:

> He wishes he could repose on a sunny bank, like young Valentine in the pretty picture that fell from a rosy cloud this morn—but the reverie of the happy youth would be rather different from his. Valentine would dream of the future, and youthful loves, and all under the inspiration of a beautiful clime! Lord Beaconsfield, no longer in the sunset, but the twilight of existence, must encounter a life of anxiety and toil; but this, too, has its romance, when he remembers that he labours for the most gracious of beings![1]

Emboldened by his party's triumph at the Southwark by-election, Disraeli announced a spring general election to be held between 31 March and 27 April.

The Conservatives' election campaign was hampered by the fact that there had been a run of bad harvests. This could not possibly be Disraeli's fault, but it did not help. Quite apart from this, their campaign was lacklustre and they had allowed their formidable party machine to deteriorate. The convention at the time was that peers did not give election speeches, which meant that Disraeli and half his cabinet were not directly involved.

Disraeli's main contribution was an open letter to the lord lieutenant of Ireland, the duke of Marlborough. It was distinctly uninspiring and must have attracted few voters. The main thrust of the letter was the risk that the Irish might want to separate from Great Britain, an issue that, at that time, did not engage most British voters.

Unlike the Conservatives, the Liberals had built up their party organisations and this put them in a stronger position than in the past. Gladstone once more headed for Midlothian, and, as before, big crowds listened to his addresses at the stations at which his train stopped. Roy Jenkins says that there were 2,000 at Grantham, 6,000 at York, and too many to count at Newcastle.[16] As usual, we should treat such round figure estimates with caution. As before, he got a tremendous reception in Edinburgh, and as he had a few weeks earlier, he campaigned with great vigour and success. As expected, he was duly elected to serve the constituency.

Many expected the result of the election to be very close, with the Conservatives perhaps having the edge, but this is not what happened. The Liberals won 353 seats, the Conservatives won 238, and the Irish Home rulers won 61. Seventy-five-year-old Disraeli must have known that it was the end of his time in government.

Disraeli accepted the result with admirable equanimity, which is more than can be said of the queen. She was very probably just letting off steam, but she pondered on the possibility of abdication rather than having to accept Gladstone as prime minister. She told her secretary, General Ponsonby, that she would consider this 'rather than send for or have any *communication* with that *half-mad firebrand* who wd soon ruin everything and be a *Dictator*. Others but herself may submit to his democratic rule but *not the Queen*. His ranting had demonstrated a most unpardonable and personal hatred to Ld B who had restored England to the position she had lost under Mr G's Gov't'.[17]

Disraeli meanwhile got on with winding up his government and organising rewards and honours. One of these was a peerage for his secretary, Montagu Corry. The queen needed a lot of persuading, but he managed it. Gladstone ungraciously compared the honour to the decision by Caligula to make his horse a Roman senator.[18] This witty criticism has been made many times over the years, but Gladstone was one of the first to say it. It was unfair as well as being unkind because Corry had given outstanding service over a long period, much of it unpaid. The queen offered Disraeli a title or honour of his choosing, but he declined the opportunity. She also told him that she hoped that they would remain close on a private basis.

Hartington was the leader of the Liberals in the Commons, and it was not absolutely clear that Gladstone would be the next prime minister. Disraeli did the constitutionally correct thing and advised the queen to send for Hartington and ask if he was able to form a government. This would have pleased her, but the Liberals had already sounded out Gladstone and his position was known. Hartington advised her that the Liberals could not form a government without Gladstone, and that Gladstone would not serve in a government unless he was the leader of it. So Gladstone it had to be.

Gladstone was asked to meet the queen at Windsor—travelling back to Buckingham Palace was not something that had occurred to her. In a chilly interview, he agreed to form a government, and soon afterwards, he submitted his cabinet list to her. This included the surprising and unwise decision that he would again be chancellor of the Exchequer. It was a demanding job and gave him too much to do. The seventy-year-old Gladstone became prime minister for the second time on 23 April 1880.

20
1880–1881

Disraeli's health had been deteriorating for many years and he looked old, but the five-years-younger Gladstone had looked much more robust. However, he too now began to show his age. He retained much of his vigour, but was susceptible to minor illnesses. Shortly after asking Gladstone to form a government, the queen told Disraeli that he had looked 'very ill and haggard, and his voice was feeble'.[1] He was, though, still capable of dominating the House of Commons and he dominated the leader of the Conservatives in the Commons, Sir Stafford Northcote. However, in its first year, Gladstone's government suffered a number of defeats on minor matters. It was shortly after this that he acquired the sobriquet 'Grand Old Man', sometimes abbreviated to 'GOM'.

Like Disraeli in 1874, Gladstone took office without a clear, coherent plan of what he wanted to do, though he knew what he wanted to undo, namely Beaconsfieldism. He wanted to withdraw from colonial commitments or at least to stabilise them, and he wanted to have what he regarded as a Christian, moral foreign policy. He also wanted to put the public finances on a sound footing. In 1874, he had handed Disraeli a £5.25 million surplus, but in 1880, he inherited an £8 million deficit. He blamed Disraeli for this, but perhaps he did not sufficiently allow for the poor harvests and trading problems, which were not his fault.

Before taking office in 1868, Gladstone had said that his mission was to pacify Ireland. Despite this, in 1880, he was unprepared for trouble in what has sometimes been called 'John Bull's other island'. During the election campaign, Disraeli had drawn attention to potential problems there, but he had ignored the warning. The agricultural depression was much worse in Ireland than in England and there was much hardship. Evictions increased fivefold between 1877 and 1880. Ireland was to play a large and very difficult part in Gladstone's extended political career. Amazingly, he only visited Ireland once in his entire life—for three weeks in the autumn of 1877. Disraeli never crossed the Irish Sea. In 1884, Gladstone admitted that he had been

Mr Punch presents lunch. The Marquess of Hartington, leader of the Liberals in the House of Commons (1875–1880), says 'here's a pretty lunch'. The Earl of Granville (with beard), Foreign Secretary 1880–1885, says 'indigestible I'm afraid, but we must make the most of it'. Behind him stands Gladstone, and behind Gladstone stands Disraeli depicted as a coloured lady. Published 29 May 1880. *Punch*

taken by surprise 'by the severity of the crisis that was already swelling upon the horizon, and that, shortly afterwards, rushed upon us like a flood'.[2]

An early problem for the prime minister was the newly elected Liberal candidate for Northampton, Charles Bradlaugh. He wanted to affirm rather than take the oath of allegiance, which included a religious reference. He said that this was because the oath would have no meaning for him. He later told a newspaper that he would take the oath but would 'regard myself as bound not by the letter of the words, but by the spirit which the affirmation would have conveyed had I been permitted to use it.'[3] Two select committees recommended that he not be allowed to take his seat, and due to his protests, he was briefly imprisoned. His Northampton seat was declared vacant.

The episode was a farce, and it was very difficult for Gladstone. He was deeply religious and he had a low regard for Bradlaugh, who, among other things, advocated birth control and republicanism. On the other hand, he believed that voters should choose their MPs, so he reluctantly backed Bradlaugh. He appeared indecisive and Lord Randolph Churchill (the father of Sir Winston) and others succeeded in making him look foolish. The Bradlaugh nonsense continued throughout the 1880–85 parliament and he finally took his seat after the 1885 general election. The sequence of events is described in the next chapter.

Gladstone made a good start in dealing with the country's finances. On 10 June 1880, he introduced a successful and well-received budget. It was his twelfth but his first for fourteen years. Nevertheless, it should have been someone else doing it. There were others able to do so. Hugh Childers did well after taking the office from Gladstone in December 1882. The minutiae of finance took far too much of Gladstone's time, which should have been spent guiding the government. The burden may have been a contributory factor in a serious medical problem. Six weeks after the budget, he suffered a severe chill that developed into pneumonia. It was six weeks before he was back to full health.

To add to his problems in his first year (and indeed in subsequent years), the queen found dealing with him distasteful. On 20 September 1880, she told Disraeli that she dealt with the government mainly through Lord Granville: '… for I never write except on formal *official* matters to the Prime Minister … I always look to you for ultimate help'.[4]

Disraeli might have retired as leader of his party, but he did not do so, nor did his colleagues ask him to step down. He took a seven-year lease on a house in Curzon Street, which was convenient for parliament. Perhaps this indicated that he was confident of several years more life and a continuing political position.

He lived rather a lonely life, but he had two interests. Firstly, he moved from social commitment to social commitment, though not hosting any of them. He was not short of invitations because hosts and hostesses were flattered by the presence of the great man. At the dinner parties and other events, he was often content to say little and just attend. He enjoyed the attention and just being there. In a brutally unkind phrase, Lytton Strachey said that he was moving 'an assiduous mummy, from dinner party to dinner party'.[5]

Disraeli's second interest was writing. In the late autumn of his life, he finished another very successful novel, this one with the title *Endymion*. He had started it in the early 1870s after finishing *Lothair*, and he had written just a little more after the Congress of Berlin. Over the course of just four months, he finished it. It was about politics in the middle of the nineteenth century and, like most of his other novels, it had a wildly improbable plot. Many of the characters were readily recognisable as being based on leading people active at the time, but Gladstone was not one of them.

The book was generally well reviewed and, like *Lothair*, it was a great commercial success. Disraeli left the financial negotiations to his secretary, Montagu Corry, now ennobled as Lord Rowton. Disraeli was sitting in the Lords when Corry passed him a note telling him that the publisher, Longmans, had agreed to an advance of the extraordinarily large sum of £10,000. This was at the time the largest ever advance for a work of fiction. The second largest is believed to be the £9,000 paid to Charles Dickens for *Dombey and Son*.⁶ Longmans recovered the advance in just a few months.

Not content with this, Disraeli started another novel. He died when he had completed nine chapters, and poignantly he laid down his pen in mid-sentence, half way through a sentence in the first paragraph of the tenth chapter. He usually gave his books the title of their main character, so it would probably have been called *Falconet*. The nine chapters were published in *The Spectator* magazine in 1905.

The fictional Falconet is an unpleasant man, and it is not hard to discern that he is based on Gladstone. The book describes him as 'essentially a prig and among prigs there is a freemasonry which never fails. All the prigs spoke of him as the coming man'. He is also described as 'having a complete deficiency in the sense of humour'. Even the name Falconet can with a little imagination be linked to Gladstone. A falconet is a small falcon and Gladstone's beaky face and intense eyes had been likened to a bird of prey. The book was not finished or published in Disraeli's lifetime, but it would have been a final insult to his nemesis. Disraeli had taken to referring to him in correspondence as AV. This was meant to indicate 'Arch Villain'.

After leaving office, Disraeli corresponded regularly with the queen, mostly not using formal channels. Instead, he accepted the services of Montagu Corry as an intermediary and she did the same with her highland servant, John Brown. She also sent him gifts, including salmon from Balmoral. He responded to her Christmas gifts with a note prefaced 'Oh! Madam and most beloved Sovereign'.⁷ On 31 December 1880, he left his treasured house at Hughenden for the last time and transferred to London. He did not know it, but he had less than four months to live.

On 15 March, Disraeli made his last speech in the House of Lords. It was a very good one supporting a vote of confidence to the queen following the recent assassination of Tsar Alexander II. Among other things, he said that he was 'the most beneficent prince that ever filled the throne of Russia'.⁸ He was certainly one of the better tsars, but one must wonder how sincere was the compliment. They had taken very different views over the Eastern Question and the Congress of Berlin. If we were to be very pedantic, we could say that it might have been sincere because he thought that all the previous tsars were even worse. Three days later, Disraeli asked a short question in the Lords and these were his last words uttered in parliament.

On 22 March, Disraeli caught a chill and it quickly turned into bronchitis. His doctor recorded that it was accompanied by 'distressing asthma, loss of appetite, fever and congestion of the kidneys'.⁹ Disraeli realised the seriousness of his condition and told his friend Philip Rose 'I shall never survive this attack. I feel it is quite impossible … I feel this is the last of it.'¹⁰ The doctors repeatedly issued misleadingly optimistic bulletins, but he was quite right. He did, though, retain his sense of humour. Told that the queen would visit him, he said: 'No it is better not. She would only ask me to take a message to Albert'.[11]

Other people did visit, though they did not get as far as his bedroom. Their number included Gladstone who called twice. He wrote in his diary: 'May the Almighty be near his pillow'.[12] On 30 March, the publisher's proofs for *Hansard* covering his last speech in the House of Lords arrived. Ignoring advice, Disraeli insisted on checking them, saying: 'I will not go down to posterity talking bad grammar'.[13] His last recorded words were 'I had rather live, but I am not afraid to die.'[14]

Gladstone was dreading the death, which he knew must come soon. It would be nice to think that Christian feeling for a respected political opponent was the reason, and his diary entry 'May the Almighty be near his pillow' provides some evidence for this. It should be remembered that he wrote the diary exclusively for himself and he did not expect others to see it. However, this was not the reason. He despised the man, and everyone from the queen downwards knew it. The real explanation was that the country, again from the queen downwards, would be watching to see if he mishandled his role in what would follow.

He made a brilliant start. Disraeli died at 4.30 a.m. Gladstone was informed at 8 a.m., and immediately afterwards, he offered his executors a public funeral. By this, he meant Westminster Abbey or St Paul's Cathedral. Just a little later, the queen telegraphed her wish for a public funeral and he was able to tell her that he had already made the offer. It did not happen because Disraeli had left firm instructions that he was to be buried with his late wife at St Michael and All Angels Church at Hughenden.

Gladstone had mixed feelings about this wish. He wrote to his son that 'there was something very touching about Disraeli's determination to be buried with his wife'.[15] However, after the 'private' funeral, he complained: 'As he lived so he died—all display without reality or genuineness'.[16] The funeral was held on 26 April and the simple service was conducted by the local vicar.

Other things were not simple. Protocol prevented the queen from coming, although she would have liked to have done so. She did, though, send a handwritten note and flowers, which were placed on the coffin. However, the prince of Wales and three of her other sons did come. Other prominent attendees included all but one of Disraeli's last cabinet, various bishops, and ambassadors from France, Russia, Germany, the US, and Turkey. Senior Liberals included Hartington, Harcourt, Rosebery, and the 15th earl of Derby. The last of these was the son of the former Conservative prime minister. He had for a long time been Disraeli's friend and he had served in his cabinets. However, they had fallen out and he had recently defected to the Liberals.

The Feud: 1846–1881

A special train brought the prominent mourners to High Wycombe from Paddington Station in London. 'God's Wonderful Railway' (GWR) did them proud. The shops in High Wycombe were closed and crowds lined the route from the station to Hughenden.

A very prominent absentee was Prime Minister William Ewart Gladstone. It appears that part of his motive was a genuine wish not to be responsible for overshadowing a 'private' event. The other part and probably the main part was that he thought that to go would be insincere. The very dubious reason that he gave for not going was overwork. This was obviously ludicrous. It annoyed the country and, not least, it annoyed the queen.

Disraeli's funeral had been while parliament had broken for Easter. Gladstone decided that tributes in parliament would not be until 9 May. The delay was among other things annoying to the queen and some others. In his defence, Gladstone said that the delay was fixed with the agreement of Sir Stafford Northcote, the leader of the Conservatives in the Commons. He also said that he was following the precedent set on the death of Lord Palmerston. This was true, but Palmerston had died during the parliamentary recess. Disraeli had not.

The technical motion before parliament was that a national memorial to Disraeli should be erected in Westminster Abbey, and it was on this motion that Gladstone would speak.

This was the part above all others that he dreaded. He was so upset at the prospect that he repeatedly prayed for guidance and he took to his bed with severe and lengthy diarrhoea, presumably induced by stress.

When the time did come to make the speech, he did it very well and his offering was well received, including by the queen. He brought in Disraeli's unique career, his loyalty to his race, his devotion to his wife, and his absence of rancour. He also praised certain qualities that he had possessed 'in a degree undoubtedly extraordinary ... his strength of will; his long-sighted consistency of purpose ... his remarkable power of self-government; and, last, but not least, his great parliamentary courage—a quality which I, who have been associated in the course of my life with some scores of ministers, have, I think, never known but two whom I could pronounce his equal.'[17] The two ministers that he had in mind were Sir Robert Peel and Lord Russell.

For several days afterwards, the diarrhoea continued, but fortunately it had not affected him while speaking in parliament. He had largely told the truth, and although some of his remarks must have been insincere, it was a job well done. His views on Disraeli's motives were kept to himself. Despite all the fine tributes, and Gladstone's were just one of them, fifty-five votes were cast against the motion to erect the memorial.

Protocol prevented the queen from attending the funeral, but she made a private visit to Hughenden Manor, the church, and the vault just a few days later. The vault was opened so that she could see the coffin with her flowers still on it. She ordered a marble memorial to be placed in the church. It was inscribed 'placed by his grateful and affectionate Sovereign and friend Victoria R.I.' The two letters denote '*Regina Imperitrix*' meaning 'Queen Empress'. She had Disraeli to thank for being able to call herself empress. The memorial is the only known example of a memorial erected by a reigning monarch to one of her subjects. She mourned Disraeli for the rest of her life and her opinion of Gladstone never altered.

The Disraeli tomb in the churchyard is a large crypt containing the remains of Benjamin Disraeli, his wife, Mary Anne, Mrs Brydges Williams, and a number of the members of Disraeli's family. The crypt was finally sealed in 1967 when the last member of the family was buried there. Mrs Brydges Williams was Disraeli's benefactress and friend. Her story is told in Chapter 13.

Hughenden Manor is owned by the National Trust and can be visited by the public. It is advisable to check dates and times in advance.

PART V

Gladstone after Disraeli:
1881–1898

21
1881–1885

Although things went badly towards the end, history tends to regard Gladstone's 1868–74 government as a considerable success. The same cannot be said of his second administration in 1880–85. Luck was not with him, and he was beset by a sea of difficulties. He mishandled quite a few of the problems that he faced, but he did have some successes. Franchise reform was prominent among them.

The queen was not the least of his difficulties. The point has already been made several times in this book, and he really did have a heavy cross to bear. During his second administration, she sent him 270 letters and 170 telegrams, many of them censorious, making unwelcome demands, or both. He sent her 1,017 letters, almost all of them detailed and very respectful.[1] She also pestered him verbally and occasionally through other people. Needless to say, it all took a great deal of his time. Being chancellor of the Exchequer as well as prime minister also took a lot of his resources, but he finally had the sense to discard this role in December 1882. Hugh Childers took over the Exchequer, and despite Gladstone's misgivings, he did it well.

The previous chapter includes an account of Charles Bradlaugh's attempt to take his seat as a member for Northampton. He was a convinced atheist and his convictions would not allow him to take the necessary religious oath. After a tremendous fuss and farcical series of events, the seat had been declared vacant. It was a problem for the devoutly Christian Gladstone, and he had been made to look foolish. His problems continued. During the course of a single parliament, the Northampton seat was declared vacant five times and Bradlaugh won all the consequent by-elections.

On one occasion, Bradlaugh affirmed, took his place on the Liberal benches, and participated in a vote. He was then unseated. Another time, he marched up to the table, took a paper from his pocket, and administered the oath to himself. At one time, four legal actions were in progress. He sued the deputy sergeant-at-arms for an alleged assault during what he contended was his illegal arrest. He was being prosecuted for blasphemy. There was an action to

[Cartoon: St. Stephen's Review Presentation Cartoon, March 24th 1888. Left panel labelled AUGUST 3RD 1881; right panel labelled MARCH 14TH 1888.]

Trials and tribulations of the atheist MP Charles Bradlaugh.

impose bankruptcy penalties on him in connection with his illegal vote, and finally his supporters were challenging the right of the House to exclude him.[2]

Gladstone might have recalled that, after the 1880 general election, Disraeli had forecast trouble and advised that Bradlaugh be allowed to take the seat. He had posthumously been proved right. Bradlaugh was elected again in the 1885 general election and this time the new speaker, Arthur Wellesley Peel, the son of Sir Robert Peel, refused to hear objections and swore him in.

Gladstone's difficulties in 1881–85 included problems with the Boers in the Transvaal. In 1881, the governor of Natal and almost 100 British troops were killed at the Battle of Majuba Hill. In consequence, there was an explosion of jingoism in Britain and a wave of demands from the queen and the country that reinforcements be sent and revenge exacted. This Gladstone did not do. Negotiations had already been taking place and they were continued.

Independence was restored to the Transvaal, subject to British supervision of its foreign relations other than with the Orange Free State, but this arrangement only lasted for three years. The queen and the British people were upset, and the Boers were given the erroneous impression that future bad behaviour by them (as the British saw it) would not be resisted. During the Second Boer War of 1899–1902, they found to their cost that this was not the case.[3]

Gladstone's conciliatory attitude towards the Boers, or weakness as many others believed it to be, was not always his approach to foreign and colonial problems. In July 1882, he ordered the bombardment of Alexandria and the occupation of

Egypt. The country was still a province of the Turkish Empire, and because of the Suez Canal, it was very important to France and Britain. France decided not to join Gladstone in his actions. The crisis was provoked by a nationalist revolt led by the Egyptian Colonel Arabi. Fifty foreigners were massacred and the British consul was injured. Arabi mounted guns, which were a threat to Royal Navy ships, and he sought to repudiate some of the country's debts.

The British action was brilliantly successful. The enemy was annihilated at Tel-el-Kebir and Arabi was captured. Gladstone funded the action by raising income tax. The events were a welcome boost to the popularity of Gladstone and his government. However, they came with the consequence of saddling the country with continuing responsibilities in Egypt and its southern neighbour. One of the repercussions of this features later in this chapter.

Bitter Irish problems featured very prominently in the latter part of Gladstone's political career, and the events in *John Bull's Other Island* plagued him throughout his 1880–85 administration. They were too numerous to receive more than a brief summary in this chapter.

In 1881, the Irish National Party, led by Charles Stewart Parnell, was making the conduct of business in the Commons difficult and at times almost impossible. At the expense of a vast amount of his time and energy, Gladstone managed to secure the passage of a Coercion Act, and he then introduced a Land Bill to the Commons. This was designed to alleviate some of the suffering in rural Ireland, but it was rejected by the Lords. The queen used her influence to prevent a continued clash between the Lords and the Commons, and it eventually became law. The bill had occupied fifty-eight sittings of the Commons and Gladstone had personally fought it through clause by clause.

In October 1881, Parnell was imprisoned in Kilmainham Gaol in Dublin. It was done as a (legal) executive decision and there had not been a trial or a conviction. Six months later, he was released following negotiations instigated and approved by Gladstone. Controversially, one of the intermediaries was Captain O'Shea MP, the husband of Parnell's mistress. He was hoping for political preferment and both his involvement and the negotiations caused considerable discontent. Parnell agreed to tone down the extremism of his parliamentary activities. His aims, though, remained unchanged.

Soon after Parnell's release, Gladstone suffered a terrible personal blow and the chances of tranquillity in Ireland suffered a major setback. Lord Frederick Cavendish was a Liberal MP and Gladstone's nephew by marriage. In May 1882, he was appointed chief secretary to the lord lieutenant of Ireland. Within a few hours of his arrival in Dublin, he was stabbed to death while walking in Phoenix Park.

Cavendish had enjoyed very friendly relations with Gladstone and his murder was a personal, as well as a political, disaster. Lady Cavendish wrote the following in her journal:

Charles Stewart Parnell.

> Uncle William ... his face ... like a prophet's in its look of faith and strength ... came up and almost took me in his arms, and his first words were, 'Father forgive them, for they know not what they do.' Then he said to me, 'Be assured it will not be in vain,' and across all my agony there fell a bright ray of hope, and I saw in a vision Ireland at peace, and my darling's life-blood accepted as a sacrifice for Christ's sake to help to bring this to pass.... I said to him as he was leaving me, 'Uncle William, you must never blame yourself for sending him.' He said, 'Oh there can be no question of that.'

Sadly, Lady Cavendish's vision of Ireland at peace did not come to pass. The murder put an end to any hopes of an early end of the Irish problem. Murders were still being committed more than a century later. In the short term, Ireland continued to cast a cloud over Gladstone's second administration.

Gladstone faced many problems and disappointments during the course of his 1880–85 administration, but he was entitled to take considerable satisfaction from his steps in securing parliamentary reform. It started in 1883 with the much-needed and effective Corrupt and Illegal Practices Act. This was followed by the closely linked Representation of the People Act 1884 and the Redistribution of Seats Act 1885. It was not easy.

The Second Reform Act, masterminded by Disraeli in 1867, had left the country with around 3 million electors. They were all men, and about 40 per cent of adult males had the vote. Gladstone's 1884 Act left the country with about 5 million electors, still all men. Very slightly, more than 60 per cent of adult males had the vote. Disraeli's Act, although very far reaching, had favoured the boroughs over the counties and had left the need for a major redistribution of seats. England was favoured over Scotland and especially over Ireland. Gladstone's Acts addressed these issues.

The 1884 Act increased the size of the electorate in Ireland by 260 per cent. Many of the new voters supported Parnell and Home Rule, and the consequences for the Liberal Party in that part of the UK were devastating. This was both foreseeable and foreseen. Roy Jenkins says that Gladstone and his supporters did this with their eyes open and rather nobly.[5]

The first of the two bills had no trouble in the Commons, but it was a different matter in the Lords. Gladstone lobbied furiously but the Upper House rejected it by 205 votes to 146. Lord Salisbury now led the Conservatives and he (then Lord Cranborne) had resigned from Lord Derby's cabinet in 1867 because he could not accept Disraeli's bill. However, many of the 205 had voted reluctantly and it was by no means certain that they would do so again.

The queen thought that the Lords accurately reflected the views of the country and that they had every right to reject the bill. Gladstone was furious and he was not willing to accept the defeat, which posed the possibility of a Lords *v*. Commons constitutional crisis. Surprisingly, the queen moderated her views and brought pressure to bear in order to get a compromise. She was pushing at an open door and an agreement was reached.

It was widely expected that the Representation of the People Act would benefit the Liberals other than in Ireland, and that the following legislation concerning the redistribution of seats would favour the Conservatives. The latter feared that after the passage of the first act, Gladstone would call a general election and that this would take place before the redistribution of seats. This would have been unfair, and they were right to resist the prospect. However, it probably would not have happened and satisfactory assurances were given. Then, with minor amendments, the passage of both bills was secured. They were both implemented before the next general election was held.

The debacle over the death of General Gordon cast a long shadow over the last part of Gladstone's term of office. He felt with justification that Gordon had been reckless and insubordinate, and had brought his misfortune on himself, but nevertheless, Gladstone and his government had in several ways and at several times badly misjudged the situation.

Following the events described earlier in this chapter, the crisis unfolded in a vast territory south of Egypt then known as Egyptian Soudan. At the time, Britain had a great interest in Egypt. A fanatical self-proclaimed Mahdi or Messiah initiated a rebellion. The Egyptian Khedive sent a military expedition to suppress it. The very large Egyptian force, which had an English commander, was very badly defeated in November 1883. The commander and thousands of Egyptians were killed.

These disastrous events caused great consternation in London. The British government decided to withdraw from the region and General Gordon was despatched to what is now known as the Sudan. Gladstone had not met Gordon and he only played a small part in his appointment. He did, though, give his approval to what others had done. Gordon's instructions were badly drafted but could be summarised as advising on how an orderly withdrawal could be achieved. He was not instructed to do whatever it was that he advised.

Gordon was not suited to the role. He was an outspoken Christian of what might be called the muscular variety, and his varied career illustrated an exceedingly adventurous streak in his character. He was not a man likely to take kindly to advising on an orderly withdrawal. He was much more likely to want to turn failure into triumph, then set about doing it. When he heard of the appointment, the leader of the Opposition, Lord Salisbury, thought that the government had taken leave of it senses.[6]

Gordon's appointment owed a lot to a press campaign that gathered much public support. The queen was very pleased. They were not sure what Gordon was going to do, but whatever it was, they admired him and thought that he was the man to do it. On 18 January, he set off in haste from Charing Cross Station in London. At the station, Foreign Secretary Lord Granville handed him his railway ticket. Just as the train was about to depart, it was realised that Gordon was not carrying any money. General Wolseley, the man who would later lead the relief expedition, handed him the money in his pockets and also his gold watch.

Gordon did exactly what his detractors feared that he might do. He set about leading the Egyptian forces and consolidating their positions. Fifty-four days later, he was besieged in Khartoum, together with his troops and civilians. The siege lasted 320 days, though for most of them it was not complete.

During this time, Gordon's behaviour was at times bizarre. He sent messages to the Mahdi trying to convert him to Christianity. He received replies that endeavoured to convert him to Islam. If he had tried, he might have been able to achieve a withdrawal, but he chose not to do this. Instead, he exuded unjustified optimism and sent absurd messages to London. Towards the end of the siege, he showed signs of wanting to be killed.

In Britain, pressure built for a relief force to be sent to rescue him, and this was strongly wished by the queen. The cabinet was split. Gladstone and half of them thought that Gordon should be left to his fate, and the other half wanted some sort of rescue. This was despite Gordon's messages saying that he did not need or want it. Gladstone stalled for a very long time, but he ultimately agreed and General Wolseley was despatched to lead it. He reached Khartoum on 28 January 1885, but Gordon and many of the others there had been killed two days earlier. Had Gladstone acted more quickly, they would probably have been saved.

To a considerable extent, the British people still admired Gordon and they were furious, few more so than their head of state. The queen sent her prime minister an outraged and ungrammatical telegram, and as a calculated insult, she did so without using the customary cipher. It was handed to him by the stationmaster at Carnforth Junction Railway Station. Her missive read: 'These news from Khartoum are frightful and to think that all this might have been prevented and many precious lives saved by earlier action is too fearful'. Gladstone's frigid and formal response read:

> Mr Gladstone has had the honour this day to receive Your Majesty's Telegram *en clair*, relating to the deplorable intelligence received this day from Lord Wolseley, and stating that it is too fearful to consider that the fall of Khartoum might have been prevented and many precious lives saved by earlier action.
>
> Mr Gladstone does not presume to estimate the means of judgement possessed by Your Majesty, but so far as his information and recollection at the moment go, he is not altogether able to follow the conclusion which Your Majesty has been pleased thus to announce.
>
> Mr Gladstone is under the impression that Lord Wolseley's force might have been sufficiently advanced to save Khartoum had not a large portion of it been delayed by a circuitous route along the river, upon the express application of General Gordon...

Gladstone's unpopularity led to an unfortunate variation on his nickname. For some time, it had been 'Grand Old Man', or just the initials 'GOM'. Now it was sometimes 'MOG', which meant 'Murderer of Gordon'. Another hostile variation, using the original 'GOM', was 'God's Only Mistake'.

The government was in disarray and on its last legs during the months following Gordon's death. Shortly after the event, it survived a vote of censure by just fourteen votes. The cabinet was disunited, and by May, ten of its sixteen members were on the brink of resignation.[7] On 9 June, the government suffered a defeat on the beer duty. Thirty-nine members of the Irish party joined six Liberals in voting against the government. A further seventy Liberals abstained. It was the last straw and Gladstone resigned.

There could not be a general election because the new electoral registers were not yet ready, so the queen sent for Lord Salisbury. Gladstone was offered an earldom, but to the queen's disappointment, he declined. He would have had less scope to cause trouble for her, as she saw it, if sitting in the House of Lords. The two had a civilised and reasonably friendly farewell interview at Windsor on 24 June. Gladstone would be back in little more than seven months.

22
1885–1893

The need, as he saw it, for Irish Home Rule completely dominated the remainder of Gladstone's parliamentary career. It follows that it dominates this chapter. In very late 1884, he had come to believe that it was necessary and that at least, in the long term, it was inevitable. He only confided in his family and some associates, but his thinking on the matter was quite well known. He did not make a feature of it during the November–December 1885 general election, which was the first held after the extension of the franchise and the redistribution of seats.

The election gave the Liberals 333 seats, the Conservatives 251, and the Parnellite Irish 86. Before the election, the Conservatives had been flirting with Parnell, and so long as the Irish stayed with them, the Conservatives had a very small majority. They continued in office. Gladstone wanted the Conservatives to give Ireland Home Rule, but this did not become their policy. They thought that it was a trap and that his motivation was wanting them to split in an inevitable dispute. They were wrong. Gladstone was sincere.

After the election, Gladstone came out unequivocally for Home Rule, much to the consternation of some of his colleagues. In January 1886, Lord Salisbury's government lost a vote on an amendment to the Queen's Speech, the subject of it not being connected to Ireland. Salisbury resigned and his grateful sovereign offered him a dukedom. He declined with the elegant words: 'His fortune would not be equal to such a dignity.... The kind words in which your Majesty has expressed approval of his conduct are very far more precious to him than any sort of title'.[1]

Gladstone accepted the queen's commission, and on 1 February 1886, he commenced his short-lived third administration. Needless to say, she was not pleased with this development. She told her secretary: 'She does not in the least care, but rather wishes it should be known, that she has the greatest possible disinclination to take this half crazy and really in many ways ridiculous old man—for the sake of the country'.[2] Lord Hartington and a phalanx of Liberals were not willing to take office in Gladstone's government because they would not support his plans for Irish Home Rule. They became collectively known as

Liberal Unionists. Joseph Chamberlain stayed with Gladstone but resigned a couple of months later.

Over the next three months, Gladstone undertook the massive task of preparing the Home Rule Bill and he introduced it to the Commons on 8 April. His speech was an effective one and lasted three hours and twenty-five minutes. The bill was lost on the second reading. Ninety-three Liberals voted against it and the voting was 343 to 313, a majority of thirty.

Gladstone asked for a general election and this was held in July 1886, only eight months after the previous one. Home Rule was the dominant issue. Many voters did not appreciate being consulted again so quickly and the turnout was very low. Nevertheless, the result was a decisive defeat for Gladstone. The Conservatives had 316 seats and the Liberal Unionists 78. Gladstone's Liberals had 191 and the Irish Nationalists 85. Lord Salisbury and the Conservatives returned to power and together with the Liberal Unionists they had a majority of 118.

Lord Salisbury's government remained in power for six years, mainly due to the Liberal Unionists mounting hostility to Home Rule. During this time, Gladstone's sight and hearing became increasing problems for him. His sight in particular became a serious handicap.

Robert Arthur Talbot Gascoyne-Cecil, a Spy cartoon from *Vanity Fair*.

Life for Gladstone, who was now an old man, was intense, but it is worth setting out the first two light-hearted verses of a poem that he sent to Margot Tennant in December 1889. This was shortly after her visit to Hawarden:

> *When Parliament ceases, and comes the Recess,*
> *And we seek, in the country, rest after distress,*
> *As a rule upon visitors, place an embargo*
> *But make an exception in favour of Margot.*
>
> *For she brings such a treasure of movement and life*
> *Fun, spirit, and stir to folk weary with strife.*
> *Though young, and though fair, who can hold such a cargo,*
> *Of all the good qualities going as Margot?*

The vivacious Margot Tennant later became the second wife of future Prime Minister Herbert Asquith.

Around the same time, Gladstone was sitting in the library at Hawarden in the company of Lord Rosebery, Lord Ripon, and John Morley. He suddenly said that it was his time for prayers and he asked Ripon and Morley to go to another room. This was because Ripon was a Roman Catholic and Morley was agnostic. The next day, Rosebery told them that Ripon had been banished because he believed too much and Morley because he believed too little.[4]

Two years later, on New Year's Eve 1891, Gladstone reflected on Disraeli, his old adversary who had died ten years previously. He was not complimentary. For all the deterioration that had occurred during his time in public life, he blamed one man only—Disraeli. Palmerston had had faults, but he had also had many principles and genuine liberal convictions. Disraeli had had no principles or convictions of any kind, except on the subject of Jews. He had not personally disliked Disraeli; he had, on the contrary, found plenty to admire in him; and he had intensively disapproved of the man who had corrupted and debauched the public life of England.[5]

Over his extremely long political life, Gladstone moved from being a reactionary Tory to a progressive Liberal, but on occasions, he expressed views close to his earlier beliefs. In 1890, during a visit to Oxford, he regretted the admission of women as students, and incredibly, he said that the duke of Wellington had been perfectly right when he said in 1830 that the constitution was incapable of improvement.[6] He further asserted that the country had never been better governed than it was in the days before the Great Reform Act.

In the two years to 1890, the Liberals took twelve seats from the Conservatives in by-elections and Gladstone's prospects were improving. However, a subsequent falling out with Parnell and a split in the Irish party had the opposite effect. In 1891, he announced a hotchpotch of radical measures that became known as the Newcastle Programme. Quite a lot of it was foisted on him and did not meet with his approval. He was, after all, nearly eighty-two years old, and he was fixated with Ireland.

The next general election was held in the summer of 1892, and Gladstone was hoping for a big win. This would enable him to get the Home Rule Bill through the Commons, and it would send a clear message to the Lords. They would know that if they rejected it, they would be overthrowing the clear will of the voters and perhaps setting up a peers *v*. people crisis. Gladstone did win, but it was not the big victory that he wanted. The Liberals had 273 seats and could count on the support of the divided 81 Irish Home Rulers. The Conservatives had 269 seats and the Liberal Unionists had 46. Including the one Socialist, Keir Hardy, Gladstone had an apparent majority of forty for Home Rule.

The queen was stuck with Gladstone for the fourth time. Astonishingly, the Court Circular recorded that she received Salisbury's resignation 'with regret'.[8] After appointing him, she recorded privately that Gladstone 'was greatly altered and changed, not only much aged, walking rather bent, with a stick, but altogether; his face shrunk, deadly pale, with a weird look in his eyes, a feeble expression about the mouth, and the voice altered'.[9] This remarkable sentence contains eight commas and a semicolon. It was not a joyful interview, and afterwards, Gladstone told his secretary that it had been 'as dismal as that which might have taken place between Marie Antoinette and her executioner'.[10]

For various reasons, it was not a happy or united cabinet, but Gladstone's final government had a respectable number of legislative achievements. Ireland, though, of course dominated its early stages. During the preparation of the bill, Gladstone was attacked by a mad cow while walking at Hawarden. It might seem funny, but it was a serious matter and he felt the effects for three weeks. The cow was subsequently shot. Afterwards, an elaborate wreath was delivered to Hawarden. The inscription with it read: 'To the memory of the patriotic cow which sacrificed its life in an attempt to save Ireland from Home Rule'.

Gladstone had intended that the Home Rule Bill would have the title 'A Bill for the Better Government of Ireland', but the queen flatly refused to utter the words 'Better Government'. The title of the bill was amended, and in the Queen's Speech, she announced that her government would introduce a 'Bill to Amend the Provision for the Government of Ireland'.

The main difference compared with the failed 1886 bill was that eighty Irish MPs would sit at Westminster, though they would only speak and vote on matters that affected Ireland. Gladstone introduced the bill with a very good speech lasting almost two and a half hours, and it received a formal first reading without a vote. The second reading passed with a majority of forty-three.

Gladstone's performance during the marathon committee and report stages was incredible, and he did it all while finding it almost impossible to read his notes. The committee stage took parts of no less than fifty-three parliamentary days, and during them, he made eighty speeches. The exhausted prime minister was on top form and attracted admiration from all parts of the House, including from those opposed to him. His bitter Conservative adversary, Lord Randolph Churchill, remarked to a prominent Liberal Unionist: 'And that is the man you deserted. How could you do it?'[11]

The bill finally passed the Commons with a majority of forty. Gladstone knew that it would almost certainly be rejected by the Lords, and this duly happened. The Conservatives, the Liberal Unionists, the establishment, the queen, and a significant part of the populations of England, Wales, and Scotland opposed it. The Lords only allocated a derisory four days to the bill. The so called 'backwoodsmen' did their duty as they saw it and came to London. A total 560 peers were entitled to vote and 82 per cent of them did. They rejected the bill by the crushing majority of 419 votes to 41.

Gladstone was defeated. It would be another twenty-eight years of strife and bloodshed before Ireland was divided on terms from which he would have recoiled in horror.

23
1893–1898

There was no prospect of Home Rule for Ireland during the next few years. Gladstone was approaching eighty-four years of age and was suffering under the handicap of failing eyesight. With only one break, he had been an MP for more than sixty years and he had an unparalleled record as a statesman. One would have expected him to take a well-earned and honourable retirement. This, though, did not happen.

Many elderly statesmen have and have had the ability to persuade themselves that they must carry on because there are things to be done that only they can do, or at least things that can best be done by them. Churchill, who went on too long before he retired at eighty, is an example. Palmerston was in reasonably good health when he died in office two days before his eighty-first birthday. Konrad Adenauer was eighty-seven when he ceased being chancellor of West Germany. Gladstone was firmly in this category, and there were things for him to do.

In the event, he did not carry on for long because he was, with only one dissenter, defeated by his cabinet. The issue was increased naval expenditure, which was wanted by the opposition, his cabinet, the queen, and the press. Gladstone thought that it could lead to a dangerous arms race with the competitive building of warships. In view of what happened in the years leading to the First World War, can we say that he was wrong?

On 28 February 1894, Gladstone had an audience with the queen and indicated that he would be resigning. He afterwards recorded:

> I had an audience of the Queen for 30 or 35 minutes today, doubtless my last in an official capacity. She had much difficulty in finding topics for an adequate prolongation: but fog and rain and [her] coming journey to Italy all did their duty and helped. I thought I never saw her looking better. She was at the highest point of her cheerfulness. Her manner was personally kind throughout.[1]

On 1 March, he presided over his last cabinet, which he subsequently dubbed the blubbering cabinet. This was because several members of it, but not himself, were visibly upset. Later that day, he spoke to the House of Commons for the last time. He never entered the Palace of Westminster again, though he remained an MP until the general election fifteen months later. During this time, he was permanently paired with a Liberal Unionist, aged ninety-one. This was Charles Villiers, who remained an MP until his death at the age of ninety-six.

Gladstone met the queen and resigned on 2 March. She did not ask his advice on who should succeed him and appointed Lord Rosebery as the next prime minister. It is widely believed that, if asked, he would have recommended First Lord of the Admiralty Earl Spencer.

Gladstone had fifty more months to live, and during this time, he was half deaf and more than half blind. He died on 19 May 1898. It is probably true to say that we will not see his like again.

In contrast to Disraeli, he had a state funeral at Westminster Abbey. The pallbearers were the prince of Wales (later Edward VII), the duke of York (later George V), Lord Salisbury, Lord Rosebery, Lord Kimberley, Sir William Harcourt, Arthur Balfour, the duke of Rutland, Lord Rendel, and George Armitstead. Perverse to the last, the queen sent a telegram to the prince of Wales asking what precedent he had followed and whose advice he had taken when he decided to act as a pallbearer. He imperiously replied that he knew of no precedent and had taken no advice.

Archibald Phillip Primrose, 5th Earl of Rosebery (1847–1929), he was the Queen's choice to succeed Gladstone. A lithograph published in Germany, 1902, in *Weltrundschau zu Reclams Universum*.

Endnotes

Chapter 1

1 Vincent, *Disraeli* (1990), p. 38.
2 Aldous, *The Lion and the Unicorn* (2006), p. 16.
3 *Ibid.*, p. 16.
4 Aronson, *Victoria and Disraeli* (1977), p. 20.

Chapter 2

1 Parry, *Benjamin Disraeli* (2007), p. 6.
2 Aldous, *The Lion and the Unicorn* (2006), p. 19-20.
3 *Ibid.*, p. 19.
4 Aronson *Victoria and Disraeli* (1977), p. 22.
5 *Ibid.*, p. 23.
6 *Ibid.*, p. 25.
7 Aldous, *The Lion and the Unicorn* (2006), p. 21.
8 Repeated in full in Mason, *The Struggle for Democracy* (2015), p. 92.

Chapter 3

1 Shannon, *Gladstone Volume 1* (1982), p. 5.
2 Jenkins, *Gladstone* (1995), p. 4.
3 *Ibid.*, p. 11.
4 *Ibid.*, p. 11.
5 Mason, *Prime Ministerial Anecdotes* (2018), p. 159.
6 *Ibid.*, p. 102.
7 Shannon, *Gladstone Volume 1* (1982), p. 9.
8 Mason, *Prime Ministerial Anecdotes* (2018), p. 81.
9 Jenkins, *Gladstone* (1995), p. 14.
10 *Ibid.*, p. 14.
11 Shannon, *Gladstone Volume 1* (1982), p. 12.
12 *Ibid.*, p. 19.
13 *Ibid.*, p. 18.

Chapter 4

1 Shannon, *Gladstone Volume 1* (1982), p. 29.
2 *Ibid.*, p. 21.
3 *Ibid.*, p. 25.
4 Jenkins, *Gladstone* (1995), p. 21.
5 *Ibid.*, p. 21.
6 Shannon, *Gladstone Volume 1* (1982), p. 32.
7 Mason, *The Struggle for Democracy* (2015), p. 108.
8 Jenkins, *Gladstone* (1995), p. 24.

Chapter 5

1 Tweedie, *Gladstone in Longman History Series* (1998), p. 5.
2 *Ibid.*, p. 5.
3 *Ibid.*, p. 6.
4 Rooke, *Gladstone and Disraeli* (1970), p. 27.
5 Matthew, *Gladstone* (1986), p. 25.
6 Shannon, *Gladstone Volume One* (1982), p. 58.
7 Aldous, *The Lion and the Unicorn* (2006), p. 9.
8 *Ibid.*, p. 10.
9 *Ibid.*, p. 11.

Chapter 6

1 Mason, *Prime Ministerial Anecdotes* (2018), p. 41.
2 Aldous, *The Lion and the Unicorn* (2006), p. 24.
3 Rooke, *Gladstone and Disraeli* (1970), p. 27.
4 *Ibid.*, p. 25.
5 Magnus, *Gladstone* (1854), p. 43.
6 *Ibid.*, p. 43.
7 Tweedie, *Gladstone in Longman History series* (1998), p. 24.
8 Magnus, *Gladstone* (1954), p. 39.
9 Jenkins, *Gladstone* (1995), p. 52.
10 Aldous, *The Lion and the Unicorn* (2006), p. 29.

Chapter 7

1 Magnus, *Gladstone* (1954), p. 54.
2 *Ibid.*, p. 54.
3 Jenkins, *Gladstone* (1995), p. 67.
4 *Ibid.*, p. 67.
5 Magnus, *Gladstone* (1954), p. 58.
6 *Ibid.*, p. 58.
7 Jenkins, *Gladstone* (1995), p. 70.
8 *Ibid.*, p. 70.
9 *Ibid.*, p. 70.
10 Hurd and Young, *Disraeli* (2013), p. 93.

11 Aldous, *The Lion and the Unicorn* (2006), p. 38.
12 *Ibid.*, p. 39.
13 Hurd and Young, *Disraeli* (2013), p. 103.
14 *Ibid.*, p. 106.

Chapter 8

1 Gimson, *Gimson's Prime Ministers* (2018), p. 95.
2 Aldous, *The Lion and the Unicorn* (2006), p. 41.
3 *Ibid.*, p. 41.
4 *Ibid.*, p. 41.
5 *Ibid.*, p. 41.
6 Shannon, *Gladstone Volume 1* (1982), p. 193.
7 Aldous, *The Lion and the Unicorn* (2006), p. 47.
8 *Ibid.*, p. 49.
9 Jenkins, *Gladstone* (1995), p. 85.
10 Hurd and Young, *Disraeli* (2013), p. 115.
11 Jenkins, *Gladstone* (1995), p. 86.

Chapter 9

1 Isba, *Gladstone and Women* (2006), p. 99.
2 *Ibid.*, p. 115.
3 *Ibid.*, p. 112.
4 *Ibid.*, p. 113.
5 Jenkins, *Gladstone* (1995), p. 308.
6 Mason, *Prime Ministerial Anecdotes* (2018), p. 93.
7 *Ibid.*, p. 81.
8 Hurd and Young, *Disraeli* (2013), p. 137.
9 Aldous, *The Lion and the Unicorn* (2006), p. 59.
10 Hurd and Young, *Disraeli* (2013), p. 137.
11 *Ibid.*, p. 138.
12 Aldous, *The Lion and the Unicorn* (2006), p. 60.
13 Jenkins, *Gladstone* (1995), p. 63.
14 Shannon, *Gladstone Volume 1* (1982), p. 213.
15 Jenkins, *Gladstone* (1995), p. 97.
16 *Ibid.*, p. 95.
17 *Ibid.*, p. 126.

Chapter 10

1 Jenkins, *Gladstone* (1995), p. 137.
2 Shannon, *Gladstone Volume 1* (1982), p. 250.
3 Magnus, *Gladstone* (1954), p. 102.
4 Hurd and Young, *Disraeli* (2013), p. 145.
5 *Ibid.*, p. 145.
6 Aldous, *The Lion and the Unicorn* (2006), p. 65.
7 Hurd and Young, *Disraeli* (2013), p. 146.

8 *Ibid.*, p. 153.
9 *Ibid.*, p. 155.
10 *Ibid.*, p. 155.
11 *Ibid.*, p. 148.
12 Shannon, *Gladstone Volume 1* (1982), p. 258.
13 Hurd and Young, *Disraeli* (2013). p. 149.
14 Jenkins, *Gladstone* (1995), p. 141.
15 Mason, *The Struggle for Democracy* (2015), p. 151.
16 Hurd and Young, *Disraeli* (2013), p. 151.

Chapter 11

1 Aldous, *The Lion and the Unicorn* (2006), p. 77.
2 *Ibid.*, p. 78.
3 Jenkins, *Gladstone* (1995), p. 148.
4 *Ibid.*, p. 149.
5 Aldous, *The Lion and the Unicorn* (2006), p. 82.
6 *Ibid.*, p. 83.
7 Hurd and Young, *Disraeli* (2013) p. 168.
8 Jenkins, *Gladstone* (1995), p. 159.
9 Magnus, *Gladstone* (1954), p. 115.
10 *Ibid.*, p. 115.

Chapter 12

1 Jenkins, *Gladstone* (1995), p. 181.
2 *Ibid.*, p. 90.
3 Aldous, *The Lion and the Unicorn* (2006), p. 96.
4 Matthew, *Gladstone* (1954), p. 123.
5 *Ibid.*, p. 123.
6 Aldous, *The Lion and the Unicorn* (2006), p. 97.
7 *Ibid.*, p. 98.
8 Matthew, *Gladstone* (1954), p. 106.
9 Aldous, *The Lion and the Unicorn* (2006), p. 99.
10 *Ibid.*, p. 105.
11 *Ibid.*, p. 106.
12 Jenkins, *Gladstone* (1995), p. 190.
13 Aldous, *The Lion and the Unicorn* (2006), p. 112.
14 Parry, *Benjamin Disraeli* (2007), p. 64.

Chapter 13

1 Jenkins, *Gladstone* (1995), p. 199.
2 *Ibid.*, p. 207.
3 *Ibid.*, p. 208.
4 Magnus, *Gladstone* (1954), p. 141.
5 *Ibid.*, p. 148.
6 *Ibid.*, p. 146.

7 *Ibid.*, p. 146.
8 *Ibid.*, p. 146.
9 Jenkins, *Gladstone* (1995), p. 241.
10 *Ibid.*, p. 242.
11 *Ibid.*, p. 241.
12 Hurd and Young, *Disraeli* (2013), p. 179.
13 Aldous, *The Lion and the Unicorn* (2006), p. 149.
14 *Ibid.*, p. 149.
15 Hurd and Young, *Disraeli* (2013), p. 181.
16 Aldous, *The Lion and the Unicorn* (2006), p. 148.
17 Magnus, *Gladstone* (1954), p. 158.
18 *Ibid.*, p. 159.
19 *Ibid.*, p. 159.
20 Mason, *Prime Ministerial Anecdotes* (2018), p. 89.
21 *Ibid.*, p. 89.
22 Mason, *The Struggle for Democracy* (2015), p. 33.
23 *Ibid.*, p. 76.
24 *Ibid.*, p. 76.
25 Jenkins, *Gladstone* (1995), p. 261.
26 Mason, *Prime Ministerial Anecdotes* (2018), p. 142.
27 Magnus, *Gladstone* (1954), p. 179.
28 Jenkins, *Gladstone* (1995), p. 261.

Chapter 14

1 Hurd and Young, *Disraeli* (2013), p. 190.
2 Magnus, *Gladstone* (1954), p. 183.
3 Jenkins, *Gladstone* (1995), p. 265.
4 *Ibid.*, p. 266.
5 Magnus, *Gladstone* (1954), p. 184.
6 Aldous, *The Lion and the Unicorn* (2006), p. 169.
7 Hurd and Young, *Disraeli* (2013), p. 203.
8 *Ibid.*, p.204.
9 Jenkins, *Gladstone* (1995), p. 271.
10 Hurd and Young, *Disraeli* (2013), p. 207.
11 Mason, *The Struggle For Democracy* (2015), p. 82.
12 Jenkins, *Gladstone* (1995), p. 273.
13 Aldous, *The Lion and the Unicorn* (2006), p. 180.
14 *Ibid.*, p. 180.
15 Jenkins, *Gladstone* (1995), p. 273.
16 Hurd and Young, *Disraeli* (2013), p. 212.
17 Jenkins, *Gladstone* (1995), p. 275.
18 Hurd and Young, *Disraeli* (2013), p. 214.
19 *Ibid.*, p. 217.
20 *Ibid.*, p. 218.
21 Magnus, *Gladstone* (1954), p. 192.
22 Jenkins, *Gladstone* (1995), p. 285.
23 Magnus, *Gladstone* (1954), p. 192.
24 Aldous, *The Lion and the Unicorn* (2006), p. 199.
25 *Ibid.*, p. 201.

26 *Ibid.*, p. 201.
27 *Ibid.*, p. 202.

Chapter 15

1 Jenkins, *Gladstone* (1995), p. 293.
2 *Ibid.*, p. 294.
3 Matthew, *Gladstone 1809–1874* (1986), p. 168.
4 Mason, *Prime Ministerial Anecdotes* (2018), p. 130.
5 *Ibid.*, p. 18.
6 Magnus, *Gladstone* (1995), p. 194.
7 *Ibid.*, p. 199.
8 *Ibid.*, p. 199.
9 Jenkins, *Gladstone* (1995), p. 299.
10 Aldous, *The Lion and the Unicorn* (2006), p. 211.
11 *Ibid.*, p. 212.
12 *Ibid.*, p. 212.
13 *Ibid.*, p. 211.
14 Hurd and Young, *Disraeli* (2013), p. 224.
15 Magnus, *Gladstone* (1995), p. 204.
16 Jenkins, *Gladstone* (1995), p. 322.
17 Hague, *The Pain and the Privilege* (2008), p. 26.
18 Jenkins, *Gladstone* (1995), p. 323.
19 *Ibid.*, p. 327.
20 *Ibid.*, p. 329.

Chapter 16

1 Magnus, *Gladstone* (1954), p. 204.
2 Jenkins, *Gladstone* (1995), p. 343.
3 Mason, *Prime Ministerial Anecdotes* (2018), p. 87.
4 Jenkins, *Gladstone* (1995), p. 341.
5 Magnus, *Gladstone* (1954), p. 206.
6 Jenkins, *Gladstone* (1995), p. 358.
7 Mason, *The Struggle for Democracy* (2015), p. 95.
8 *Ibid.*, p. 95.
9 *Ibid.*, p. 95.
10 *Ibid.*, p. 93.
11 Jenkins, *Gladstone* (1995), p. 353.
12 Hurd and Young, *Disraeli* (2013), p. 229.
13 *Ibid.*, p. 231.
14 Aldous, *The Lion and the Unicorn* (2006), p. 226.
15 *Ibid.*, p.226.
16 Hurd and Young, *Disraeli* (2013), p. 233.
17 *Ibid.*, p. 233.
18 Magnus, *Gladstone* (1954), p. 230.
19 Aldous, *The Lion and the Unicorn* (2006), p. 231.
20 *Ibid.*, p. 234.
21 Jenkins, *Gladstone* (1995), p. 374.

22　*Ibid.*, p. 376.
23　Aldous, *The Lion and the Unicorn* (2006), p. 241.
24　Jenkins, *Gladstone* (1995), p. 376.
25　Aldous, *The Lion and the Unicorn* (2006), p. 243.
26　*Ibid.*, p. 243.
27　*Ibid.*, p. 245.
28　Jenkins, *Gladstone* (1995), p. 379.
29　*Ibid.*, p. 379.
30　Aldous, *The Lion and the Unicorn* (2006), p. 244.
31　Jenkins, *Gladstone* (1995), p. 380.

Chapter 17

1　Hurd and Young, *Disraeli* (2013), p. 238.
2　Aldous, *The Lion and the Unicorn* (2006), p. 256.
3　Jenkins, *Gladstone* (1995), p. 382.
4　*Ibid.*, p. 390.
5　Weintraub, *Disraeli* (1993), p. 536.
6　Hurd and Young, *Disraeli* (2013), p. 240.
7　Weintraub, *Disraeli* (1993), p. 546.
8　Hurd and Young, *Disraeli* (2013), p. 240.
9　*Ibid.*, p. 246.
10　Aldous, *The Lion and the Unicorn* (2006), p. 258.
11　*Ibid.*, p. 260.
12　Magnus, *Gladstone* (1954), p. 236.
13　*Ibid.*, p.233.
14　Jenkins, *Gladstone* (1995), p. 395.

Chapter 18

1　Aldous, *The Lion and the Unicorn* (2006), p. 267.
2　*Ibid.*, p. 267.
3　*Ibid.*, p. 267.
4　*Ibid.*, p. 270.
5　Jenkins, *Gladstone* (1995), p. 400.
6　*Ibid.*, p. 403.
7　*Ibid.*, p. 403.
8　*Ibid.*, p. 405.
9　Weintraub, *Disraeli* (1993), p. 565.
10　*Ibid.*, p. 568.
11　*Ibid.*, p. 590.
12　*Ibid.*, p. 577.
13　Aldous, *The Lion and the Unicorn* (2006), p. 286.

Chapter 19

1　Weintraub, *Disraeli* (1993), p. 600.
2　*Ibid.*, p. 600.

3 *Ibid.*, p. 600.
4 *Ibid.*, p. 601.
5 Jenkins, *Gladstone* (1995), p. 425.
6 Hurd and Young, *Disraeli* (2013), p. 295.
7 *Ibid.*, p. 298.
8 *Ibid.*, p. 298.
9 Jenkins, *Gladstone* (1995), p. 425.
10 *Ibid.*, p. 424.
11 *Ibid.*, p. 424.
12 Aldous, *The Lion and the Unicorn* (2006), p. 299.
13 *Ibid.*, p. 299.
14 *Ibid.*, p. 300.
15 Weintraub, *Disraeli* (1993), p. 621.
16 Jenkins, *Gladstone* (1995), p. 431.
17 Weintraub, *Disraeli* (1993), p. 625.
18 Hurd and Young, *Disraeli* (2013), p. 308.

Chapter 20

1 Jenkins, *Gladstone* (1995), p. 439.
2 Magnus, *Gladstone* (1954), p. 274.
3 Mason, *The Struggle for Democracy* (2015), p. 114.
4 Magnus, *Gladstone* (1954), p. 279.
5 Hurd and Young, *Disraeli* (2013), p. 314.
6 Weintraub, *Disraeli* (1993), p. 632.
7 *Ibid.*, p. 649.
8 Hurd and Young, *Disraeli* (2013), p. 314.
9 Aldous, *The Lion and the Unicorn* (2006), p. 317.
10 Hurd and Young, *Disraeli* (2013), p. 314.
11 *Ibid.*, p. 315.
12 Weintraub, *Disraeli* (1993), p. 657.
13 *Ibid.*, p. 655.
14 Aldous, *The Lion and the Unicorn* (2006), p. 319.
15 Jenkins, *Gladstone* (1995), p. 459.
16 *Ibid.*, p. 459.
17 Magnus, *Gladstone* (1954), p. 280.

Chapter 21

1 Jenkins, *Gladstone* (1995), p. 469.
2 Mason, *The Struggle for Democracy* (2015), p. 115.
3 Magnus, *Gladstone* (1954), p. 286.
4 *Ibid.*, p. 302.
5 Jenkins, *Gladstone* (1995), p. 488.
6 Magnus, *Gladstone* (1954), p. 310.
7 Jenkins, *Gladstone* (1995), p. 515.

Chapter 22

1 Jenkins, *Gladstone* (1995), p. 543.
2 Magnus, *Gladstone* (1954). p. 342.
3 *Ibid.*, p. 382.
4 *Ibid.*, p. 379.
5 *Ibid.*, p. 381.
6 *Ibid.*, p. 383.
7 *Ibid.*, p. 384.
8 *Ibid.*, p. 398.
9 *Ibid.*, p. 398.
10 *Ibid.*, p. 398.
11 Jenkins, *Gladstone* (1995), p. 603.

Chapter 23

1 Jenkins, *Gladstone* (1995), p. 616.